Library of
Davidson College

International Law: Process *and Prospect*

by
Anthony D'Amato

Transnational Publishers, Inc.
Dobbs Ferry, New York

Library of Congress Cataloging-in-Publication Data

D'Amato, Anthony A.
  International law.

  Includes index.
  1. International law. I. Title.
JX3091.D36 1986   341   86-19335
ISBN 0-941320-35-9

© Copyright 1987 by Transnational Publishers, Inc.

All rights reserved. No part of this publication may be reproduced in any form or by any electronic or mechanical means including information storage and retrieval systems without permission in writing from the publisher.

Manufactured in the United States of America

CONTENTS

Acknowledgments	iv
Introduction	v
Chapter One. Is International Law Really "Law"?	1
Chapter Two. Force or Enforcement?	27
Chapter Three. "Territorial Integrity" and "Political Independence"	57
Chapter Four. Use of Force Against Nuclear Installations	75
Chapter Five. Human Rights as Entitlements	89
Chapter Six. Human Rights as Norms of Customary International Law	123
Chapter Seven. The Commercial and Political Desirability of Human Rights	149
Chapter Eight. Territorial Apartheid	165
Chapter Nine. The Individual Versus the State	193
Chapter Ten. Nicaragua and the Academic View of International Law	223
Postscript. International Law as a Career	233
Index	247

Acknowledgements

Chapter 1: "Is International Law Really 'Law'?" 79 *Northwestern Law Review* 1293 (1985), copyright 1985 by Anthony D'Amato. Chapter 2: Co-Authored with Robert B. Von Mehren and prepared for the Hudson Institute in 1963, under the title "The Legality of the Use of Force Short of War." Chapter 3: Written for the present book. Chapter 4: Part of this chapter is an editorial, "Israel's Air Strike Upon the Iraqi Nuclear Reactor," 77 *American Journal of International Law* 584 (1983), reprinted by permission. Chapters 5 and 6: Most of the material in these chapters comes from "The Concept of Human Rights in International Law," 82 *Columbia Law Review* 1110 (1982), copyright 1982 by Anthony D'Amato. Chapter 7: Part of this chapter is "Are Human Rights Good for International Business?" 1 *Northwestern Journal of International Law and Business* 22 (1979), reprinted by permission. Chapter 8: Parts of this chapter are from "The Bantustan Proposals for South-West Africa," 4 *Journal of Modern African Studies* 177 (1966), reprinted by permission, and 1 *New England Law Review* 59 (1966), reprinted by permission. Chapter 9: Most of this chapter is written for the present book, but the last part on the *Tel-Oren Case* is from an editorial, "Judge Bork's Concept of the Law of Nations is Seriously Mistaken," 79 *American Journal of International Law* 92 (1985), reprinted by permission. Chapter 10: Most of this chapter is an editorial, "*Nicaragua* and International Law: The 'Academic' and the 'Real,'" 79 *American Journal of International Law* 657 (1985), reprinted by permission. POSTSCRIPT: From *American University Journal of International Law and Politics*, vol. 1, no. 1 (1986), copyright 1986 by Anthony D'Amato.

INTRODUCTION

If you take a map of Africa and superimpose it upon a similar map of fifty years ago, a rather remarkable result occurs. The names of the countries are different now, but the borders of the countries are pretty much the same. What's remarkable about that is the fact that the old borders were largely arbitrary—invented in the capitals of Europe by negotiation from time to time among the colonial powers, and not necessarily reflecting tribal or other political divisions within Africa itself. When the nations of Africa threw off colonialism and became independent, why didn't they change the old boundaries?

What may be more important about a boundary is not that it is arbitrary, but that it is there. Its very existence proclaims a set of legal expectations; to change it is to introduce instability and probably armed conflict. Many rules of international law are like boundaries: what's important is not what the rule is, but that there is a rule.

In the first chapter of this book, I attempt to deal with whether international law exists and whether it is real; a philosopher might call this the ontology of international law. Here we may find that international law functions the way national boundaries do. More than that, both international law and national boundaries define what a "nation" is, and hence are intrinsically part of international reality. A "nation," I shall suggest, is a bundle of entitlements; one of the most important of those entitlements is jurisdictional competence within the territory demarcated by the nation's boundaries.

But any discussion of "law," whether international or domestic, has its darker side, its antithesis: physical force. All of law is an attempt to curb and channel the use of force so that people and nations will settle their differences by means other than resort to violence. Law, to use a phrase of Abraham Lincoln, is the faith that right makes might. The enormous conceptual problem facing students of international law is to study how international law can curb and channel transnational violence in a system in which, unlike the domestic legal system, there is no central enforcement authority, no court system of compulsory and unlimited jurisdiction, and no legislature. The international law of the use of force is of course a huge subject; in chapters 2 to 4, I try to deal with some of its important aspects.

But even as the student of international law begins to grapple with the legal regulation of force, another intellectual challenge of historic, indeed revolutionary proportions, presents itself: how to accommodate the law of individual human rights in an international legal system that is apparently addressed to nations and not to individuals. This problem forms the springboard for Chapters 5 through 7.

Finally, Chapters 8 through 10 deal with particular matters of current concern, though in a rather abstract way. The concept of territorial apartheid, which may be of increasing relevance to the situation in South Africa, is studied in Chapter 8 by examining the equities of a scheme of over twenty years ago for "homelands" in Namibia, then called South-West Africa. The specifics, of course, are not relevant to South Africa today, but the method of analyzing considerations of justice and equity may be useful. Chapter 9 addresses the broad problem of individual vs. the state. And Chapter 10 takes a current matter of headline importance in international law—the case of *Nicaragua v. United States*—to raise a broader issue. A philosopher might call it the issue of the epistemology of international law. What I try to look at, in a preliminary way, is the question of how much weight we can accord to what governmental officials say that international law is. What governments say about international rules is, of course, relevant to a student's examination of what those rules are, but is it the whole story? This inquiry, of course, reflects back to the first chapter on what international law is, and to the chapters in between on how we might find out what it is.

On a more personal level, a Postscript is included that addresses the question of a career in public international law. The challenges facing any person who would like to work as a lawyer in international law are nearly as formidable as the problems in the often insane arena of international politics.

I would like to acknowledge the financial assistance of the Northwestern University School of Law which has awarded me several summer research grants, and the editing assistance of Marjorie A. Moore of the staff of Transnational Publishers, Inc.

1

IS INTERNATIONAL LAW REALLY "LAW"?

Many serious students of the law react with a sort of indulgence when they encounter the term "international law," as if to say, "well, we know it isn't *really* law, but we know that international lawyers and scholars have a vested professional interest in calling it 'law.'" Or they may agree to talk about international law as *if* it were law, a sort of quasi-law or near-law. But it cannot be true law, they maintain, because it cannot be enforced: How do you enforce a rule of law against an entire nation, especially a superpower such as the United States or the Soviet Union?

I. The "Enforcement" Argument

One intriguing answer to these serious students of the law is to attempt to persuade them that enforcement is not, after all, the hallmark of what is meant, or what should be meant, by the term "law." As Roger Fisher observed, much of what we call "law" in the domestic context is also unenforceable.[1] For example, where the defendant is the United States, such as in a case involving constitutional law, how would the winning private party enforce his or her judgment against the United States? Upon reflection, we see that the United

---

1. *See* Fisher, "Bringing Law to Bear on Governments," 74 *Harv. L. Rev.* 1130 (1961), excerpted in B. Weston, R. Falk, and A. D'Amato, *International Law and World Order* 125-30 (1980).

States, whenever it loses a case (and these cases are very frequent—the myriad cases involving income taxes, social security benefits, welfare, and the like), only complies with the court's judgment because it wants to. The winning private party cannot hold a gun to the head of the United States to enforce compliance, even if there were a natural meaning to the term "head of the United States." We can go even further than Professor Fisher did: Every criminal law prosecution is a case of an individual pitted against the state (or the "people" of the state). What is to stop the state from saying, "You were acquitted by the jury, but that was a travesty of justice, so we're going to imprison you anyway"? How does the defendant, in handcuffs, stop the state from going ahead? In some countries, at some times, we have heard of dictators or military regimes proceeding with the imprisonment and execution of defendants who were acquitted by their own courts. In terms of power, there is nothing to stop the United States from disregarding adverse judgments of its own courts. In this sense, therefore, a great deal of what we normally call "law" in the United States is unenforceable by private parties arrayed against the state.

It is no objection to this line of reasoning, by the way, to dismiss it as farfetched. If one objects that the United States, in any event, routinely complies with adverse judgments of its own courts, then the international lawyer can answer that the same is true of rules of international law. As Louis Henkin put it, "Almost all nations observe almost all principles of international law and almost all of their obligations almost all of the time."[2]

But a more substantial critique of Professor Fisher's analogy between cases involving the government as a party and international-law cases is that *most* domestic litigation, after all, does *not* involve the government as a party. Most cases involve one citizen against another ("citizen" including artificial persons such as corporations), and as to *those* cases the law is enforced by the full sovereign powers of the state against the losing litigant. This majority of cases, then, tends to define what we mean by "law;" it constitutes the paradig-

---

2. L. Henkin, *How Nations Behave* 47 (2d ed. 1979). This statement in a sense follows tautologically from the fact that there is an international system of legal rules. Clearly, the rules that have evolved over time are the ones that nations have found to be in their collective self-interest; this is simply a Darwinian process applied to customary international law. Professor Henkin's statement, however, while tautological, is not vacuous; after all, nations might have instead evolved into a nonrule anarchical system.

matic instance of law. Therefore, the argument goes, the minority of cases that do involve the state or the United States as a party are, in a sense, parasitic upon the paradigmatic instance. We tend to regard this latter minority of cases as "law" only because they share certain attributes with the generality of cases. But if we look hard at this minority of cases where the government is a party, we must concede that they are not really "law" because, at bottom, they are unenforceable. They only appear to be law when looked at uncritically. In short, this line of argument *concedes* Professor Fisher's major premise—that international-law cases are similar to domestic cases where the government is a party—but denies his minor premise, that such cases are instances of "law." Hence, international law is no more "law" than is constitutional law or even criminal law. As John Austin stated, both constitutional and international law are merely "positive morality."[3]

One might object and say that it is frivolous to exclude the vast body of constitutional law and criminal law cases from what we mean by "law." If you say that, then you see the force of Professor Fisher's argument. You are well on your way to accepting the "reality" of international law. But I have presented the skeptical argument against Professor Fisher's view because I want to be rigorous and not have to rely on an argument by analogy, which is ultimately the kind of argument that Professor Fisher has used.

Let us then consider a second line of reasoning against the proposition that enforcement is the hallmark of law. This argument is not associated with any particular writer, because it relies on early conceptions of law and also on the philosophy of law itself. If we consider what law is *not*, we soon realize that it is *not* a rationale for the application of force. It is not a system of "might makes right" in the sense that the state constantly has to compel people, at gunpoint, to behave in a certain way. If you look through a volume of cases, or even a volume of statutes or annotations, you will find that most of the matters therein concern the working-out of private arrangements in a complex society. Most of "law" concerns itself with

---

3. J. Austin, *The Province of Jurisprudence Determined* 127 (Hart ed. 1954). Austin, however, did not know much about classic international law; he was somewhat taken in by writers who included only treaties as international law. The term "international law" itself was, after all, invented by Austin's contemporary, Jeremy Bentham, and Bentham was philosophically inimical to unwritten law. *See* J. Bentham, *An Introduction to The Principles of Morals and Legislation* 326 n.1 (2d ed. Oxford 1948) (1st ed. Oxford 1789).

the interpretation and enforcement of private contracts, the redress of intentional and negligent harms, rules regarding sales of goods and sales of securities, rules relating to the family and the rights of members thereof, and other such rules, norms, and cases. The rules are obeyed not out of fear of the state's power, but because the rules by and large are perceived to be right, just, or appropriate. No state could possibly compel people to obey all these rules at gunpoint; there would not be enough soldiers and policemen to hold the guns (a sort of extreme Orwellian vision of society); they would have to sleep sooner or later, and then anarchy might break out.

Even more fatal to this view of extreme enforcement is that the state would need many rules to channel the behavior of the enforcers themselves. For instance, how would all these police officials and soldiers know what rules they must enforce, and who would make sure that they enforced the rules as written? We would need another phalanx of soldiers to police the enforcers.[4] And on top of that, another layer of officials pointing the guns at the heads of the gun-pointers. The whole process would break down of its own weight. Indeed, Orwell in his novel, *1984*, avoided the question of how to coordinate and control the activities of the officials of the state he described. He simply referred to the state in the abstract as exercising monolithic power over the citizenry, finessing the real problem of how to organize such a state so as to control the controllers.

If law is not, by and large, a body of rules that are enforced at gunpoint, what is an individual rule of law? Is it, as the nineteenth century positivists maintained, a command of the state that is backed by the state's enforcement power?[5] To be sure, some "laws" might be just that: A dictator issues a command for his personal indulgence or whim, and if he has sufficiently satisfied his close advisers and the military in other areas, they will probably enforce his command. But most laws will not have this characteristic. Indeed, looking at the matter more microscopically, what is it that *forces* a judge to decide the case before her on the basis of precedent and statutes? Is another judge holding a gun to her head? Does she examine whether the law will be enforced to see whether it is law? How does she know, in advance of her own decision, what will be enforced?

---

4. The argument is elaborated and extended in A. D'Amato, *Jurisprudence: A Descriptive and Normative Analysis of Law* 7-8, 151-53 (1984) [hereinafter cited as A. D'Amato, *Jurisprudence*], and in D'Amato, "Legal Uncertainty," 71 *Calif. L. Rev.* 1, 39 n. 78 (1983).

5. *See* A. D'Amato, *Jurisprudence, supra* note 4, at 118-22 (tracing the command theory of law from Hobbes through Bentham and Austin).

This point came up in the famous case of *Marbury v. Madison*,[6] familiar to generations of American law students but often misinterpreted. In that case, Chief Justice Marshall's "bottom line" was that the Supreme Court had no original jurisdiction to issue writs of mandamus. In short, there was no power to enforce that which the plaintiff demanded. If "law" were coincident with enforceability, then, since under Marshall's reasoning there was not power of enforcement in the Supreme Court because it lacked *jurisdiction*, nothing Marshall said in his opinion would have had any legal significance. To put it another way, lacking a "remedy," the plaintiff would have no "right," not even a right to get a decision from the Court on the question of "right."

But Marshall took an entirely different tack. He *began* with the question: Does the plaintiff have a right? He then asked the second question: If the plaintiff has a right, does he have a remedy? And his third question was: If the plaintiff has a remedy, can the relief issue from this Court? By putting the questions in this order, Marshall did the opposite of what the positivists would require. By dealing first with the question of "right," Marshall was able to address that question wholly apart from whether there was a remedy or whether the remedy was available from the Supreme Court. As all law students know, Marshall answered his own question that there was indeed a right, and secondly, there being a right meant that the plaintiff had a remedy. By going through this reasoning, Marshall was able to establish the groundwork for his path-breaking assertion of judicial review of questions of constitutionality. He held that, in the face of a right and remedy, the congressional statute purporting to grant that remedy to the Supreme Court as a matter of original jurisdiction violated the Constitution. Marshall would not have been able to make his assertion of judicial review if he had begun and ended his opinion with the simple sentence, "We have no jurisdiction; case dismissed." Hence, we see that in a case where by the Court's own admission it lacked jurisdiction and the power of enforcement, nevertheless the Court was able to establish a point of fundamental substantive significance.

Marshall's persuasiveness was dependent upon a consensus at the time he wrote his opinion that there could be such a thing as a "right" without a real remedy. This was part of a larger conviction in those

6. 5 U.S. (1 Cranch) 137 (1803).

days that the "law" itself was not something that only works when a policeman is standing by ready to enforce it physically. Law indeed is something that is opposed to force. Right is not the same thing as might. In continental countries, the word for "law" is, as translated, the word "right." In law, there is a fundamental element of right, of justice, dating back to Cicero's and St. Thomas' equation of "right reason" with the natural law (the latter being those reasonable rules that accommodate the peaceful affairs of persons in a society).[7]

Under this argument that we are developing, the relation of force to law, of might to right, is a contingent and not a necessary relation. We can imagine a society under law where there is no force. People obey the laws, and no one disobeys. There is no need, in this idyllic utopia, for enforcement, because there is universal willing compliance. Surely we cannot claim that such a society does not have "law." It is clear that the society is one that is under law, and that the contingent use of force is simply not necessary. To take an example closer to home, suppose that in some state of the Union there has not been a kidnaping since that state entered the Union. Would we say that the law against kidnaping in that state is not a law? Certainly no one would argue that if a law is so successful that it never needs enforcement, it is not a law. Thus, we can conclude from this hypothetical that enforcement is not intrinsic to, is not necessary to, the idea of law.

But you might object that enforcement must potentially be present, even if it is not invoked. In other words, in the state that has no kidnaping, it is nevertheless true that if someone commits this crime—or even contemplates committing it—the potential for enforcement is ever-present. It is this potential for enforcement, after all, that the positivists insist upon when they draw our attention to the necessary connection between a rule of law and its enforcement.

To take care of this objection, we may simply modify our previous hypothetical of the idyllic utopia. Assume not only that they have never had a need to enforce their laws, but also that they have no enforcement machinery—no police, no jails, no sheriffs, no marshals.

---

7. "Natural law" is not something handed down from on high, nor is it the a priori speculations of "right reason." Rather, it may best be described in modern terms as those systemic rules that have survived through evolution over time as best fitting the mutual needs of a society. An example of this approach, though not in those terms, is found in J. Finnis, *Natural Law and Natural Rights* (1980). For a categorical historical perspective, see D'Amato, "Lon Fuller and Substantive Natural Law," 26 *Am. J. Juris* 202 (1981).

They can still have a system of laws, as complex as you please, even without the potential for enforcement.

Yet you might now object that we cannot prove something about the nature of law, an all-too-human institution, by postulating the existence of a utopia where the inhabitants never break the law. Can we modify our utopia to make it seem more realistic? Suppose occasionally someone breaks the law, but is ostracized from society. Suppose one who breaches a contract is considered a moral renegade who should not be entrusted with any further business dealings. These expressions of sharp social disapproval, and occasionally of ostracism, may work to discourage the few people who would disobey the law. They may not always work, but they may be potent enough to deter most of the people (a minority to begin with) who might consider breaking the law. Thus, our not-perfect utopia now consists of a regime where almost all of the laws are obeyed almost all of the time, where occasional disobedience is met with sharp social disapproval, and where occasionally, despite the "mechanism" of social disapproval, occasional violations of the law occur.[8] Is this not, nevertheless, a legal system?

A positivist might happen to object to this concept as follows: The idea of social disapproval, and sometimes social ostracism, is the same thing as a sanction. It constitutes a way of enforcing the law. Hence, by introducing this social-disapproval factor into the utopia, we have simply underscored the original point—that law (except in idyllic utopias which do not exist) depends upon potential enforcement.

But if that is the positivist's position, then the international lawyer should gladly concede the point. For international law recognizes that the social-disapproval factor operates as a sanction. A nation among the community of nations which violates the law, for example, by disregarding a treaty obligation, would certainly be subject to social disapproval by the other nations. In this sense, international law is really "law."

Now it is perhaps the positivist's turn to beat a hasty retreat. The positivist may now want to retract the equation of social disapproval with "sanction," for fear of including international law under the

---

8. *See* M. Barkun, *Law Without Sanction* (1968); *cf.* Reisman, "Sanctions and Enforcement," in *International Law Essays* 381, 383-89 (1981) (group and community norms provide a "civic" sanction, distinguishable from a state-imposed public sanction).

term "law." Instead, the positivist will retreat to the original position that physical or even violent enforcement is necessary to make law "law," and hence international law is not "law." We may, however, suspect that the positivist is reshaping definitions in order to *exclude* the international-law case, rather than to arrive at a general definition of law.[9] Consistent with this position, the positivist will have to argue that any legal system in which social disapproval functions as the sole sanction (for example, in a peaceful tribal society) does not have "law." "Law" is present only when, in addition to social disapproval, there is physical coercion stemming from the sovereign power of the state. But what if there is no *need* for this physical coercion? The positivist must then conclude that there is no law.

Such a position would be difficult to defend, for if there is a society where people are so law-abiding that they get along only with the social-disapproval sanction, that society manifests a rather good case of "law." It is strange to insist that, for there to be law, physical coercion must also be used even if there is no need for it.

Yet the serious student of law may not be satisfied with the preceding argument in its entirety. We want to ask what happens if the need for physical coercion should arise. In the international system, at least, we have states which occasionally break the rules of international law and which seem not to be deterred by expressions of social disapproval from the other states. This is a reality of international life. Therefore, unlike the tribal society where social disapproval may constitute an effective sanction, international society needs a physical sanction to underscore its legal rules. Otherwise, the rules will occasionally be flouted. Perhaps they will be ignored most often when the "chips are down," which is exactly when they most need to be enforced. How can we call such a system, dependent for its support on so feeble a mechanism as social approval, a "legal" system?

It is hard to discern the logic behind the preceding objection, even while it is easy to understand it. We all recognize, and regret, that rules of international law are flouted on occasion, and we are all too aware of the fact that an outraged world public opinion simply is

---

9. This is analogous to H. L. A. Hart's exclusion of international law from "mature" legal systems, because it lacks a "rule of recognition" (Hart's equivalent of the positivist's command-backed-by-sanction). *See* H. L. A. Hart, *The Concept of Law* 208-31 (1961); D'Amato, "The Neo-Positivist Concept of International Law," 59 *A.J.I.L.* 321 (1965) (natural-law critique of Hart).

incapable of discouraging the violation. Should our conclusion then be that the rules of international law are not "law" as we know the term, because as we know the term the "law" involves the concept of physical enforcement? Yet, even in asking this, we acknowledge that physical enforcement is not a *necessary* characteristic of law (our "utopian" examples). And we also acknowledge that, even in domestic cases, where the state is one of the parties, we cannot meaningfully speak of physical enforcement (Professor Fisher's argument). These two arguments destroy most of the logical force of our position that international law is not really law, and yet we may cling to that position.

Some early writers on the law of nations attempted to meet the enforcement objection head-on, by asserting that rules of international law are indeed enforced by the mechanism of war. A nation that violates the rules will be the object of a "just war" initiated precisely to punish the transgressing nation and to enforce the validity of the rules.[10] This argument today sounds like an archaic ploy, for we know enough about wars to have learned that the "transgressing" state may occasionally win if it has the physical power to do so. Physical might bears no necessary connection to international right. Interestingly, the concept of a "just war" has become, if possible, even more archaic under the collective security mechanisms of the League of Nations and its successor the United Nations. These bodies, in principle at least, are designed to stamp out acts of aggression wherever they occur. In other words, they are not set up for the purpose of enforcing international law, but simply for the purpose of enforcing international peace. It follows that if the peace is unjust, it will be enforced anyway. The United Nations seems to call for a "cease fire" in disregard of the merits of the local conflict, and it appears to be less concerned with enforcing international law than with enforcing a prohibition against the use of force no matter what the justification.

Yet there is something in the notion of a "just war" that may help us to fashion a more compelling case for the proposition that international law is really "law" than the other arguments we have examined. I will try to show in Part Three that what I will label as reciprocal-entitlement violation is a mechanism akin to the old "just

---

10. *See* 2 L. Oppenheim, *International Law* 177-79 (H. Lauterpacht 7th ed. 1952); M. Walzer, *Just and Unjust Wars* (1977).

war" notion that underlies a realistic enforcement mechanism for international law.

At present, we may conclude tentatively as follows:

(1) The fact that some states disobey periodically some rules of international law does not itself mean that those rules are not rules of "law," because even in domestic society some people (e.g., criminals) break the law from time to time.

(2) On the other hand, the fact that most states obey most rules of international law most of the time is not enough to call those rules "legal" because we are especially concerned with "important" cases where states may get away with violating rules of international law. If states can violate rules with impunity when it is in their national interest to do so, how can we call those rules "law"?

(3) We recognize, even though it makes us somewhat uncomfortable, that international law is more properly analogized to domestic cases where the state is a party than to domestic cases where one citizen sues another. Under this conception, we concede that our usual notions of "enforcement" are not appropriately applied to the state. But because we recognize as "law" those domestic cases involving the state as a party, we should also recognize as "law" those international controversies involving states as parties.

(4) We further concede that physical coercion is not a necessary component of "law." However, we are reluctant to conclude that it is totally unnecessary, because we have seen too many cases where a nation violates international law and gets away with it due to the lack of an effective enforcement mechanism.

(5) Hence, we are somewhat, though not totally, persuaded that international law can properly be labelled "law" for most purposes. But we may remain unconvinced, at this point, that it is *really* "law."

II. The "Verbal" Argument

Let us for the moment look at the question whether international law is really law from an entirely different angle. Suppose we were to read all the communications that governments officially make to one another: letters, speeches, proclamations, treaties, agreements, diplomatic initiatives, and so on. Suppose we read these with an eye toward whether the language contained in these communications refers to "law" and is "legal" language. In brief, we would be engaging in a "content analysis" of these communications to see whether what is being asserted and claimed therein can properly be called "legal."[11] We will find, indeed, much of the content of intergovernmental communications is self-consciously grounded in legal terminology. There should be nothing surprising about this, considering the fact that lawyers typically help draft these documents and speeches. We will find, indeed, that the more important the communication the more likely it is cast in legal terms, and the more likely it is that lawyers have played a role in drafting it.

We might then want to argue that, given the reality of this legal language, it would be rather absurd to maintain that "law" is *not* involved in these intergovernmental communications. If the relevant actors call it "law," who are we to say that they are all wrong? Rather, is it not our job, as observers or scholars, to employ the terms the way the relevant actors intend those terms to be employed? Thus, the very utilization of legal language in intergovernmental communications is an argument for the proposition at least that governments resort to "law" in their attempts to influence each other; or refer to "law" in an attempt to appear to be legal and thus ward off disapproval of other states.

We might want to add to this argument the position taken by the "policy-oriented jurisprudence" of Myres McDougal and his colleagues, including Harold Lasswell, Michael Reisman, Lung-chu Chen, and others.[12] We might collect on a library shelf their voluminous works and ask, "What have they written about?" If our answer is not "law," what is it? To be sure, when we take their books down from the shelf and look into them, we begin to get an extraordinarily broad definition of "law." The concept is so broad, indeed, that we wonder if there is anything which they can properly call "non-law." They cite works from the social sciences, from the humanities, as well as works on international law and international politics. Their idea of international law is that it is a process of authoritative decision-making, but then they seem to view "authoritative" so broadly as to

---

11. *See* P. Stone, D. Dunphy, M. Smith and D. Ogilvie, *The General Inquirer* (1966); cf. D'Amato, "Psychological Constructs in Foreign Policy Prediction," 11 *J. Conflict Res.* 294 (1967) (content analysis of writings of foreign policy actors to derive predictive "general constructs" of such behavior).

12. For a good summary statement, with bibliographical references, *see* McDougal & Reisman, "International Law in Policy-Oriented Perspective," in *The Structure and Process of International Law: Essays in Legal Philosophy Doctrine and Theory* 103 (1983).

encompass just about any decision made by any international decisionmaker.[13] Finally, they disassociate law from enforcement. Legal rules, according to Professor McDougal, "exhaust their effective power when they guide a decision-maker to relevant factors and indicate presumptive weightings."[14]

According to the policy-oriented jurisprudence school, therefore, international law is nothing other than international communication. Under the first argument I made in this Part, the prevalence of legal language in international communication indicates that nations are talking about, and believe they are talking about, "law" in the positions they take vis-à-vis each other. Under the second McDougal-type argument, international communication itself is "law" irrespective of its being couched in legal terms. Taken together, both of these positions may convince the reader that international law is really law.

In the past, I was intrigued by the law-as-communication approach.[15] Recently, I have become uneasy with it, in part because it proves too much. *Any* international contention couched in legal language (or even, following McDougal, not couched in legal language) becomes "law." Yet surely the "law" is not everything. It does not include contradictory positions, although McDougal comes perilously close to this in his notion of the complementarity of customary prescriptions.[16] If international "law" says that nations may or may not attack one another, that the high seas are free to all and closed to all, that genocide is both permissible and prohibited, then I would conclude that there is no international "law" worth talking about on these points. (Someone who disagreed with me would probably say that the "verbal" argument I have outlined here compels the conclusion that there *is* international law, but that its content is incoherent.)

The other misgiving I have about the verbal argument is that scholars are, after all, not precluded from criticizing the propriety of the

---

13. *See, e.g.*, M. McDougal, H. Lasswell & L. Chen, *Human Rights and World Public Order* 161-363 (1980).
14. M. McDougal, *Studies in World Public Order* 887 n.109 (1960).
15. *See, e.g.*, D'Amato, "The Relation of Theories of Jurisprudence to International Politics and Law," 27 *Wash. & Lee L. Rev.* 257 (1970); cf. D'Amato, "What 'Counts' as Law?" in *Law-Making in the Global Community* 83 (N. Onuf ed. 1982) (attempting to put the law-as-words approach in perspective).
16. For a critique, with references to Professor McDougal's writings, see A. D'Amato, *The Concept of Custom in International Law* 220-26 (1971).

use of language by other persons. Even though international communications are couched in legal terms, an observer does not have to conclude that the use of those legal terms is proper. In the insurance business, contracts between insurance companies are called "treaties," even though this is not the use of the term that international lawyers recognize. An international lawyer is not precluded from criticizing the terminology of "treaties" if that criticism throws some light on what insurance companies are really doing. For example, does the use of the term "treaty" imply that rules of international law relating to treaty interpretation should be followed in disputes among insurance companies, instead of domestic contract rules? The answer is no, and thus the term "treaty" can be criticized as misleading. Similarly, we might properly criticize the resort to legal terminology in international communications if we can show that it is not really "law" that is being invoked.

We may therefore conclude at this point by saying, simply, that the prevalence of legal language in international communications *adds* to our previous conclusions that international law is properly called "law" for most purposes and in most contexts. We still, however, reserve final judgment on the question whether it is really "law."

III. The "Reciprocal Entitlements" Argument

I believe that a conclusive argument can be fashioned that international law is really law, by showing that international law is enforceable in the same way that domestic law is enforceable. Of course, I cannot make the claim that international law is always enforced. Rather, what I shall proceed to do is to take a closer look at what we mean by enforcement, and then show that it is applicable equally to the domestic and to the international legal systems.

When we examine the concept of enforcement of law, we find that law can be enforced in many ways. For example, a parent might frown upon a child who does not brush his teeth, or might express stern disapproval. This tends to "enforce" the law, although as we saw earlier it is not a satisfactory concept when we think of enforcement.[17] For it is too easy for the child, or the nation, to decide to violate the law and pay the mild price of incurring social displeasure.

---

17. *See supra* pp. 3-4.

Thus, we want to narrow the concept of enforcement. Perhaps a good way to begin to narrow it is to exclude all modes of "enforcement" that are extrinsic to the legal system itself. Social disapproval, for instance, is extrinsic to the legal system, as is social approval. These are external mechanisms for enforcing, or more accurately reinforcing, the law, but we know intuitively that they are not provided by or required by the law itself. (If the law *required* them, then you would have the regressive problem of how to force people to socially disapprove of a miscreant's behavior.)

When we look at the legal system itself, we find that it typically provides for deprivations, for disabilities. When a person disobeys the law, the law "punishes" him in some way. The possibility of punishment, in turn, is supposed to deter a rational person from violating the law in the first place.

Enforcement thus consists of some form of legally imposed sanction. A monetary fine is an example of a punishment that is not physical. Physical punishments include being deprived of your freedom, for example by being incarcerated or being forced to perform some kind of community service as part of your "sentence." In the extreme, you may be deprived of your life if convicted of a capital crime.

In this entire spectrum of legally imposed sanctions for violation of the law, we find that the law has removed one or more of your entitlements. I could use the word "rights" here—for example, your rights to life, to liberty, and to property. But the word "entitlements" is more precise, because it denotes legally recognized rights. If you claim a right that the law does not recognize (for example, a woman's claim to the right to vote before the constitutional amendment of 1920 providing for universal suffrage), you do not have an "entitlement." Since we are talking about enforcement mechanisms intrinsic to the legal system, it is more precise to speak of entitlements than to speak of rights.

In all cases of law violation, the law responds by depriving you of one or more of your entitlements. You have a legal entitlement to liberty; you lose it if you commit a crime punishable by incarceration. You have a legal entitlement to your bank account; you lose it if you have failed to pay your taxes or if someone obtains a judgment against you and attaches it. You have an entitlement to performance under a private contract that you make with someone else; if you fail to perform your part of the bargain, a court may decide that you have forfeited your entitlement under the contract. Some of these entitlement deprivations that you suffer because you have violated the law can be effectuated against you without any need for physical enforcement. Your bank account can be taken away from you by a bookkeeping entry made in the bank pursuant to a court order. Your marriage can be legally dissolved by a court decree without your willing compliance or participation. Thus, when we think of legal enforcement, we need not imagine the use of physical force against the person of the law-violator, although, of course, in some cases physical force is appropriate. The deprivation of either your entitlement to liberty, or your entitlement to life, may result from your conviction of a major crime.

Furthermore, there would be no possibility of enforcement by entitlement deprivation if people were not assigned some entitlements in the first place. If you had no entitlements, you would obviously suffer no loss if the law deprived you of some of them. (There is no "law" in the "jungle.") However, we find in all legal systems without exception the legal recognition of certain rights of the people, which we call entitlements. At a minimum, there is recognition of life and liberty. With a set of entitlements, therefore, each person is vulnerable to removal of some of them by the law. Legal systems typically enforce their own rules by removing one or more entitlements of persons who violate the rules.

If the account I have just given of the function of entitlements in the enforcement of law is persuasive, and if it fully captures the more diffuse notion of enforcement, then we next can turn to the international legal system to see how the process of entitlements and entitlement-deprivations works to provide for the enforcement of legal rules.

Let us imagine a primitive international situation. Two nations are at war with each other, but are weary of it and are interested in the possibility of peace. The problem now is how to send a peace ambassador from one nation to the other. The war between them is so total and brutal that no one wants to be an emissary for fear of being killed by the other side. We assume that this is the first "case" of resolving the conflict between the two nations so there are no prescribed methods of establishing peace.

Perhaps nation A could dispatch a particularly brave person who would carry a letter saying, "don't kill the bearer of this letter, as we are attempting to set up communications with you, and we promise to give safe conduct to any person you choose to send to us who has a letter from you. Moreover, as evidence of our good faith, you can hold the bearer of this letter hostage while your emissary is en route to us." Such a letter, of course, would not guarantee that its bearer would be safe. All we know is that, in some instances, letters such as this one actually worked.[18] We don't know much about those instances where the letter was ineffective and its bearer was killed. But in those cases where the letter worked, a primitive entitlement—a limited ambassadorial immunity—between the two nations was set up.

This single entitlement, however, is precarious, for the only remedy for entitlement violation by one nation is that of a reciprocal violation by the other nation of the same entitlement. Thus, suppose nation A is furious with the peace terms brought by nation B's emissary, and responds by killing the emissary. In effect, nation A has opted to resume total war. Nation B, it is true, can retaliate by killing the emissary it is holding, but nation A presumably had already taken this possibility into account and decided to "sacrifice" its own emissary. The two nations have thus destroyed the only entitlement that existed between them. They revert to a lawless state of war, from which extrication will now be harder given the unfortunate experience with the emissaries. Clearly the entitlement of diplomatic immunity would have had a better chance to survive had there been a second and different entitlement between the two nations. Then a threat by one nation to destroy the diplomatic immunity could be countered by a threat to destroy the other unrelated entitlement.

Thus, stability has a better chance the more entitlements there are. It is not the purpose of this chapter to discuss historically how entitlements arose among nations, or how they became more complex and differentiated. Yet we might briefly consider the perspective of a new nation (perhaps a nation that has just received its independence from a colonial power).

Our new nation receives at its birth a host of entitlements. It has not chosen nor selected any of these entitlements; instead they are, so to speak, thrust upon the new nation. The first entitlement is of fundamental importance: the entitlement of statehood, which means,

---

18. Cf. G. Schwarzenberger, *The Inductive Approach to International Law* 75-78 (1965).

in the international system, that our new nation is a geographic entity entitled to exert its own legal jurisdiction in the area within its boundaries and to claim the inviolability of those boundaries against all other states. The legal sanctity of its borders signifies that our new state is a state in a community of states, and not merely a gang of thieves subject to the untrammelled degradations of other neighboring gangs. Indeed, it appears that the very definition of a state, or nation, involves an entitlement to the sanctity of its borders. Without such boundaries, the entity is hardly a "state." Yet, the boundaries are boundaries only by virtue of their recognition by all the other states in the system.

In sum, still considering this first entitlement, our new nation depends for its very identity upon the recognition of other similar states in the community of states. I am not talking about de jure recognition; rather, all that is necessary is a sense in the international community that the new state is enclosed by international boundaries, and those boundaries, like all boundaries, are lines that differentiate the internal affairs of the state from the external affairs and cannot be crossed at will by military forces in either direction. This notion of a boundary is so fundamental that the Vienna Convention on the Law of Treaties specifically excepts boundary-establishing treaties from the normal rules of *rebus sic stantibus*,[19] and the World Court in its leading decision in the *Continental Shelf Cases* made it clear that the normal generation of customary international law cannot affect ownership of territory (in those cases, the submerged land areas) absent a showing of consent from the owner.[20]

Our new state might, therefore, look upon the international law of the sanctity of its boundaries as a gift of a valuable entitlement. But the entitlement carries with it reciprocal duties, so that it is not necessarily a gift. The entitlement provides that our new nation must respect the borders of all the other states. Suppose our new nation is very powerful militarily, and expansionist-minded; it might want to extend its boundaries at the expense of its neighboring states. In that case, the entitlement of sanctity of boundaries is, in the first instance, more of a curse than a gift. (Later on, if the new state has

---

19. Vienna Convention on the Law of Treaties, art. 62, *adopted* May 12, 1969, 8 *I.L.M.* 679, 702 (1969).
20. *North Sea Continental Shelf* (W. Ger. v. Den., W. Ger. v. Neth.), 1969 I.C.J. 3. This case has been widely misinterpreted, and thus the statement in the text is supported by an extensive argument given below, in Chapter 6.

succeeded militarily in extending its dominion, it might then want to establish the principle of sanctity of international boundaries, so as to secure its own gains.) Obviously, we cannot know, a priori, whether a new state likes or dislikes any particular entitlement. And that is indeed the point: the new entitlements that accrue to the new state at its birth are those that the international system has imposed upon the new state. If pressed to make a judgment whether the host of entitlements as a whole are a blessing or a curse to the new nation, we would conclude that, on the whole, the system of entitlements is beneficial to the new nation. This conclusion follows from the simple observation that international entitlements did not descend from God, but rather they evolved slowly over time to serve the collective self-interest of all the states. It is unlikely, therefore, that a system of rules that serves the collective self-interest would be inimical to the individual interests of any given state. Nevertheless, it is possible that *some* of the entitlements would be contrary to the interest of our new nation. If so, there is nothing our new nation can do about it. The list of entitlements is a given; they are thrust upon our new nation without its initial consent.

At least, there is no provable manifestation of initial consent by the new nation. But there is an inferred consent which stems from our new nation taking its position among the community of nations. By asserting the inviolability of its borders from external attack, our new nation defines itself as a state that has internationally recognized boundaries. Indeed, it is hard to think of what our new nation would be if it did not have those boundaries, and therefore the inference of its consent to statehood is very powerful. Our new nation also has the entitlement to send ambassadors to other states who want to receive them; and even before the first treaty is concluded giving those ambassadors diplomatic protection, there is an international entitlement that they have initial diplomatic immunity to proceed to other countries to negotiate such treaties. Moreover, our new nation is the beneficiary of the whole set of entitlements regarding its capacity to enter into binding treaties with other nations, and to have those treaties construed and applied according to the customary international law regarding the interpretation of treaties. Additionally, our new nation, at birth, benefits from the entitlement that all nations are free to use the high seas, to send satellites into outer space, to claim for themselves a territorial sea, an underlying continental shelf, and an exclusive economic zone. It may be that our new nation does not border upon any ocean, or if it does so border, that there is no underlying continental shelf. All the international entitlements say is that if a nation does border on an ocean it is entitled to claim an exclusive territorial sea, and if it has a continental shelf it is entitled to claim certain exclusivities with regard thereto. The full list of entitlements embraces areas such as the entitlement to protect nationals abroad, the protection of the laws of war and rules regulating the conduct of hostilities, rules regarding the exertion of extraterritorial jurisdiction, and among other topics the following: international servitudes, succession of states, international rivers, lakes, canals and straits, polar regions, rights and duties of states in outer space, nationality and status of ships, piracy, slavery, international traffic in narcotics, nationality and statelessness, rights of aliens, asylum, extradition, international communications including satellites and "jamming" of broadcasts, immunities of states and their agencies and subdivisions, protection of human rights, diplomatic and consular privileges and immunities, status and privileges of international organizations, status of armed forces on foreign territory, limits of criminal jurisdiction, enforcement of foreign judgments and commercial arbitrations, treaties (entry into force, modification, termination), pacific blockade, reprisals, arms shipments, relations between belligerents and neutrals, etc. The point of making such a list is that for our new nation, all the specific entitlements in these subject-matter categories work two ways: first, to benefit our new nation to the extent that it has any interest in claiming any specific entitlement; and second, to impose upon our new nation the duty to respect those same entitlements when they are asserted against it by other nations.

Taken as a whole, these entitlements define what it is to be a "nation" or "state" in the modern world.[21] To be sure, these are the legal definitional parameters of a nation, but a nation is admittedly a legal fiction. As a construct of international law, a nation is nothing more nor less than a bundle of entitlements, of which the most important ones define and secure its boundaries on a map, while others define its jurisdictional competency and the rights of its citizens when they travel outside its borders.

Some writers have tried to base all these competences on the

---

21. *See* Chapter 5, *infra*.

"consent" of the nation.[22] They are thus compelled by their own logic to assert that a new nation is not bound by any particular rule of international law until it has consented to that rule.[23] The new nation is then in a preferred position; it can pick and choose among the rules those that it likes. This pick-and-choose position is clearly wrong as a matter of historical fact as well as logic. Historically, existing nations have never allowed new nations to pick and choose, nor have new nations asserted a *tabula rasa* position.[24] Logically, if a new nation tried to assert such a position, the reaction of the other nations might well be that the new nation's *rights* as well as its duties are up for grabs, thus placing the new nation in a perilous position vis-à-vis its boundaries and other basic legal entitlements. Perhaps some such calculus has operated to dissuade any new nation from making the claim that these writers assert.

"Consent" is an elusive notion for yet another reason. If international law is truly grounded in each nation's consent, then what is to stop a nation from withdrawing its consent at any time? Specifically, when a nation finds a particular rule of international law disadvantageous to it, it could simply withdraw consent—even up to the very moment of application of the unwanted rule. The result would be to wipe out the notion of "law." Of course, some writers, focusing on consent, claim that international law is illusory anyway.[25] That claim begs the question, for if international law is real, as I have been arguing, then "consent" does not explain its application to states. What the writers are trying to say is that consent is such a

---

22. *See, e.g.*, G. Tunkin, *Theory of International Law* 123-33 (1974); G. Van Hoof, *Rethinking the Sources of International Law* 76-82 (1983). For a critique of "consent" theories, see A. D'Amato, *supra* note 16, at 187-99. Even the writers who insist upon consent will accept *tacit* consent; yet it is a short move from tacit consent to inferred consent to legally inferred consent, *i.e.*, that given all the other elements that constitute a norm of international law, consent ultimately is inferred. To the extent that writers espouse consent out of a notion of the sovereignty of national *will* (an insistence based on positivist theory), none of them has ever answered the following question: What happens if a state, having given its consent to a rule, wants to change its mind? Such a change of mind would appear logically to be precluded by consent theory (at least, if that theory purports to explain how nations become obligated), and yet would seem to be required by the predominance of the will.

23. *See, e.g.*, Van Hoof, *supra* note 22, at 78. Accord E. Zoller, *Peacetime Unilateral Remedies: An Analysis of Countermeasures* 6 (1984).

24. A. D'Amato, *supra* note 16, at 191-92.

25. *See, e.g.*, Watson, "Legal Theory, Efficacy and Validity in the Development of Human Rights Norms in International Law," 1979 *U. Ill. L.J.* 609, 632-35; *cf.* Tieya, "The Third World and International Law," in *The Structure and Process of International Law, supra* note 12, at 955 (recognizing continued validity of international law, but noting changes due to emergence of Third World interests).

powerful explanatory mechanism that international law as a result is not real. This puts a theoretically false cart before the horse.

If one wants to insist upon finding a role for the concept of consent, it may be useful to view consent in the following way: A nation is a bundle of entitlements which define what the nation is. In choosing to exist as a nation, the nation has consented to the bundle of entitlements. However, this scholastic exercise in logic, the sort that Pascal liked to satirize, is only necessary if someone is actively worried about the concept of consent and its role in international law. The simple conclusion follows that a nation is coextensive with its international legal entitlements.

This conclusion in turn illustrates why, as a matter of its very identity, a state should act in such a manner as to preserve its entitlements. Yet, its identity as a state, its "bundle of entitlements," is dependent upon the acquiescence of all the other states in the system. Since every state has the same bundle of entitlements—otherwise there would be legal inequality among states, a proposition that has never seriously been advocated—the other states in the system have an obvious interest in acquiescing in the entitlements of any given state. In this manner, a new state starts out, as we have seen, with its full complement of entitlements.

But just as all the states in the international legal system have a collective interest in acquiescing to all the entitlements for any given state in the system, they also have an interest in preserving the entitlements per se. For ease of illustration, let us consider the previously mentioned entitlement of diplomatic immunity. All the states in the system have an interest in the preservation of this particular entitlement. The existence of this entitlement, like other entitlements, helps define what a state is and what the international legal system is. The system would be something different, perhaps diminished, if the entitlement of diplomatic immunity were undermined.

To preserve this entitlement, the states in the system collectively will allow certain actions to be taken against any given state which violates the entitlement of diplomatic immunity. Prior to 1979, it would have been difficult to come up with a single example of a state which directly violated that entitlement. In nearly every case up to 1979 in which a diplomat's life or liberty was threatened, the host state immediately took action against those persons who threatened the diplomat. If the host state itself wanted to expel the diplomat, it

21

would arrange for the diplomat's return. But in 1979, after some radical students occupied the American Embassy in Tehran, the government of Iran took the unprecedented step of ratifying the action and holding the American diplomatic personnel hostage. This was a case of a deliberate violation of international law, the violation of the entitlement of diplomatic immunity. To allow it to go unremedied would constitute a threat to the existence of that entitlement in the international legal system.

What legal recourse did states have to prevent the erosion of such an entitlement? An obvious move would be to allow the United States to violate Iran's similar entitlement by arresting diplomatic and consular officials of Iran who were physically present in the United States at the time of the takeover of the American embassy in Iran. While this tit-for-tat strategy is generally regarded as legal under international law, it is not always a particularly effective strategy.[26] As we saw previously in the idealized example of two states at total war, the tit-for-tat strategy would simply eliminate the incipient ambassadorial-immunity entitlement and plunge the states back into the chaos of total war. Today, under a more developed international legal system, the tit-for-tat strategy might not have as negative an outcome, but it nevertheless could operate to erode rather than to preserve the entitlement in question. For instance, if the United States had jailed all Iranian diplomatic and consular officials, such an action at least in theory could be interpreted not as an attempt to punish Iran for its initial act but rather as a recognition that Iran's act was correct and that in fact diplomats are not entitled to immunity—I say "in theory" because this example may appear to be farfetched. But

---

26. For a recent, provocative explication of the tit-for-tat strategy, see R. Axelrod, *The Evolution of Cooperation* (1984). *See also* A. Rapoport, *Strategy and Conscience* 48-57 (1964); A. Rapoport, *Fights, Games, and Debates* 166-79 (1960). The most complete analysis of the legality of countermeasures under international law is E. Zoller, *supra* note 23. However, it is not clear whether Professor Zoller confines her conclusions to countermeasures which do not violate an independent norm of international law (i.e., those which may simply violate a state's treaty commitments or other such obligations owing to a particular state). In the *Case Concerning the Air Service Agreement (U.S. v. France)*, appended to Professor Zoller's book, the Arbitral tribunal concludes:

> Under the rules of present-day international law, and unless the contrary results from special obligations arising under particular treaties, notably from mechanisms created within the framework of international organisations, each State establishes for itself its legal situation vis-a-vis other States. If a situation arises which, in one State's view, results in the violation of an international obligation by another State, the first State is entitled, within the limits set by the general rules of international law pertaining to the use of armed force, to affirm its rights through counter-measures.

Id. at 166-67.

since the content of international law depends upon the recognition of what the entitlements are by all the states in the system, the action I have just hypothesized by the United States and Iran might well be interpreted as a new understanding of the entitlement of diplomatic immunity, i.e., that such immunity exists no longer. Consider the following more realistic example of the same theoretical process: nation A announces a territorial sea of 300 miles from its coastline; nation B argues that A has illegally infringed upon the high seas by attempting to expropriate part of it, and in retaliation, nation B proclaims its own 300-mile territorial sea. Despite what nation B said, the action it took tends to reinforce A's claim. Thus, rather than challenging A's claim to a 300-mile territorial sea, B has reinforced it. A new rule, giving coastal states a much larger area of jurisdiction over the high seas will evolve. And the old entitlement—that the high seas were open to all nations—will partly be eroded by these new claims for an extensive territorial sea. Thus, the tit-for-tat strategy, in this example, not only fails to deter the original entitlement violation but in fact reinforces it.

The United States, in fact, did not retaliate by jailing Iranian consular and diplomatic officials, although that action was considered and reported in the press.[27] Instead, the United States took steps that were also justified under international law and which constitute a more sophisticated (though, as we shall see, perhaps more dangerous) method of enforcement. The United States "froze" approximately thirteen billion dollars of Iranian deposits in American banks and in various European banks where the United States, through American corporations, had the power to act.[28] If it were not for the initial Iranian act of holding the American diplomats hostage, the United States would be unjustified under international law in violating the Iranian entitlement to the use of its own bank deposits abroad. Indeed, by freezing the Iranian assets, the United States was effectively confiscating the interest those assets would have earned.[29] This was a direct deprivation of Iranian property by the United States. Yet there was no condemnation of the American action by the international

27. See New York Times, Dec. 13, 1979, at § A1, col. 5.
28. See Nickel, "Battling for Iran's Frozen Billions," Fortune, Dec. 15, 1980, at 117.
29. At the time the $13 billion was blocked, interest rates were approximately 15 percent. The assets were blocked for slightly over one year. At compound interest, this amounts to interest earned, and unpaid, of over two billion dollars. When the hostages were returned to the United States, the United States agreed to pay, in partial settlement, interest of $800 million to Iran, as reported in The New York Times. Jan. 21, 1981, at § A9, col. 1.

community; instead, the American action in violating a different Iranian entitlement from the one that Iran violated in the first place (diplomatic immunity) was tolerated by general silence, whereas governments from all over the world expressly condemned Iran's seizure of the American embassy. The workings of international law are rarely as explicit as scholars might like them to be, but I believe we are entitled to infer from the reaction of the community of nations that they did not perceive a threat to the shared entitlement of keeping state-owned deposits in foreign banks as a result of the American action, but rather regarded the U.S. action as a temporary infringement of an Iranian entitlement for the limited purpose of enforcing the original entitlement of diplomatic immunity.[30] Thus, the international community implicitly accepted the legality of a strategy that violates an offending nation's entitlements in order to repudiate that nation's initial offence. In the Iran-United States case, the strategy worked well, for the American diplomatic personnel were all safely returned to the United States, and the United States lifted the freeze on Iranian assets.

Of course, I am not attempting here to support my theory of a reciprocal-violation-of-a-different-entitlement by the single case of the American hostages in Tehran. The pattern is a general one and can be substantiated by numerous examples.[31] Moreover, the tit-for-a-different-tat pattern "makes sense" in a legal system that does not have a central court of compulsory jurisdiction, a world legislature, and a world police force.[32] The absence of these institutions does not

30. Two judges out of the fifteen on the World Court felt that the blocking of Iranian assets should be set off against any reparations owing to the United States, but all fifteen members of the Court agreed that Iran's initial detention of the American diplomatic and consular personnel was unlawful. See *United States Diplomatic and Consular Staff in Tehran* (U.S. v. Iran), 1980 I.C.J. 3, 51 (Morozov, J., dissenting); *id.* at 58 (Tarazi, J., dissenting).

31. See generally E. Zoller, *supra* note 23.

32. The employment of a different countermeasure raises the question of proportionality of response. International law has not evolved a specific measure of proportionality, but it is at least clear that the countermeasure cannot be wholly disproportionate to the initial delict. The *Air Service Case*, in E. Zoller, *supra* note 23, at 167, calls attention to the possibility of a wholly different countermeasure, and states that it should be measured in terms of quality as well as quantity in order to judge proportionality. Interestingly, the social science literature bears out the effectiveness of quantitatively non-measurable responses so long as there is an ordinal ordering of preferences. As Axelrod demonstrates, *supra* note 26, at 17-18, the payoffs of the two players need not be comparable, nor symmetric, nor measurable on an absolute scale, and there is no need to assume rationality on the part of the players. The only ordering of preferences is that a nation prefers there to be no rule violation, and prefers taking a countermeasure in the event of a rule violation rather than letting the violator get away with a rule violation. In turn, taking countermeasures, in an iterated series (which for international purposes can extend over the centuries) is a stable and robust strategy for deterring the initial delict. Nations in their interactions seem to have evolved a tit-for-tat or a tit-for-a-different-tat strategy

mean that international law isn't really law; rather, it simply means that international law is enforced in a different way.

There is a danger in relying on the enforcement of international law by allowing a retaliatory deprivation of the offending nation's entitlement. The danger is the potential escalation of entitlement violations, ultimately leading to international anarchy. In the idealized case where there was only one entitlement, its destruction put the nations back into anarchy. The same result is possible if in the modern world there is runaway destruction of many entitlements. But the fact that law can become ineffective doesn't mean that it isn't law in the first place. Some people expressed fear when President Richard Nixon faced impeachment that he might order the military to seize Congress and the Supreme Court and proclaim himself immune from any attempt to dislodge him as President. While this may not have been a very realistic fear, if such a scenario had occurred, it would mean that constitutional law had deteriorated; but it would not mean that no constitutional law existed prior to Nixon's seizure of the reins of government. Similarly, while international law could destroy itself through a runaway series of violations of entitlements, until then it polices itself by the meta-rule I have described: that it is legal to deter the violation of an entitlement by threatening a counter-violation of the same or a different entitlement. This latter enforcement action is the "physical sanction" provided by the international legal system, just as the rules regulating police, prison officials, sheriffs, etc., are its domestic legal equivalents.

IV. Conclusion

International law is enforced by the process I have described as reciprocal-entitlement violation. The violation may be of the same entitlement or, more likely nowadays, of a different entitlement. But it is on the whole an effective process—as effective for the international legal system as is the enforcement of most laws in domestic systems via the state-sanctioned deprivation of one or more entitlements held by individual citizens or corporations. Occasionally peo-

in their numerous interactions over the centuries, and this probably accounts for the stability of international legal rules. The tit-for-a-different-tat strategy is actually codified in the Vienna Convention on the Law of Treaties, art. 60, *supra* note 19, at 701, allowing a party to suspend *any* treaty obligation or obligations if the other party commits a material breach of any of its obligations.

ple or states will break laws despite the presence of enforcement machinery, but that does not mean that there were no laws to begin with. Nor, as I have tried to argue, should we swing to the opposite side of the spectrum and say that enforcement has nothing to do with whether laws exist. We don't need to take such an extreme position with respect to international law because there is, in fact, enforcement, resulting in a stable system of international entitlements. It is impossible to understand why nations do or refrain from doing the things they do without understanding what entitlements are included in the bundle and how nations act to preserve their full complement of existing entitlements. In this sense, international law is a very realistic component of the picture that political scientists try to draw of how nations behave. The "serious students of law" who claim that international law isn't really "law" make the same mistake that some political scientists make in ignoring norms in order to be "scientific" in their "descriptions." A state cannot be described without reference to its entitlements, nor can its actions be fully understood without reference to the steps it takes to preserve those entitlements.

2

FORCE OR ENFORCEMENT?*

There seems to be an enormous conceptual confusion in theories about law in general, but most importantly in theories of international law, between *force* and *enforcement*. I use the word "conceptual" here because what we *see* is one thing but how we conceive of it is something else entirely. Let us suppose that we see *A* hitting *B* over the head with a stick. *A* is clearly engaged in a use of force; that is what we see. Yet the legal analysis only begins with what we see. Legally, we have to ask whether *A* is *justified* in hitting *B* over the head with a stick. This is not the same as asking whether *A* has a *reason* to use the stick; *A* may indeed have a reason, such as the claim that *B* insulted him, or that *B* did not call him "sir," or that *B* was late to work, or any of thousands of similar such reasons. "Justification" is a much more restrictive concept. *A* might be justified in hitting *B* if *B* had just pulled out a knife and was in the act of trying to stab *A*; this is the well-known justification of self-defense. Or if *A* is a policeman and *B* has just committed a felony and is resisting arrest, then under proper circumstances *A* might be justified in hitting *B*. One rough test we might employ in asking whether *A* is justified in hitting *B* is to ask whether *B* in turn would be justified in hitting back. If *A* is a policeman, *B* would not be justified; nor would *B* be justified if *B* had initiated the encounter by threatening *A* with a knife. Of course, this rough "test" is not really a test, since we'd have to

---

*This chapter was co-authored in part with Robert B. von Mehren.

know *A*'s justification before we can determine whether *B* in turn is justified in resisting. But it does give us some general *sense* of the equities involved.

These issues come up when we see a nation using military force against another nation. If nation *A* drops bombs on nation *B*, nation *A* will invariably have a reason to do so; whether it is justified is a different question. In early 1986 the United States dropped bombs for a period of a couple of hours on Libya; the reason given was Libya's support of terrorists, some of whom had purportedly killed Americans in Europe. Was this use of force justified?

If, as some people charged, the United States dropped the bombs on Libya because the United States disliked Khadaffi (the ruler of Libya) and in addition because the United States wanted to project a "cowboy" image, then it would have been an unjustified use of force. Would it have then been illegal under international law? The answer is yes, given the United Nations Charter of 1945, the Kellogg-Briand Pact of 1928, and other multilateral agreements representing an international consensus against the unjustified transboundary use of force. Clearly this wasn't always the international law rule. But it is the rule today. An unjustified use of military force against another nation is illegal. The other nation would be justified in retaliating, and that retaliation would not legally be a justification for counter-retaliation.

Thus the question is whether the United States' raid on Libya was *justified*. Not any reason will do; the reason has to be of a kind that is cognizable under international customary law. And here we get to the distinction between force and enforcement.

The use of force, I contend, is only legal under international law if it is an *enforcement* action or if it is undertaken in self-defense. All other uses of force are ruled out by the U.N. Charter and other instruments evidencing customary international law.

Self-defense might itself be considered a kind of *enforcement* action. It's an immediate attempt to repel an unjustified aggressive use of force. For example, we wouldn't consider the felon, in my earlier example, to be justified in resisting the policeman's use of force against him, since the policeman's action (we assume) was justified. So, self-defense really only comes into play when there is an unjustified attack. Hence, in this sense, self-defense is a species of enforcement action—it is a use of force designed to protect against, and repel, an invader who has invaded illegally.

Force or Enforcement?

In any event, *enforcement* is the alternative to naked force. The latter is illegal under international law. Hence, for conceptual clarity I urge the adoption of the idea that the only legal use of transboundary military force by nations in the world today is for purposes of *enforcement*.

Enforcement of what? Of international law, clearly. Unless there is a violation of a norm of international law, there can be no enforcement action. The state that resorts to force when there is no violation of international law is therefore acting illegally. Thus, in the Libya case, the only justification open to the United States to drop bombs on Libya was the claim that Libya was violating international law by supporting terrorists.

Would that have been a good claim? Clearly, if a *government* itself supports and directs terrorist acts, that government is engaged in an undeclared war against other states and their citizens. There is no doubt that such a government has violated international law. In the Libya case, the only issue is a factual one: Did the government of Libya direct and support acts of international terrorism? If so, Libya violated international law.

Assuming the facts could be shown that Libya directed and supported acts of international terrorism, then the United States' response was an act of *enforcement*. That does not answer the question entirely of whether the United States acted legally, but at least it gets us fairly far in our analysis. To recapitulate, we've seen that the United States' act in dropping bombs on Libya was in response to a violation of international law by Libya (assuming the facts could be shown), and hence would be justified, if at all, under the rubric of the term *enforcement*.

But once an act is categorized under the rubric *enforcement*, there are then certain legal tests we have to apply to that act that stem from the notion of enforcement. These tests circumscribe the use of force. Some of these tests are:

(1) Was the enforcement carried out by the appropriate party? (In the Libya case, should the enforcing party be the United Nations instead of the United States? Or a coalition of states?)

(2) Was the enforcement proportional to the harm? (No one would contend that Libyan sponsorship of isolated acts of terrorism would justify the United States to drop nuclear weapons on Libya and destroy the entire country and its inhabitants. Hence there is clearly a question of proportionality in all of these cases of enforcement.)

(3) Was the enforcement of limited duration? (The raid on Libya was over in a matter of hours.)

(4) Was there an attempt to use enforcement to effect a change in the territorial integrity or political independence of the country that was attacked?

These questions of enforcement tie in to the previous chapter on reciprocal entitlement violations. International law is not a system of law that is centrally enforced; rather it is, in a sense, "democratically" enforced. An entitlement violation can engender a reciprocal entitlement violation. Sometimes the reciprocal violation is a use of force, in which case we can call it an enforcement action.

Let us now consider the classic cases of "justification" for the use of force: self-defense, self-help, and to "get even." These cases will throw light on the legal parameters of enforcement action at the same time that they help shade in the scope of justification.

When is the transboundary use of military force justified under customary international law? The most obvious justification is self-defense. But, we must ask, self-defense of what? Of territory, certainly. But what of ships or aircraft over the high seas? Or of nationals abroad? Or of their property abroad? Or of "vital interests?"

Related to self-defense is self-help. When is forcible self-help allowable under customary international law? And what about helping others? Suppose military force is needed to prevent a nation from committing genocide against its own citizens. Would that be a situation negating the normal prohibition on transboundary military force not in self-defense?

I. Self-Defense

A. Of Territory

1. *Self-defense of territory against armed attack*: It seems clear that in the present state of international law, a nation can legally use force in its self-defense. The Charter of the United Nations provides in Article 51:

> Nothing in the present Charter shall impair the inherent right of individuals or collective self-defense *if an armed attack occurs*

against a Member of the United Nations, until the Security Council has taken the measures necessary to maintain international peace and security. . . . [Italics supplied.]

In applying this doctrine of self-defense a threshold question arises as to what constitutes "armed attack". "Armed attack" suggests territorial trespass. Thus, aid to revolutionary groups is probably not a case of "armed attack," as we shall examine more closely below. However, an attack by "volunteers" or bands or irregulars can amount to an "armed attack," if these groups are shown to be in complicity with the government of the state from which they operate.

The doctrine of self-defense does not permit an excessive response to an "armed attack." The magnitude of the response must be related to the magnitude of the attack, and to be legal the response must be proportionate to the force applied by the attacker. Daniel Webster's formulation in the *Caroline* case, which has been repeated by countless writers and governments since 1842, and has been invoked by the Nuremberg and Tokyo Tribunals, requires "nothing unreasonable or excessive" in the self-defense action, "since the act, justified by the necessity of self-defense, must be limited by that necessity, and kept clearly within it."[1] Japan initially defended its invasion of Manchuria in 1931 to the League of Nations as arising out of the need for self-defense. But even if it is assumed that the Japanese in 1931 were justified in their initial use of force, it is impossible to regard their later operations as measures of self-defense.[2] The publicists seem to be of the same opinion with respect to the Goa operation by India in 1961. Self-defense can only go so far; after that, it is aggression.

The entire concept of self-defense and its limitation of reasonableness amount to simple common sense. Since a defense is an action to repel an aggression, any defense out of proportion to the initial one becomes an aggression of its own.

2. *Self-defense of territory against force short of armed attack*: It is somewhat difficult to imagine situations where physical force short of armed attack is applied against the territory of a state. One possibility might be that, during a natural disaster, a foreign state would attempt to jam essential radio communications. The general view of the commentators is that, since no armed attack is involved, the

1. VI *Works of Daniel Webster*, 250-61 (12th ed. 1860).
2. *See* Brierly, *Law of Nations*, 316 (5th ed. 1955).

affected state cannot forcibly respond and justify its response by the rights of self-defense. This view reads Article 51 of the Charter of the United Nations as restricting the doctrine of self-defense to cases of armed attack. A contrary interpretation might be urged on the ground that Article 51 simply recognizes the right of self-defense and, hence, cannot be read to be a limitation on that right. It stresses the term "inherent right," arguing that such a right in principle cannot be limited.[3]

In any event, any response against force short of armed attack would be subject to the doctrine of proportionality and could not be legal if the response were excessive.

3. *Self-defense of territory against threat of force*: The international law of the 19th century may have permitted anticipatory self-defense ("pre-emptive strike") in certain circumstances. The exchange between Webster and Ashburton concerning the *Caroline* case would seem to leave open the possibility that in some situations the gun could be legally "jumped." However, the majority of commentators are now of the view that Article 51 of the United Nations Charter has made it illegal to "jump the gun" and fire first in anticipation of an armed attack. They reason that there is nothing in the Charter which justifies jumping the gun. If there is a broader right of "self-defense" than that specifically recognized by Article 51, there would have been no need for Article 51. When the Charter was drafted, they argue, there is weighty evidence that the United Nations was intended to have a monopoly on the use of force in international relations, and that the Article 51 exception was to be as narrow as possible. More importantly, in a nuclear world of "bluff," it may be impossible to tell whether a nation intends an immediate armed attack. Moreover, the requirements of proportionality suggest that the use of armed force in return for a serious bluff by the other side would clearly be excessive. Preparations for attack can be countered by preparations to resist effectively. A threat of nuclear attack can be countered with a like threat. But no reading of Article 51 could countenance answering a nuclear threat with all-out nuclear attack.

The real issue, if the majority view of Article 51 is accepted, may be the meaning of "armed attack" as those words are used in the Article. For example, is the launching of a rocket toward a state an

---

3. *Compare* Brownlie, "The Use of Force in Self-Defence," 37 *British Yearbook Int'l Law* 183, 239-41 (1961) with Stone, *Legal Controls of International Conflict*, 244 (2d rev. ed. 1959).

armed attack upon that state? Is a declaration of war or an ultimatum an armed attack, or does the attack begin only when it penetrates the frontier? Are isolated, sporadic incursions by armed bands armed attacks?

The first of these examples raises the question whether a rocket launching is an unequivocal attack or whether it might be a bluff with the launching state intending to destroy the rocket before it reaches the frontier. The second example is complicated by the fact that the declaration of war or ultimatum would in itself be a violation of Article 2(4) of the Charter. However, the basic legal question insofar as Article 51 is concerned would still be whether the situation was such that the declaration or ultimatum was the commencing of an armed attack or merely a bluff. Certainly, if it were the former, the aggrieved state should be able to meet the attack at its borders and perhaps just before its borders have been violated. The final example raises the question whether an armed attack must be a continuous series of events or whether episodic raids are armed attacks. When Israel, subjected to fedayeen raids, attacked Egypt, many United Nations members thought that such raids did not constitute an "armed attack" within Article 51, because of their discontinuous or isolated nature. The majority felt that the invasion of Egyptian territory was disproportionate to the previous attacks suffered. In the view of the majority, the previous attacks could have been resisted individually, but "preventive" action against Egypt violated the proportionality doctrine. Israel's reply was that the series of small raids added up to one big raid, and thus Israel's large-scale attack was proportionate to the harm it suffered.

Discussion of the Caroline Case

The episode that is known in international law as the *Caroline* case began in 1847. A rebellion in Canada against the British Crown was in its dying stages. Some Canadian insurgents obtained American support in Buffalo, New York. A body of about 1,000 persons, mostly Americans, took over Navy Island lying in the Niagara River on the Canadian side of the border, and used it as a base for raids on the shore. The steamer *Caroline* was used to ship arms and supplies to the group on the Island. The American authorities having done nothing about all this, the British commander across the river decided that the only way to cut off the traffic in supplies was to destroy the *Caroline*. When the *Caroline* was resting between supply trips at Fort Schlosser in New York, several boatloads of English soldiers slipped up to it in the nighttime, boarded it, and started shooting at the defenseless crew, which promptly abandoned ship. Two Americans were shot and killed (two others were taken prisoner temporarily in Canada). The English soldiers set fire to the boat, cut it loose, and sent it over Niagara Falls.

Much diplomatic correspondence ensued, many points of law were raised, and the case came to a head when one McLeod, one of the soldiers who asserted that he had participated in the raid, was caught in the United States and tried for murder and arson. Although he was eventually acquitted, his trial rekindled interest in the *Caroline* affair and led to the famous exchange between Webster and Ashburton.

In 1842, Daniel Webster, then Secretary of State, addressed a diplomatic note to the British government setting forth the American position that the British were responsible unless the British government could show a

> necessity of self-defense, instant, overwhelming, leaving no choice of means, and no moment for deliberation. It will be for it to show, also, that the local authorities of Canada, even supporting the necessity of the moment authorized them to enter the territories of the United States at all, did nothing unreasonable or excessive; since the act, justified by the necessity of self-defense, must be limited by that necessity, and kept clearly within it. It must be shown that admonition or remonstrance to the persons on board the *Caroline* was impracticable, or would have been unavailing; it must be shown that daylight could not be waited for; that there could be no attempt at discrimination between the innocent and the guilty; that it would not have been enough to seize and detain the vessel; but that there was a necessity, present and inevitable, for attacking her in the darkness of the night, while moored to the shore, and while unarmed men were asleep on board, killing some and wounding others, and then drawing her into the current, above the cataract, setting her on fire, and careless to know whether there might not be in her the innocent with the guilty, or the living with the dead, committing her to a fate which fills the imagination with horror. A necessity for all this, the Government of the United States cannot believe to have existed.

Lord Ashburton, then British Foreign Minister, replied and, remarkably, accepted all the principles stated by Webster, but argued that the facts of the case fitted into such a framework. For example, the act was not excessive—the boat was set adrift so that the American property in the port would not be burned, and the attack took place at nighttime for the greatest efficiency of the attack and the least loss of life.

Thus, there was agreement on the law (setting a powerful legal precedent, albeit a verbal one) and disagreement of the facts. Ashburton satisfied Webster by apologizing for the fact that the act necessitated a violation of American territory. The matter was amicably concluded as part of the over-all Webster-Ashburton agreements.

4. *Self-defense of territory after change of title*: This question might be raised in this way. Assume that State *A* has been involved in a dispute with State *B* over a border area. *A* has occupied the area with its troops and the two countries have submitted the issue of the ownership of the area to a competent international tribunal. That tribunal ultimately awards the territory to *B*. After *A* is informed of the award, it refuses to pull its troops out and *B* decides to use force to expel them.

It is arguable here that *B* has been subjected to an "armed attack" by *A* within the meaning of Article 51 by *A*'s refusal to withdraw its troops after the award. This argument would proceed by urging that *A* attacked *B* when it first violated *B*'s territory by, as the tribunal found, illegally occupying territory which legally always belonged to *B*, and that this attack continues until *A* withdraws. The counter-argument might be that, conceding the initial attack by *B*, mere failure to withdraw is not a new attack nor does the old attack continue so as to permit *A* to avail itself of Article 51.

A related case was presented by the Argentine invasion of the Falkland Islands (Malvinas). Here, title to the Falklands was the subject of a long-standing dispute between the United Kingdom and Argentina, and diplomacy at the United Nations was proceeding with glacial slowness. Finally, Argentina decided to invade the islands. The United Kingdom responded, and in a war of brief duration drove the Argentine forces away. Whether this was a genuine case of "self defense" depends upon whether one accepts the British position as to sovereignty over the islands. But even if it was not a case of self-defense, nevertheless the world community ultimately sided with the

British, on the grounds that Argentina had no right to use military force to conquer territory whose title was the subject of peaceful negotiations. In this latter respect, perhaps the British counterattack was a justifiable example of self-help, of which more will be said below.

B. *Of Ships and Aircraft*

The principles discussed above relating to the self-defense of territory apply to ships and aircraft. The theory expressed in United Nations debate that the fedayeen raids on Israel were not "attacks" within Article 51, might lead to the conclusion that an isolated attack on a ship or aircraft does not justify the exercise of the right of self-defense. In any event, the doctrine of proportionality would probably restrict the response to one made by the craft being attacked or by other craft in the area at the time of the attack and would limit the magnitude of such responses to that reasonably required to defend against the attack. The mounting of a large scale unrelated riposte would run afoul of the principle of proportionality.

C. *Of Nationals or Property Abroad*

The problem whether the doctrine of self-defense extends to the defense of nationals or property threatened on the territory of another sovereign raises the issue of the meaning of "self." In the past, the predominate Western view of international law has included within the national interest for the purpose of self-defense citizens and property abroad. The use of force to put down the Boxer Rebellion of 1900 is an instance of intervention to protect nationals. For other examples, see United States Solicitor of the Department of State, *Memorandum on Right to Protect Citizens in Foreign Countries by Landing Forces* (3d ed. 1933). This history may be a barrier to "universal" acceptance of international law today.

The United Nations Charter appears to have altered the situation and made it difficult to argue that the old doctrine still survives. Article 2(4) prohibits the threat or use of force against the territorial integrity or political independence of any state. If State *A* harms the nationals of State B who are residing in A, it would not seem that A has violated Article 2(4). It may have caused a "threat to the peace" under Article 39, but this would be a matter for the Security Council and not for self-defense. However, if B "intervenes" in A to protect its nationals, there is a question whether B itself has violated Article 2(4). We will consider questions of this kind in the following two chapters.

It should be noted, however, that on numerous occasions in recent years, the argument has been advanced that self-defense applies to the protection of nationals or property abroad.

Britain, during the Suez intervention, maintained that it was acting to safeguard British lives. This argument did not get very far in the United Nations. Two years later the United States made a similar contention when sending troops to Lebanon. There was considerable evidence at the time that American lives were not seriously in danger in Lebanon. In the Cuban crisis, the United States government appears to have acquiesced to a limited degree in the proposition that an invasion of Cuba which would result in the loss of life of Soviet citizens in Cuba might provide the grounds for Russian military intervention on a greater scale. On the other hand, the Report of the Commission of Investigation into the Greek frontier incidents indicates that maltreatment of the Slavs in Greece did not absolve the Yugoslavs for their support of the frontier attacks.[4]

An argument could be advanced that intervention to protect nationals might be legal in some cases. If nation A is physically unable to protect the citizens of B within its territory (e.g., from riots or revolutions), B's intervention for the limited purpose of protecting its nationals—a job which A would presumably do if it could—would arguably not contravene A's "political independence," safeguarded by Article 2(4) of the Charter. Furthermore, it could be argued that such a limited foray to protect B's nationals would not violate A's "territorial integrity" under Article 2(4). One might contend that "territorial integrity" is not quite the same as territorial inviolability, and that "integrity" may be preserved even though there is a limited armed foray into a state's territory by another state. Thus Article 2(4) might not be considered a barrier to such action, as we shall see in subsequent chapters. Article 2(3) requiring the settlement of inter-

4. *U.N. Security Council Official Record* 2d year, IX Spec. Supp. No. 2, at 110 (S/360/Rev. 1 (1947)).

national disputes "by peaceful means" would also not in itself be a barrier since, on the assumption that A would protect B's nationals if it had the power to do so, there is no "dispute" between A and B.

Yet this line of argument carries overtones of a justification for self-help which itself may no longer be legal. Any time an opening wedge for "intervention" is allowed, there is a possibility of abuse. One of the underlying assumptions pervading the United Nations system was not to allow nations unilaterally, on pretext of safeguarding their nationals abroad, to open the way for ultimate aggression.

The United States appears to have explicitly recognized the new principles, at least with respect to Latin America, by adhering in 1948 to the Charter of the Organization of American States. This Charter provides in Article 15:

> No State or group of States has the right to intervene, directly or indirectly, for any reason whatever, in the internal or external affairs of any other State.

Article 17 provides:

> The territory of a State is inviolable; it may not be the object, even temporarily, of military occupation or of other measures of force taken by another State, directly or indirectly, on any grounds whatever.

D. Of Vital Interests

In the 18th and 19th centuries, the majority opinion among publicists appears to have been that a nation is entitled to use force for "self-preservation," and that a nation is competent to judge for itself what interests are vital to its self-preservation.

In 1934, the United States and British governments denied that Japan had the right to take action in China by virtue of her special interests there.[5] And in 1935, the League Council disregarded the Italian argument that its Ethiopian action was necessary to protect

---

5. *See* Willoughby, *The Sino-Japanese Controversy and the League of Nations*, 623-56 (1935).

vital interests, and that Italy had the right to decide the limits of self-defense for itself.[6]

Since the establishment of the United Nations, it now seems clear that "self-defense" is no legal justification for redress of violations of a nation's "vital interests." This conclusion flows from Article 2(3) and 2(4) of the Charter and is supported by United Nations practice. Protection of vital interests was one of the main claims made by Britain in its invasion of Egypt in 1956. The Colombian delegate summed up the United Nations consensus: "the use of force or armed intervention to secure rights, even lawful rights, has been strictly prohibited" by the United Nations Charter.

II. Self-Help

A. To Secure Justice

Prior to 1920, self-help to secure justice was accepted as legal more often than not in the literature. The lack of international organizations seemed in itself to require self-help and the objective of securing justice was appealing. This doctrine extended to matters such as the collection of debts.[7] It even extended to intervention in another state's affairs for the benefit of that state's own nationals, called "humanitarian intervention."[8] President Theodore Roosevelt wrote in 1904:

> Brutal wrongdoing, or impotence, which results in the general loosening of the ties of civilized society may finally require intervention by some civilized nation, and in the Western Hemisphere the United States cannot ignore its duty.[9]

Discussion of the Corfu Channel Case

The *Corfu Channel Case* was decided by the International Court of Justice in 1950. The facts divide the case into two segments. First,

---

6. *A.J.I.L.* 1-40 (1936 Supplement).
7. *See* Drago, "State Loans in their Relation to International Policy," 1 *A.J.I.L.* 695 (1907).
8. Stowell, *Intervention in International Law*, 51-62 (1921).
9. Moore, *Principles of American Diplomacy*, 262 (1918).

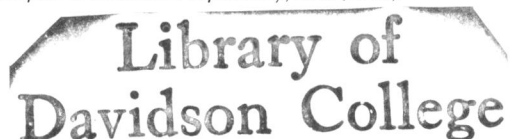

British warships in 1946 cruised through the Corfu Channel and, while in Albanian territorial waters, were seriously damaged by exploding mines. The Court held with respect to this part of the case that there is a right of innocent passage of warships through the Corfu Channel in peacetime because the strait connects two portions of the high seas and is an international waterway.

The second aspect of the case is relevant here. A few weeks after the British ships had been damaged, the British government informed Albania that the British navy would sweep the channel of the mines. Albania protested, but England went ahead and swept the channel, guarding its sweepers with an imposing array of cruisers and war vessels.

The key question faced by the Court with respect to his aspect of the case was whether the British minesweeping operation was legal under international law. Great Britain rested its case on two arguments: (1) It had to intervene in Albanian territorial waters in order to secure evidence to determine whether the mines were actually laid by Albania; if it did not intervene, the "evidence" might have been destroyed by Albania; and (2) the mine sweeping was justified as a measure of self-protection or self-help.

The Court's opinion said, as to these two points:

> The Court cannot accept such a line of defence. The Court can only regard the alleged right of intervention as the manifestation of a policy of force, such as has, in the past, given rise to most serious abuses and such as cannot, whatever the present defects in international organization, find a place in international law. Intervention is perhaps still less admissible in the particular form it would take here; for, from the nature of things, it would be reserved for the most powerful States, and might easily lend to perverting the administration of international justice itself.
>
> The Court cannot accept this defence either. Between independent States, respect for territorial sovereignty is an essential foundation of international relations. The Court recognizes that the Albanian Government's complete failure to carry out its duties after the explosions, and the dilatory nature of its diplomatic notes, are extenuating circumstances for the action of the United Kingdom Government. But to ensure respect for international law, of which it is the organ, the Court must declare that the action of the British Navy constituted a violation of Albanian sovereignty.

It is interesting to note that the Court's opinion contains no mention of the United Nations Charter and completely rejects the voluminous literature of the 19th century justifying certain policies of intervention. Most importantly, the Court suggests that, even if there be a gap in the United Nations Charter ("defects in international organization"), resort to force in self-help is illegal. In other words, customary international law apart from the Charter may have evolved by 1945 to prohibit many uses of force which the Charter itself prohibits. Yet to some extent, the Court's 1950 opinion 35 years later seems idealistic. It seems premised upon an effective Security Council if not an effective United Nations. Britain's acts from today's vantage point seem reasonable, proportionate to the harm, and hence—were it not for the Court's opinion—legal.

B. To Get Even

1. *Reprisals*: A reprisal is by strict definition an illegal act. Under earlier principles of international law, a reprisal could sometimes be legal, if it met certain conditions and were justified by the prior illegal act of the state against which the reprisal was directed. Subsequent to the establishment of the United Nations, however, it seems that reprisals can no longer be considered legal. Article 2(3) of the Charter requires states to "settle their international disputes by peaceful means," and under Article 33(2), the Security Council may "call upon" them to do so. Whether there is a category of use of force which is so minor that it can be viewed as legal under the Charter is considered in the discussion of pacific blockade below.

In the days when reprisals might have been legal, there existed certain rules circumscribing their use. Today, these rules may be said to add a special dose of legal obligation to the nation which decides to violate the law in the first instance by resorting to reprisals. (In this sense they are analogous to the 1949 Geneva Convention on the Protection of Civilian Persons in Time of War, even though war by 1949 was illegal.)

The rules limiting reprisals were these: (1) The occasion for the reprisal must be a previous act contrary to international law; (2) the reprisal must be preceded by an unsatisfied demand; (3) if the initial demand for redress is satisfied, no further demands may be made;[10] and (4) the reprisal must be proportionate to the offense.

Discussion of the Naulilaa, the Tampico and the Corfu Incidents

Naulilaa Incident: This incident gave rise to rules (1), (2) and (4) stated above.

In October 1914, while Portugal was neutral in World War I, a party of German officials crossed over into Portuguese Angola to discuss the purchase of supplies. A misunderstanding in interpretation arose; a Portuguese official seized the bridle of a German's horse and the rider struck the official. Another German drew a gun, the Portuguese fired and three Germans were killed. The German government made no demand for satisfaction upon Portugal, but in alleged reprisal German troops destroyed certain forts and posts in Angola. Fourteen years later, the Arbitral Tribunal found the reprisal illegal. The Portuguese act did not violate international law, being due to a misunderstanding. The German government did not make any prior demand. And the reprisal consisting of six acts was disproportionate to the incident of Naulilaa.

Tampico Incident: In 1914, a Mexican squad arrested at Tampico without cause a paymaster and two seamen of the U.S.S. Dolphin. The men were released shortly thereafter, and General Huerta, head of Mexico's provisional government, made a personal apology. But the United States Admiral in the area also demanded that the Mexicans salute, in a special ceremony, the United States flag by firing 21 guns. Huerta replied that he would do this only if the United States fired a like salute, gun for gun. The United States declined. President Wilson sought and obtained a joint congressional resolution to use United States forces "to enforce his demand for unequivocal amends for certain affronts and indignities."[11] United States marines thereupon landed at Vera Cruz and sized the customhouses. An army force later relieved the marines and occupied the city for several months. This was, effectively, the end of the matter.

---

10. This is one important difference between reprisal and war. In war, under The Classical Theory, A is not legally obliged to lay down its arms if B is ready to comply with A's request made before the war began.

11. 2 Hyde, *International Law*, 1662-78 (1955).

The joint congressional resolution disclaimed "any purpose to make war upon Mexico." Such disclaimers are legion in the history of reprisals. This makes sense: the nation making the reprisal elects to proceed by way of reprisal rather than by way of declaration of war. But as Thomas Jefferson wrote, reprisals have always resulted in a state of war when directed against a state strong enough to make that response.[12]

Corfu Incident: This is the most recent "classic" case of a reprisal. The Italian representative on the commission which in 1923 was marking out the frontier between Albania and Greece was shot, together with three of his assistants, by Greek bandits. Mussolini at once had his fleet bombard Corfu, killing several civilians. He occupied the island and demanded indemnity. Frightened, Greece paid 50,000,000 lire directly to Italy. The League of Nations was not prepared to take action directly against Italy on behalf of a small power.

A Commission of Jurists in 1924 said that under the Covenant of the League, it is for the Council to decide whether coercive measures which are not intended to constitute acts of war are inconsistent with the Covenant. In this, the Jurists are generally thought to have abdicated their responsibility for answering the question put to them.[13]

2. *Pacific blockade*: "Pacific blockades" were common in the 19th century. Scholars were divided, however, on whether any blockade could be "pacific." The majority view was that a pacific blockade was characterized by the limitation that it could not legally be enforced against third states. But most "pacific blockades" were enforced against third states.[14] Writers who said that a "pacific blockade" was a contradiction in terms, held that such blockades were illegal acts. However, if undertaken by way of "reprisal" for prior illegal offenses, then the blockade was often considered justified.

Pacific blockades were supposed to be subject to the following requirements. They had to be (1) declared by competent authority; (2) instituted after notification of the time and place they were to take effect; (3) used only after failure of negotiations; (4) reasonably ef-

---

12. *See Jefferson's Works*, 628.
13. *See*, in general, Wigmore, "The Case of *Italy v. Greece*," 18 *Illinois Law Review* 131 (1923).
14. *See* 2 Oppenheim, *International Law*, 148 n. 2 (7th ed. 1952).

fective (*i.e.*, no "paper blockades");[15] and (5) not excessive (*i.e.*, ships which broke the blockade could be sequestered, but not confiscated).[16]

The legal status of a pacific blockade today is a difficult question. It may turn on facts such as these: Does the blockade apply to ships of third countries or only to those of the blockaded country; does the blockade actually involve the use or threat of force; are the ships blockaded carrying weapons or merely goods?

Whether a pacific blockade is legal under the United Nations Charter turns upon Articles 2(3) and 2(4). The former requires United Nations members to settle their disputes "by peaceful means in such a manner that international peace and security, and justice, are not endangered." Is a pacific blockade a "peaceful means" or is a blockade of any type a warlike act? Even if such a blockade is a "peaceful means," will not resort to it endanger international peace?

Article 2(4) requires United Nations members to "refrain in their international relations from the threat or use of force against the territorial integrity or political independence of any state, or in any other manner inconsistent with the Purposes of the United Nations." Since a pacific blockade usually involves either the threat or use of force,[17] Article 2(4) would be contravened if the blockade were directed against territorial integrity or political independence or in a manner inconsistent with the purposes of the United Nations.

The Cuban quarantine of 1963 probably did not infringe the "territorial integrity" part of Article 2(4). The ships blockaded were those of third powers, not those of Cuba, and thus Cuban territorial integrity was not involved. Even if the ships blockaded had been Cuban ships, it is hard to see how Cuban territorial integrity would have been compromised, unless we accept the now discredited fiction that a ship is a floating island. If however, a pacific blockade were to be enforced within the territorial seas of the blockaded state, that could be a temporary infringement of territorial integrity, as it is a general rule of international law that the territorial sea is an inherent part of a nation's territory, for practically all purposes. For further discussion of whether a temporary infringement of territorial integrity violates Article 2(4), see the next two chapters.

---

15. *Declaration of Paris*, 1856, Rule 4).
16. *See* Grob, *Relativity of War and Peace*, 247-66 (1949); Hogan, *Pacific Blockade, passim* (1908).
17. Conceivably, a nation's ships might assemble in an area, blocking up ports or passageways but not threatening offensive forceful action against other vessels.

A pacific blockade might come closer to violating a nation's "political independence," by blocking its access to other states or by applying economic pressures so severe that freedom of political choice is lost. The concept of "political independence" has been formulated by McDougal and Feliciano as follows:

> Impairment of 'political independence' as an attack upon the institutional arrangement of authority and control in the target state . . . involves substantial curtailment of the freedom of decision-making through the effective and drastic reduction of the number of alternative policies open at tolerable costs to the officials of that state.[18]

A blockade would curtail alternatives. Whether the curtailment would be substantial might depend upon the scope and effectiveness of the blockade.

Lastly, it is uncertain whether a pacific blockade would be inconsistent with the "Purposes of the United Nations". The United States delegation at the drafting of the Charter said that this final phrase was intended to state in the broadest terms an all-inclusive prohibition against the use of force, and to ensure that there should be no loopholes.[19] However, it is clear that Article 51 providing for self-defense in the case of armed attack is a "loophole," and other as-yet-unthought-of loopholes may emerge as necessary to safeguard the Purposes of the Charter. One loophole might be argued to be pacific blockade. In the Cuban quarantine, President Kennedy stated that the purpose of the blockade was to maintain international peace and security by preventing an occasion for nuclear war. The first "purpose" of the United Nations is listed in Article 1(1) as the maintenance of international peace and security.

Another relevant article is Article 2(1): "The Organization is based on the principle of the sovereign equality of all its Members." A "principle" is a means to the effectuation of the organization's purposes. In this sense, one might argue that a pacific blockade would compromise a means (nation's sovereign equality) to the United Nations ends, and thus be "inconsistent with the Purposes of the United Nations" under Article 2(4). On the other hand, it can be argued that

---

18. McDougal and Feliciano, "Legal Regulation of Resort to International Coercion: Aggression and Self-Defence in Policy Perspective," 68 *Yale Law Journal* 1057, 1102 (1959).
19. *U.N.C.I.O. Doc.* v. 4, at 334-35 (Committee 1, Commission 1).

the principle of sovereign equality is satisfied if the blockaded nation is allowed to mount a reciprocal blockade.

A pacific blockade might violate the 1958 Geneva Convention on the High Seas, although this would be an argument by implication, and would depend in part on whether the ships being blocked carried commercial goods or weapons. The Convention states that a warship is not justified in boarding a foreign merchant ship on the high seas unless there is reasonable ground for suspecting piracy, slave trade, or that the ship is in fact not a foreign ship. By implication, other forcible acts are banned.

If enforced, a pacific blockade might violate the rule in the *I'm Alone Case*. In this case, an international commission of two members was established to consider and report on the sinking of the "I'm Alone," a Canadian rum-runner, on the high seas by the United States Coast Guard. The commission found, in a report rendered in 1935, that the sinking was "not justified by any principle of international law."[20] The United States accepted the report and paid the Canadians $50,000 in settlement.

Discussion of the Venezuela Blockade

In 1902 President Castro of Venezuela refused to settle certain claims of nationals of Germany, Great Britain, and Italy against Venezuela. These powers decided to set up a blockade of all vessels moving to Venezuela. Germany wanted a "pacific blockade" in order to by-pass a provision of the German Constitution calling for consent of the Bundesrat to all declarations of war. Great Britain refused to institute a "pacific blockade" on the ground that the Declaration of Paris of 1856, which laid down rules of blockade, was a statement of maritime law in time of *war*, and that the Declaration specifically provided that blockades, in order to be binding against third parties, must be made in time of war and not in time of "reprisals." In other words, Great Britain's view was that the blockade had to be a war blockade in order to be enforced against all nations. Germany accepted the British position, and asked the Bundesrat for a blockade. Germany's decision seems to have been based, at least in part, on

---

20. The report found that, on the basis of the facts, the doctrine of "hot pursuit" did not apply.

the position of the United States, which had indicated to the German ambassador that a pacific blockade would not be binding on the United States. Hence, in order to achieve an effective blockade, Germany said that a state of war existed between it and Venezuela.[21]

Germany, England, and Italy blockaded Venezuela, after Castro refused to give in to their demands. They notified all nations that any attempt to penetrate the blockade would result in seizure and detention of the offending vessel for trial in a prize court with probable ultimate confiscation of ship and cargo. The blockade lasted about two and a half months and ended after mediation by the United States.

The United States at no time protested the blockade against its ships. By merely labeling the blockade a "war blockade," Germany and England apparently succeeded in having the United States take the position of a neutral in time of war. The reality of the matter was, of course, that the United States made a political decision to acquiesce in the blockade rather than to oppose it. It did so because the latter course would have created a substantial risk that the European powers would land marines in Caracas and seize Venezuelan territory. President Theodore Roosevelt thought that an interference with freedom of the seas was to be preferred to a possible seizure of land in violation of the Monroe Doctrine.[22]

3. *Embargo*: An embargo is a forcible detention of *A*'s ships which are in *B*'s ports by *B*. It has also come to mean the detention of *A*'s ships in *A*'s ports by *B*.

If *A*'s ships are in *A*'s ports, the preceding discussion relating to pacific blockade would be applicable. If *A*'s ships are in *B*'s ports, *A* would not be justified under Article 2(3) and the conventional interpretation of 2(4) in using force against *B*. An embargo by *B* would

---

21. It is interesting to compare the German reasoning and decision of 1902 with the American quarantine of Cuba in 1962. In commenting on the Cuban blockade, Abram Chayes, Legal Adviser, Department of State, said:
> But there was a further over-riding limitation in the traditional rules: they were part of the Law of War which says that only a belligerent in wartime can invoke the right to blockade or search for contraband. Unless nations were at war, there could be no justification for any interference at all with ordinary maritime commerce. Thus some have maintained that everything done in the October crisis would have been 'legal' if only the United States had declared war on Cuba. This may be attractive as a syllogism, but it doesn't have very much to do with law.

Chayes, "Law and the Quarantine of Cuba," 41 *Foreign Affairs* 550, 552 (1963).

22. *See* Basdevant, "L'Action Coercitive Anglo-Germano-Italienne Contra le Venezuela 1902-1903," 11 *Revue Générale de Droit International Public* 362-458 (1904).

be a clear case of a situation or dispute which comes under Chapter VI, Pacific Settlement of Disputes, of the United Nations Charter and must be settled by peaceful means, or, if it gives rise to a threat to the peace, by the Security Council.

C. Indirect Aggression

"Indirect aggression" may be thought of as the aiding and abetting (but not controlling or directing) of non-nationals in their fight against their own or a foreign government, *e.g.*, supplying arms to rebels, or permitting them to train on one's territory. The Peace Through Deeds Resolution of the United Nations General Assembly condemns "any aggression, whether committed openly, or by fomenting civil strife in the interest of a Foreign Power."[23] The basic question is whether a particular set of facts amounts to true indirect aggression.

If the nation supplying arms to the rebels exercises any degree of control over their activities, then to the extent of such degree of control the nation is itself committing aggression. It is threatening or using force, contrary to Article 2(4), unless the rebels are engaged in a full-sized civil war in their own nation. In such a case, it is arguable that, if the rebels could properly be recognized as a government, the use of force would be in support of *their* "political independence."

The supplying of arms to rebel groups arguably contravenes Article 2(3) of the Charter, which calls upon members to "settle their international disputes by peaceful means in such a manner that international peace and security, and justice, are not endangered." But this article does not seem to have exerted much pressure on United Nations Practice.

The factual situation may be complicated if a nation has a long-standing policy of selling arms to any group which has the money to buy them. The sale of arms historically has been outside the reach of norms of international law. If a nation sells arms to all purchasers, must it discriminate against rebel groups? Not only is it difficult to assert such a legal prohibition, but it is also relatively easy for the selling nation in any event to sell to third parties who then broker the sales to the rebel groups.

---

23. *G.A. Res.* 380, 5th Sess. (1951).

Discussion of Early Cases

The growing complexity of "wars of national liberation" and "guerilla warfare" (where classic distinctions between combatants and civilians are blurred) makes it increasingly difficult to discern the international law of indirect agression. Three early United Nations cases indicate some of the pre-Vietnam considerations.

Greek Frontier: A United Nations Investigation Commission reported in 1947 that Yugoslavia had trained Greek refugees within the borders of Yugoslavia and had supplied them with arms and hospital facilities. It also found that Albania had set up camps for Greek refugees at which political and military instruction was given, and from which the refugees were clothed and transported to the border. It found that Bulgaria had allowed the refugees to cross over its territory to Greece on the way from Yugoslavia. The report and subsequent General Assembly resolutions found that this situation was contrary to Article 2(4), and that the indirect aid was illegal.

Guatemala: In 1954 Guatemala asked the Security Council to put a stop to aerial aggression and mercenary invasions of Guatemala coming from the direction of Nicaragua and Honduras. The Guatemalan representative insisted, however, that there was no dispute between his country and the others (presumably to ward off any outright war). The mercenaries were at best only in small part Guatemalan rebels. The Guatemalan appeal said that "open aggression has been perpetrated by the Governments of Honduras and Nicaragua at the instigation of certain foreign monopolists" (*i.e.*, the United Fruit Company). But the insistence on no dispute between Guatemala and these countries, and the appeal to the Security Council simply to stop the aggression, indicate an indirect aggression fact situation. The Soviet delegate insisted that an aggression had been committed, although no aggressor was named. The only resolution passed by the Security Council "Call[ed] for the immediate termination of any action likely to cause bloodshed and request[ed] all Members of the United Nations to abstain, in the spirit of the Charter, from rendering assistance to any such action."[24] This resolution had no immediate practical results, and in fact the Guatemalan government was overthrown. However, it does indicate an official view that it is illegal to "render assistance" to actions against a member gov-

---

24. *U.S. Sec. Coun. O.R.* 9th year, 675th meeting 40-41.

ernment, and thus indicates a trend of international law towards illegality of indirect aggression.

Lebanon: Lebanon complained to the Security Council in 1958 that the United Arab Republic was engaged in indirect aggression. This consisted, it was charged, in infiltration of armed bands, participation in terrorist acts by U.A.R. nationals, and large-scale supply of arms from U.A.R. to subversive elements in Lebanon, training of those elements in Syria, all covered by a propaganda wave calling for the overthrow of the Lebanese government. These charges were enough for the United States to send marines, at the request of the Lebanese government. The U.A.R. argued, in part, that arms can always be obtained during periods of unrest and that in any case the U.A.R. was not responsible for their availability. A subsequent United Nations Observer Group in the Lebanon investigation failed to confirm indirect aggression.

D. Removing Troops

If the troops of nation *A* are on the territory of nation *B*, either through invitation or as a carry-over from a war, nation *B* has a right to have the troops removed, either under notions of trespass, or under Article 2(4) of the Charter on the claim that political independence has been violated. The illegality appears to be much stronger if the troops are there for illegal objectives.

In cases involving withdrawal of World War II occupation forces or withdrawal of former colonial governments, United Nations resolutions have called for withdrawal in relatively mild terms: *e.g.*, British troops in Greece in 1946, Soviet troops in Iran in 1946, British and French troops in Lebanon and Syria in 1946, and French troops in Tunisia in 1958. In the Hungarian case of 1956, very strong resolutions were passed by the General Assembly condemning the presence of Soviet troops after Hungary had denounced the Warsaw Pact.

E. Necessity

1. *Natural disasters*: A nation acting in good faith is probably justified in taking forcible preventive action against an immediate natural

disaster on a neighboring nation's territory (*e.g.*, sudden flooding or forest fires), providing it uses a reasonable amount of force, gives notice as soon as possible, and knows that the other state could not provide a timely remedy.[25]

2. *Land blockade*: A land blockade is a denial of entry to territory by a nation which wholly or partly surrounds another. There is probably no legal right to resort to forcible self-help by land blockade. The blockading nation, however, is not violating the United Nations Charter, since a land blockade is not a resort to force but merely a denial of access to territory, which a sovereign state may do.[26] Consider the Berlin crisis (unclear whether international law apart from treaty could be said to apply to a city).

III. Defend or Help Others

A. *Invitation*

If nation A sends its troops into nation B at the request of the government of B, and its troops carry out military activities, then A, in responding to the invitation, has not committed any illegal act against B. See, *e.g.*, United States troops in Lebanon in 1958, British troops in Jordan in 1958, and Soviet missiles and personnel in Cuba in 1962. Extremely difficult fact situations can arise, however. The Soviet Union presently has troops engaged in fighting in Afghanistan. The Soviet Union claims it responded to an invitation by the government of Afghanistan, but other observers say force and threats of force were used by the Soviets against government officials in order to procure the invitation.

B. *Treaty*

A treaty may contain an invitation to send in troops. The legality of troops sent into a country pursuant to a treaty is the same as in the case of "Invitation" discussed above.

---

25. See Rodick, *The Doctrine of Necessity in International Law* (1928).
26. See, *e.g.*, *Right of Passage Case (Goa)*, I.C.J. *Reports*, 1960, 110-15 (Dissenting Opinion of Sir Percy Spender).

A classic case of invitation to intervene by treaty is contained in the Platt Amendment whose provisions were made part of the 1903 treaty between the United States and Cuba. This Amendment said:

> The Government of Cuba consents that the United States may exercise the right to intervene for the preservation of Cuban independence, the maintenance of a government adequate for the protection of life, property and individual liberty, and for discharging the obligations with respect to Cuba imposed by the Treaty of Paris on the United States, now to be assumed and undertaken by the Government of Cuba.[27]

A treaty abrogating this right was concluded in 1934 as part of the Good Neighbor Policy.[28]

IV. Group Action

A. Regional and Collective

1. *Collective self-defense*: There is a right to collective self-defense in the event of armed attack under Article 51 of the Charter of the United Nations. This right continues "until the Security Council has taken the measures necessary to maintain international peace and security." It is probable that rules and limitations applying to individual self-defense—e.g., proportionality, necessity for armed attack, etc.—also apply to collective action. The United States support in the 1980s to the "contras" in Nicaragua, and the mining of Nicaraguan harbors, was said to be in furtherance of the collective self-defense of El Salvador, Honduras, and the United States. One of the most difficult issues involved was the question of proportionality—was the United States response proportionate to Nicaragua's support of rebel groups in El Salvador?

2. *Collective self-help*: Collective self-help was probably legal prior to the United Nations Charter when used for a proper purpose. For example, the collective action to put down the Boxer uprising was treated as legal. That 1899 uprising in China led in 1900 to armed

---

27. 33 Stat. 2248 (1903).
28. 48 Stat. 1682 (1134).

intervention by Russia, Britain, France, Germany, Japan, Italy, Austria and the United States. Troops of these countries collectively put down the uprising and restored the safety of the legation buildings by 1901. Neither side considered that this was a war; third powers were not asked to assume the attitudes of neutrality. The intervention was considered a legal assertion of force by the intervening powers and by the Chinese Emperor and the local viceroys who disclaimed responsibility for the Boxer movement.[29]

V. The Evolution of the Law of Force

It is appropriate to note by way of conclusion to this chapter that a dramatic change has taken place in the last decades in the view of international lawyers towards the legality of the use of force. Prior to the establishment of the United Nations, there was a large body of literature, including decisions of international tribunals, which supported the concept that the use of force short of war in appropriate circumstances was legal. Thus, for example, nearly all books and articles written in the 19th century and the early 20th century dealing with this problem treat at great length the rules and concepts relating to reprisals, pacific blockade and related matters.

With the establishment of the United Nations in 1945, substantial doubt was cast upon the older precedents supporting the legality of the use of force short of war. There is considerable authority that the Charter preempts all principles of international law relating to the use of force and that the propriety of any use of force must, at least in the first instance, be tested against the Charter.

It is interesting to note that the semi-official position of the United States with respect to the Cuban missile crisis at least impliedly recognized the acceptance by the United States of the principle that the Charter is the significant test of legality. Abram Chayes, Legal Adviser to the Department of State, during the Cuban Missile Crisis, in an article, *Law and the Quarantine of Cuba*,[30] stated that the overriding object of international law is to keep and defend the peace. He then proceeded to argue the legality of the Cuban blockade entirely on

---

29. *See* Grob, *Relativity of War and Peace*, 64-72 (1949).
30. 41 *Foreign Affairs* 550 (1963).

the basis of considerations relating to the Charter and to the United Nations without reference to doctrines such as that of pacific blockade, which might have been used in support of the American position.

The position expressed by Mr. Chayes is consistent with that of perhaps a majority of publicists, who argue that the Charter of the United Nations is now the controlling consideration and that the Charter is primarily directed towards the preservation of peace rather than the promotion of justice. They see as the primary danger in the world today not the injustices which one state may perpetrate against another, but the danger of a large-scale war. This probably reflects a true reading of the intention of perhaps a majority of the delegates who signed the United Nations Charter in 1945.

A provocative and contrary position has been expressed by Professor Julius Stone in, for example, his work *Aggression and World Order*.[31] Stone sees as a primary danger that small states will take advantage of a legal prohibition against the use of force to do things which they otherwise would not, all to the detriment of the larger and more powerful states. Recent history, of course, bears him out. Stone feels as a practical matter that the large states cannot forego the argument that the use of force in a just cause is, at least under some circumstances, legal. The question remains as to how the justice of any particular cause can be determined.

A further objection to Professor Stone's position is that he tacitly assumes that what is "right" is "legal." Irrespective of jurisprudential considerations, international practice has shown that the argument that justice equals legality is unpersuasive. If nation A thinks that nation B's actions are justified, A will seldom question the legality of B's actions. But nation C, which thinks that B's actions are not justified, will raise a legal objection. In this instance, C will not generally be convinced by an argument that B's actions are legal "because" they are justified. Rather, C will charge, for example, that B's actions violate Article 2(4) of the United Nations Charter. And B, in turn, will not get very far adopting Professor Stone's position that in this case Article 2(4) should be overlooked because of overriding considerations of justice or morality.

But despite the difficult legal arguments associated with Professor

---

31. *Aggression and World Order*, 22 (1958).

Stone's position, claims of justice in the real world have a staying power that transcends legal arguments. Increasingly the world community has looked upon grave violations of human rights as matters equal in importance to the prohibitions against transboundary uses of force contained in the United Nations Charter. What if nation *A* embarks upon a policy of genocide against a minority group of its own citizens? (This admittedly extreme case should test the theories we are considering.) Will nations *B* and *C* stand idly by in the event that the Security Council is blocked by a great-power veto from doing anything about the genocide? Rather, *B* and *C* are likely to consider military intervention in *A*, "taking the law into their own hands," due to the failure of the United Nations to intervene. And the more the veto blocks the Security Council from acting in real cases of human-rights deprivations that continue to arise, the more international law will begin to by-pass the United Nations Charter and begin to forge a new set of principles that mediate between the use of force and the protection of human rights.

But the new principles will undoubtedly borrow a great deal from the "classic" law regarding the use of transboundary force short of war. That is why this chapter has been devoted primarily to the classic rules and reasons, even though inevitably reference to post-United Nations events and arguments had to be made. The following two chapters focus respectively on the historical meaning of Article 2(4) and on a single case (the Israeli raid upon an Iraqi nuclear reactor) that offers a frontal challenge to the Article 2(4) analysis.

3
"TERRITORIAL INTEGRITY" AND "POLITICAL INDEPENDENCE"

Whenever any transboundary use of military force occurs in the world, invariably the first legal source that is cited is Article 2(4) of the United Nations Charter. The language of Article 2(4) therefore is perhaps the most important rule of principle of international law in the modern era. The importance of each and every word in that Article is beyond disputation. My purpose here is to investigate the meaning of two of the critical terms in that Article; namely, "territorial integrity" and "political independence."

I will employ historical research of a certain kind in this endeavor. My general thesis is that the words of Article 2(4) acquired their meaning from previous usage in international instruments and documents that were accessible to the signatories to the Charter of the United Nations. In other words, I do not consult a dictionary to find the meaning of the key terms; nor do I consult Shakespeare, or works of fiction, or usage in domestic legal systems, or the writings of political philosophers. I do not rely on such sources because there is no reason to attribute the usage of the terms in those sources to the delegates at San Francisco who adopted Article 2(4) as part of the United Nations Charter. But there is good reason to charge the delegates with knowing the prior use in international law of the terms of art they employed in Article 2(4). And even apart from this implied attribution of knowledge, customary international law itself gives meaning to words as they come down throughout the years. In short, the framers of Article 2(4) were not writing on a blank slate. They were employing words that had achieved meanings through customary usage and accretion.

I do not claim that the sole meaning of Article 2(4) can be derived from historical researchers such as this one. For there are at least two other sources of meaning that rise to equal prominence. One is the "contextual" meaning of Article 2(4) as part of the United Nations Charter. For example, if part of the meaning of 2(4) is dependent upon the ability of the United Nations to use the enforcement machinery of Chapter Seven of the Charter, then our interpretation of 2(4) must be revised in light of the failure of the superpowers to agree on the employment of that enforcement machinery. A second prominent source of meaning is the meaning that has been attributed to 2(4) since it became part of the Charter in 1945. The use that the United Nations and member states have made of 2(4) since 1945 is arguably an important determinant of its present meaning. But neither of these two areas are my present concern. I shall deal only with the historical approach, carrying it down to 1945, for it has been the most neglected of the three approaches to the meaning of the crucially significant language of Article 2(4).

Article 2(4) reads as follows:

> All Members shall refrain in their international relations from the threat or use of force against the territorial integrity or political independence of any state, or in any other manner inconsistent with the Purposes of the United Nations.

The language seems to be all-encompassing, but appearances can be deceptive. For instance, would Israel's air strike upon a nuclear reactor within Iraq be in violation of Article 2(4)? The Israeli planes dropped bombs on Iraqi territory and damaged an Iraqi facility. The planes violated Iraqi airspace. But was it a violation of 2(4)?

Clearly there was a use of force. The question is whether the force was directed against Iraq's territorial integrity or political independence. As to the former, certainly there was a use of force directed against Iraq's *territory*, but is that the same thing as "territorial integrity?" And what about "political independence?" Should we inquire whether Iraq was any less independent after the raid than before? Finally, what about the prohibition on use of force that is in any manner inconsistent with the purposes of the United Nations?

These questions are addressed in the specific context of the Israeli raid in the next chapter.

For present purposes, let us keep the questions regarding "territorial integrity" and "political independence" in mind as we look at the historical meanings of these terms.

I. Treaties of Guaranty

One of the earliest uses of the terms we are investigating occurred in the Treaty of Paris of 30 March 1856, among Great Britain, Austria, France, Prussia, Russia, Sardinia, and Turkey:

> Article VII. Their Majesties engage, each on his part, to respect the Independence and the Territorial Integrity of the Ottoman Empire; Guarantee in common the strict observance of that engagement; and will, in consequence, consider any act tending to its violation as a question of general interest.[1]

Clearly this treaty constitutes an important gloss upon the term "territorial integrity." The parties obviously had in mind a guarantee of the preservation of the Ottoman Empire, thus indicating that if other states attempted to take away portions of that Empire the signatories might react in concert against such an attempt. Hence the notion of "territorial integrity" begins to take on a meaning equivalent to *preventing the permanent loss of a portion of one's territory*. Under such a meaning, the Israeli raid upon the Iraqi nuclear reactor would *not* be a use of force against Iraq's territorial integrity, because Israel neither attempted to take nor succeeded in permanently taking away any portion of Iraq's territory. As for the term "independence," in the above quoted Treaty the term seems to be parallel to, and add very little to, the term "territorial integrity."

Later treaties of guaranty seemed to bear out the rough equivalence of independence and territorial integrity. The Treaty of Christiania of 2 November 1907 among Germany, France, Great Britain, Norway and Russia stated in its preamble:

> Animés du désir d'assurer à la Norvège, dans ses limites actuelles

---

1. *State Papers* (Eng.), vol. XLVI, at 18.

et avec sa zone neutre, son indépendance et son intégrité territoriale . . .

The parties agreed to safeguard Norway's integrity "si l'intégrité de la Norvège est manacée ou lesée par une puissance . . ."[2]

However, a contemporary treaty seemed to suggest that when the word "independence" was used alone, it was not incompatible with a notion of intervention. In the Havana Treaty (United States–Cuba) of 2 May 1903, Article 3 states:

> The government of Cuba consents that the United States may exercise the right to intervene for the preservation of Cuban independence . . ."

Intervention might also have been implied in the United States–Panama Treaty of 18 November 1903 in Article 1: "The United States guarantees and will maintain the independence of the Republic of Panama."

It is not clear whether "territorial integrity" here would exclude the notion of intervention. In a non-aggression treaty between Lithuania and the U.S.S.R. of 28 September 1926, Article 2 states that the parties "undertake to respect in all circumstances each other's sovereignty and territorial integrity and inviolability."[3] Would there be need for the term "inviolability" if "integrity" excludes intervention? In fact, "inviolability" seems the stronger word: It would imply forbidding a brief attack such as Israel's raid on the Iraqi nuclear reactor. Where "integrity" is used alone, without "inviolability," an attack such as the Israeli raid might not be intended to be forbidden.

II. Article 10 of the League of Nations Covenant

The many historical treaties of guaranty in a sense fused and coalesced into Article 10 of the Covenant of the League of Nations, which was a kind of collective security pact:

> The Members of the League undertake to respect and preserve as

---

2. (Article 2). Martens, N.R.G., 3rd ser., i at 14 and ii at 9.
3. 60 L.N.T.S. No. 1410, at 145.

"Territorial Integrity" and "Political Independence"

against external aggression the territorial integrity and existing political independence of all Members of the League. . . .

Article 10 of the Covenant probably originated in the mind of Woodrow Wilson. In October 1914, Colonel Edward M. House, writing to Walter H. Page, brought up Wilson's idea that a guarantee of territorial integrity would be necessary in the peace settlement.[4] In December 1914, Wilson typed out three elements of a proposed Pan-American Pact: (1) mutual guarantee of political independence under republican forms of government; (2) mutual guarantees of territorial integrity; (3) (related to munitions).[5] This Pan-American Pact proposal had earlier roots in Wilson's original Far-Eastern and Latin-American policies in 1913.[6] The ideas underlying the Pan-American pact proposal found their way into Wilson's first draft of the Covenant.[7]

F. P. Walters writes that in January 1916, Wilson "had suggested that all the States of the Western hemisphere should unite in guaranteeing to one another absolute political independence and territorial integrity; and he always insisted on the inclusion of a similar pledge in the Covenant."[8] In May of 1916, Wilson delivered his major address on the League before the League to Enforce Peace:

> We believe these fundamental things: . . . that the small states of the world have a right to enjoy the same respect for their sovereignty and for their territorial integrity that great and powerful nations expect and insist upon.[9]

He said that the people of the United States wish their government to move along these lines:

> Second, an universal association of the nations to maintain the inviolate security of the highway of the seas for the common and unhindered use of all the nations of the world, and to prevent any

---

4. Burton J. Hendrick, *The Life and Letters of Walter H. Page*, vol. 1, 414-15 (N.Y., 1922-26).
5. Charles Seymour, ed., *The Intimate Papers of Colonel House*, vol. 1, 209-10 (Boston, 1926-28).
6. Harley Notter, *The Origins of the Foreign Policy of Woodrow Wilson*, 620 (Baltimore, 1937).
7. *See* Robert Lansing, *War Memoirs*, 199-201 (Indianapolis, 1935).
8. F. P. Walters, *A History of the League of Nations* (London, 1952).
9. Wilson, *Public Papers: New Democracy*, vol. 1, part 2, 187 (N.Y., 1926).

war begun either contrary to treaty covenants or without warning and full submission of the causes to the opinion of the world—a virtual guarantee of territorial integrity and political independence.[10]

In this latter formulation, the notion of territorial integrity and political independence, in the sense of a treaty of guaranty, embodies three interesting notions:
  (a) freedom of the seas
  (b) guarantee of treaties of peace
  (c) no undeclared wars or wars without attempt at conciliation.

Yet it is not clear that Wilson thought of these points as indispensable to the notion of territorial integrity and political independence, for in his Fourteen Points the final point did not refer to them:

> XIV. A general association of nations must be formed under specific covenants for the purpose of affording mutual guarantees of political independence and territorial integrity to great and small states alike.[11]

This idea of Wilson's made its way, as we have seen, into Article 10 of the Covenant. There was nothing in the Phillimore Plan resembling Article 10.[12] But the House draft of July 16, 1918, had as its article 20:

> The Contracting Powers unite in several guarantees to each other of their territorial integrity and political independence, subject, however, to such territorial modifications, if any, as may become necessary in the future by reason of changes in present racial conditions and aspirations, pursuant to the principle of self-determination and as shall also be regarded by three fourths of the Delegates as necessary and proper for the welfare of the peoples concerned; recognizing also that all territorial changes involve equitable compensation and that the peace of the world is superior in importance and interest to questions of boundary.[13]

In this version, it appears that the phrase beginning "subject, how-

---

10. Id. at 187-88.
11. Wilson, *Public Papers: War and Peace*, vol. 1 (address to Congress, January 18, 1918).
12. David Hunter Miller, *The Drafting of the Covenant*. 10 (N.Y., 1928).
13. Id., vol. 2, 10.

ever," was not thought of automatically as included in the notion of territorial integrity and political independence, simply because House thought it necessary to spell it out. If the House version had found its way into the Covenant, the concept of self-determination would have become linked with the notions of territorial integrity and political independence. In any event, the House draft does point up two additional factors to be taken into account in any subsequent analysis of territorial integrity and political independence:

(d) self-determination exception

(e) equitable compensation for territorial changes.

Wilson's first draft, in the summer of 1918, was similar to House's:

> Article III. The Contracting Powers unite in guaranteeing to each other political independence and territorial integrity; but it is understood between them that such territorial readjustments . . . [similar to the phrase in House's version following "territorial modifications"].[14]

These notions of modification of the principle of status quo did find their way into the Covenant, but only into an unobtrusive and feebly worded Article 19.

An interesting view is David Hunter Miller's reaction to Lansing's draft of January 31, 1919. Lansing wrote:

> That the members of the League of Nations should by mutual covenants undertake:
> (1) To refrain from invading and to protect from invasion the sovereign rights and territories of one another . . . .[15]

Miller writes: "Lansing speaks of the differences between this draft and his earlier draft as being 'of a more or less minor character.' As to this I point out that this draft provides for mutual covenants 'to protect from invasion,' a provision going much farther than anything in Article 10 of the Covenant."[16] Miller here may have been expressing a rather common reaction to Article 10: Since Article 10 was couched in the historical language of treaties of guarantee, noth-

---

14. Id., vol. 2, 12.
15. Id., vol. 2, 80.
16. Id., vol. 2, 81.

ing very specific was assumed to follow from it. But if the word "invasion" were included, then the difference would be great indeed. This point of view, if correct, underlines the importance of the later use of the term "force against" the territorial integrity and independence in Article 2(4) of the Charter. The specificity it imparts may cause a change in kind and not simply in degree.

Some support for this view is found in Sir Robert Borden's (Canada) criticism of the proposed article 10:

> Subsequent articles contemplate the possibility of war between two or more signatories under such conditions that the other signatories are not called upon to participate actively therein. If, as a result of such war, the nation attacked occupies and proposes to annex (possibly with the consent of a majority of the population) a portion of the territory of the aggressor, what is to be the operation of this article?[17]

Borden's view suggests that Article 10 is something less than a rule that the invasion of another nation's territory is illegal. This view coincides with the feeling when the United Nations Charter was drafted that what was required was a prohibition against the use of force, not a mere collective guaranty pact as in the Covenant.

It will be recalled that Article 10 provides that members will respect and preserve "as against external aggression the territorial integrity and existing political independence . . ." In an important article published in 1929, Hans Kelsen commented on this wording.[18] First, he points out that territorial integrity and political independence can be violated by means other than aggression. For example, *A* leases territory to *B*, and upon expiration *B* refuses to leave. Or, *A* delivers administrative rights over a territory to *B*, and *B* extends its sovereignty over the territory. While these cases apply more strongly to Article 10 of the Covenant because of its requirement of "external aggression," they may find parallels in Article 2(4) of the Charter if in some way these changes are effected without the use of force.

Kelsen adds that in the above examples, should *A* decide to attack *B* in order to get back its territory, *A*'s aggression would be to *reestablish* a territorial integrity, and thus not be in violation of Article

---

17. Id., 358.
18. *See* Hans Kelsen, "Legal Technique in International Law," 10 *Geneva Studies*, No. 6 (Geneva, 1929).

10. The trouble with this observation is that such a claim is often if not always heard in cases of boundary disputes, most recently having been asserted by Iraq as justification for its invasion of Iran in 1980. Yet the claim does point up a difficulty with the notion of "territorial integrity" that apparently cannot be solved by the use of words or formulas, but rather depends on a universal consensus that at some given time a certain map of the territories of all nations is accepted as embodying the clear status quo.

Argentina's invasion of the Falkland Islands in 1982 was widely perceived as violating Article 2(4) despite Argentina's claim that it was merely trying to get back its own territory. Many commentators have said either that since Great Britain was in de facto control of the Falkland Islands, Article 2(4) must therefore prohibit the use of force to recapture one's own territory, or that Article 2(4) constitutes a prohibition against attack on territory that is either *de jure* or *de facto* under another nation's control. But we cannot really deduce such consequences with confidence, inasmuch as Great Britain remained in control of the Falkland Islands for over 100 years. Would the same result follow if Great Britain had only been in de facto control for 100 days?

III. The Notion of "Force Against"

The Covenant's Article 10 did not, as we have seen, employ the notion of "force against" or "aggression against" territorial integrity or political independence, as does the later Article 2(4) of the United Nations Charter. The question then arises whether the later language of the Charter alters the meaning of "territorial integrity" or "political independence" by the inclusion of the term "force against." Some limited light may be thrown on this question by examining treaty language in the 1930s and 1940s.

The notion of using the phrase "territorial integrity and political independence" as the object of a prepositional phrase "force against" or its equivalent seems to have first come into use in 1931 and 1932 in a series of bilateral treaties concluded by the U.S.S.R. and other powers. These were all non-aggression treaties, differing in wording. The treaties with Afghanistan and France refer only to territorial integrity, so these may be considered first:

The non-aggression pact between Afghanistan and the U.S.S.R. of 24 June, 1931, Article 3, reads in part:

> The Contracting Parties shall not tolerate and shall prevent in their territory the organizations and activities of groups of persons and the activities of private persons that might be prejudicial to the other Contracting Party or prepare the overthrow of its form of government or make an attempt on the *integrity of its territory* or proceed to the mobilisation or recruitment of armed forces to be used against it.[19]

This new idea of an "attempt on the integrity" of territory is thus formulated amidst several other proscriptions which might or might not be included within its general scope. The following phraseology is deserving of closer scrutiny in the non-aggression pact between France and Russia of 29 November 1932:

> Article V. Each of the High Contracting Parties undertakes to respect in every connection the sovereignty or authority of the other Party over the whole of that Party's territories as defined in Article I [i.e., "territories which are placed under that Party's sovereignty or which it represents in external relations or for whose administration it is responsible"], not to interfere in any way in its internal affairs, and to abstain more particularly from action of any kind calculated to promote or encourage agitation, propaganda or attempted intervention designed to prejudice its *territorial integrity* or to transform by force the political or social regime of all or part of its territories.
>
> Each of the High Contracting Parties undertakes in particular not to create, protect, equip, subsidise or admit in its territory either military organisations for the purpose of armed combat with the other Party or organizations assuming the role of government or representing all or part of its territories.[20]

Although this wording does not include directly the idea of "force against" territorial integrity, it does raise the issue that agitation, propaganda, or attempted intervention can be an action against a nation's territorial integrity. Moreover, the second paragraph might be read to spell out what is meant by actions "designed to prejudice its territorial integrity" because it is a particularization of the pre-

---

19. 157 *L.N.T.S.* No. 3611, 371. Italics added.
20. 157 *L.N.T.S.* No. 3615, 418. Italics added.

ceding paragraph. If so, this includes the idea of duty to restrain use of territory for foreign non-governmental subversion. It is coupled with a broad notion of what constitutes "territory" (quote from article I).

Between January and May 1932, the U.S.S.R. signed three more non-aggression pacts. Finland was the other party in the treaty of 21 January 1932: In Article 1, the parties agreed to the inviolability of frontiers and to refrain from any act of aggression.[21] Then, Article 2 proclaimed:

> Any act of violence infringing the *integrity* and inviolability of the *territory*, or directed against the *political independence* of the other contracting party, will be regarded as an aggression.

This introduces the notion of an "act of violence" against territorial integrity or political independence. It is not clear whether "inviolability" is seen as part of the notion of "integrity" or as a separate idea; its inclusion could have been merely the result of making the treaty more explicit.

On 5 February 1932 the U.S.S.R. concluded a similar treaty with Latvia:

> Article 1. Each of the High Contracting Parties undertakes to refrain from any act of aggression directed against the other, and also from any acts of violence directed against the *territorial integrity* and inviolability or the *political independence* of the other Contracting Party, regardless of whether such aggression or such acts are committed separately or together with other Powers, with or without a declaration of war.
> Article 2. Each of the High Contracting Parties undertakes not to be a party to any military or political treaties, conventions or agreements directed against the *independence, territorial integrity* or political security of the other Party, nor to any treaties, conventions, or agreements aiming at an economic or financial boycott of either of the Contracting Parties.[22]

This treaty brings up the idea of treaties directed against territorial integrity or political independence. It is hard to imagine any treaties which do not affect these categories in some manner.

---

21. 27 *A.J.I.L.* Supp. 171 (1933). Italics added.
22. 148 *L.N.T.S.* No. 3408, 113; 27 *A.J.I.L.* Supp. 182 (1933). Italics added.

Article 1 of the non-aggression treaty with Estonia of 4 May 1932 reads:

> Both high contracting parties mutually guarantee the inviolability of the frontiers existing between them . . . and undertake to refrain from any act of aggression against each other or from any act of violence directed against the *integrity* and inviolability of the *territory* or against the *political independence* of the other contracting party independent of the fact whether such aggression or such action is undertaken separately or together with other Powers and whether or not war be declared.[23]

In the above quoted treaties, "acts of violence" are used instead of the word "force," which was to appear later in 2(4) of the Charter. However, these are only English translations. A thorough examination of this question would take into account all foreign language differences.

Another important use of these terms occurred in the Havana Protocol of July 1940, the "Declaration of Reciprocal Assistance and Cooperation for the Defence of the States of America":

> . . . . any attempt on the part of a non-American state against the *integrity* or inviolability of the *territory*, the sovereignty or the *political independence* of an American state shall be considered as an act of aggression against the states which sign this declaration . . .
> In case acts of aggression are committed or should there be reason to believe that an act of aggression is being prepared by a non-American nation against the *integrity* or inviolability of the *territory*, the sovereignty or the *political independence* of an American nation, the states signatory . . . will consult. . . .[24]

This formulation repeats the "attempt against" formula of the U.S.S.R.–Afghanistan Treaty, and also uses the notion of an "act of aggression . . . against"—a formulation that appears to be of little benefit since the word "aggression" raises a multiplicity of problems. However, the importance of the Havana Protocol in the history of the phrase under consideration is that it probably brought its use in

---

23. *A.J.I.L.* Supp. 165 (1933). Italics added. *See also* Poland, id., 188.
24. United States Department of State, *Conference Series* 71 (1940-42). Italics added.

the new format to the attention of the American states and thus helped prepare the way for its acceptance in Article 2(4) of the Charter.

The Act of Chapultepec of March 3, 1945, used the notion of "force against," but also, curiously, added a clarificatory statement:

> Part I. Third. Declaration . . . that every attack of a state against the *integrity* or inviolability of *territory*, or against the sovereignty or *political independence* of an American state, shall . . . be considered as an act of aggression. . . .
> In any case, invasion by armed forces of one state into the territory of another, trespassing boundaries established by treaty and marked in accordance therewith, shall constitute an act of aggression.[25]

This second paragraph, introduced by the term "in any case," is rather important testimony to the fact that, almost contemporaneously with the adoption of the United Nations Charter, an international instrument indicated its uncertainty whether "attacks" against "integrity . . . of territory" or "political independence" encompassed all transborder acts of armed force.

IV. The Travaux Préparatoires of Article 2(4)

Against the entire legal background described so far, the framers of the United Nations Charter began their negotiations that led to the signing of the Charter in San Francisco in 1945.

The tentative proposals put forth by the United States in 1944 that eventuated in Article 2(4) had no mention of the phrases "territorial integrity" or "political independence."

> V-1. All States, whether members of the international organization or not, should be required (a) to settle disputes by none but peaceful means, and (b) to refrain from the threat or use of force in their international relations in any manner inconsistent with the purposes envisaged in the basic instrument of the organization.[26]

Russell comments that "an earlier draft had obligated members 'not

---

25. 39 *A.J.I.L.* Supp. 108 (1945). Italics added.
26. Ruth B. Russell, *A History of the United Nations Charter*, Appendix (Wash., 1958).

to use force . . . except under the authority of the international organization.' This phraseology had been questioned as affecting the right of self-defense."[27]

The formal Dumbarton Oaks proposals had as the precursor of Article 2 Section 4:

> All members of the Organization shall refrain in their international relations from the threat or use of force in any manner inconsistent with the purposes of the Organization.[28]

Commenting on this section, the Right Honorable Peter Fraser said on 3 May 1945:

> There is in the Dumbarton Oaks plan no clear statement that the security of the individual members of the organization is the objective. . . . New Zealand would wish that in the Charter we are about to draft there should be placed in the core of the undertakings which members will assume the unequivocal pledge to resist all acts of external aggression against any member of the organization . . . I should add that while the *territorial integrity and political independence* of each member should be preserved against external aggression, changes in the status quo should at the same time be possible, although not under *force or threat of force.*[29]

The Deputy Prime Minister of Australia, Francis M. Forde, was even more explicit:

> In the Charter should also be inserted a specific undertaking by all members to refrain in their international relations from *force or the threat of force against the territorial integrity or political independence* of another state.
>
> The application of this principle should insure that no question relating to a change of frontiers or an abrogation of a state's independence could be decided other than by peaceful negotiations. It should be made clear that if any state were to follow up a claim to extended frontiers by using force or the threat of force, the claim-

---

27. Id., 296 n. 23.
28. United States Department of State, *Dumbarton Oaks Documents on International Organization* 5-16 (Publ. 2257, 1945).
29. New Zealand Department of External Affairs, *New Zealand and the San Francisco Conference* 4-5 (Wellington, 1945). Italics added.

ant would be breaking a specific and solemn obligation under the Charter.[30]

What apparently was in this speaker's mind was that "territorial integrity" meant that frontiers could not be extended, while "political independence" meant that a "state's independence" could not be "abrogated" (probably with Hitler's conquests in mind). Bolivia's proposals spelled out these terms a little more, but added to their vagueness at the same time:

> [The Charter should have] a double and reciprocal guaranty among its members: the first, concerning the territorial inviolability of the states, the legal validity of acquisitions of territory which may originate in acts of force or other means of compulsion not being recognized; and the second, concerning respect for the political independence of the states and the right which they possess to develop freely in their internal life, without the intervention of any other state.[31]

Here of course the word "inviolability" instead of "integrity" is used. Perhaps the delegate of Bolivia was unaware of any possible difference, although years later the argument was made that fedayeen raids against Israel, while they might have violated the latter's territorial inviolability, did not violate her integrity, since the raids did not demonstrate a purpose of conquest.

An even broader and more vague notion of what integrity and independence mean is found in Brazil's version of the fourth paragraph of Article 2:

> All members of the Organization shall refrain in their international relations from any intervention in the foreign or domestic affairs of any other member of the Organization, and from resorting to threats or use of force, if they are not in accord with the methods and decisions of the Organization. In the prohibition against intervention there shall be understood to be included any interference that threatens the national security of another member of the Organization, directly or indirectly threatens its territorial integrity, or

---

30. 1 *U.N.C.I.O. Docs.* 174. Italics added.
31. 3 *U.N.C.I.O. Docs.* 578.

involves the exercise of any excessively foreign influence on its destinies.[32]

If protection from "excessively foreign influence" is what Brazil thought "political independence" required (and thereby voted to accept the final version of 2(4)), then the phrase is broad enough to include the whole range of items making up proposals for a definition of "aggression" put forth by the U.S.S.R. in the last thirty years.

There were two distinct goals that animated that which became Article 2(4). The first was to have the Article become a collective security pact. New Zealand, the foremost advocate of this approach, was thus acting consistently with the usage of the terms "territorial integrity" and "political independence" found in treaties of guaranty and in Article 10 of the League's Covenant. The second was to have the Article be a prohibition against the unilateral threat or use of force, a position championed by the United States. In a profound sense, the two goals were inconsistent. The New Zealand approach would allow any nation to come to the forcible aid of any other nation that was attacked, whereas the United States position was to bar any such unilateral action. The United States believed that it was the United Nations itself which had the exclusive right to police breaches of collective security.

However, incompatible or not, the two approaches merged in the ultimate language of Article 2(4). New Zealand's terms "territorial integrity" and "political independence" found their way into Article 2(4), but the article itself clearly reflected the United States' aim of barring unilateral threats or uses of force. New Zealand's goal of having a collective security pact was decisively defeated, with many delegates in many places explaining that the United Nations itself was the equivalent of a collective security pact and hence New Zealand's position—which would have set up a separate self-enforcing collective security pact under Article 2(4)—would have subverted the purposes of the United Nations. At the same time, it would appear that the United States did not understand the long history behind the terms "territorial integrity" and "political independence." The United States delegates apparently thought that *all* transboundary threats or uses of force were prohibited by Article 2(4). The United

---

32. 3 id. at 237.

States delegate to Committee 1 of Commission I reportedly "made it clear that the intention of the authors of the original text was to state in the broadest terms an absolute all-inclusive prohibition; the phrase "or in any other manner" was designed to insure that there should be no loopholes."[33] But history since 1945 has proved to be richer than the imaginations of the delegates to the San Francisco conference. If the United States delegate just quoted had been asked whether a bombing raid by one nation over the territory of another nation would violate the newly drafted Article 2(4), she probably would have answered emphatically in the affirmative. Yet, just to take and end with this simple example, a good case can be made that the Israeli raid on the Iraqi nuclear reactor was a violation of neither Iraq's territorial integrity nor its political independence (as those terms have come down through history until coming to rest in Article 2(4) of the Charter), and moreover was not in any other manner inconsistent with the purposes of the United Nations because one of those purposes—contained in Article 11—is "disarmament and the regulation of armaments." As we shall see in the next chapter, Israel can justifiably claim that stopping nuclear weapons from getting into the hands of the Iraqi government was not at all inconsistent with this major purpose of the United Nations.

---

33. 6 *U.N.C.I.O. Docs.* at 342, Doc. 810, I/1/30, June 6, 1945.

4

USE OF FORCE AGAINST NUCLEAR INSTALLATIONS

In Chapter 2 we saw a number of instances where claims of justification have been or can be made regarding the use of transboundary military force. But a distinctly new category emerged in international law after the events of the morning of June 7, 1981. At that time, Israeli planes using conventional weapons engaged in a "surgical strike" upon an Iraqi nuclear reactor near Baghdad. The attack occurred without warning at a time when the personnel were mainly away from the plant—three lives were reputedly lost, and the Israeli planes returned to base without incident. Is it possible that we have a new justification for the use of force in international affairs—destroying another nation's emerging capability to make or prepare to make nuclear weapons?

If we do, there is a considerable burden of showing that conventional prohibitions against the unilateral transboundary use of force are overcome when the target is a nuclear reactor. Certainly the immediate response of the Security Council was to condemn the Israeli raid as violative of international law. Its resolution of June 19, 1981, "*strongly condemn[ed]* the military attack by Israel in clear violation of the Charter of the United Nations and the norms of international conduct."[1]

There is, however, a serious—and fascinating—problem for inter-

---

1. *U.N.S.C. Res.* 487, 36 *U.N. Sec. Counc. O.R.* (2288th mtg.), U.N. Doc. S/RES/487 (1981), reprinted in 75 *A.J.I.L.* 724 (1981).

national lawyers in figuring out how much weight to give to recommendations of the Security Council or General Assembly. Books have been written about this subject, but there has been no consensus. International law surely would be a much easier subject to study and master if U.N. resolutions could be treated as definitive statements of rules of international law. But, as has often been pointed out, the U.N. is not a world legislature, and its resolutions are not the functional equivalent of statutes. Instead, there are two basic problems with determining the international-law "weight" to be given to any U.N. resolution, and both of these apply to the just-quoted resolution of the Security Council on the Israeli raid.

First, there is the problem that a number of states vote for resolutions in order to satisfy allies or to "trade" U.N. votes on other matters, but do so with no conviction that the resolution they are supporting has any legal weight. Indeed, delegates to the U.N. have from time to time explained that their vote for or against a resolution was not an expression of their conviction that the resolution expressed or failed to express a valid rule of international law.[2]

Second, a resolution can sometimes signify the opposite of what it says. This occurs because of a subtle process that is connected with the first reason I've just given. Since sponsors of resolutions *know* that the resolutions do not definitively state an international-law position, they can vote in its favor to appease the world community while at the same time secretly applauding the nation that the resolution condemns. The closest analogy I can think of to this process is exemplified in stories that appear in the newspapers from time to time about a judge handing down a sentence in a notorious case of white-collar crime. Following a blistering lecture from the bench that the defendant has abused his position of trust, has let society down, has profited a thousand times as much as the bank robber who is convicted of a felony, and that the conviction of said defendant should stand as a supreme example of deterrence to other would-be white-collar criminals, the judge hands down a sentence of three-months to a model prison and promptly commutes the sentence because it is a first-time offence. Should readers of the newspaper conclude that the judge is a staunch foe of white-collar crime, or that this is simply one more case where white-collar crime is let off with

---

2. *See* B. H. Weston, R. A. Falk, and A. A. D'Amato (eds.), *International Law and World Order*, 94-101 (1980).

a slap on the wrist? The obvious answer applies to the Security Council resolution we have just examined. The Security Council strongly condemned Israel in *words*, but omitted any mention of punishment. No reparations were called for. No damages were asked. No enforcement machinery under the Charter was set in motion. Can anyone doubt that Israel might well look upon the resolution as a gentle pat on the wrist?

How, then, can the student of international law interpret such a resolution? Does it stand for a *condemnation* of Israel, or for implicit *support* of Israel? I don't think we can really decide. Therefore, we should move to a more traditional analysis of Israel's raid, and not attempt to derive a simple or easy answer from the Security Council's resolution.[3]

Sometimes the best way to conceptualize a problem in international law is to imagine what the arguments would be if they were made before an international court of competent jurisdiction. That way, we can begin to lay the groundwork for what the judicial conclusion might be, and thus get an idea of the content of the rule of international law that should be or would be applied to the matter. Accordingly, let us imagine what the arguments would be at such a hypothetical court.

Counsel for Israel might begin with the argument that a state of war exists between Iraq and Israel and that it has been Iraq since 1948 that has rejected any armistice sought by Israel. Hence it follows from the existence of a war that Israel has the right to take military action against Iraq.

The trouble with this argument is that war itself is illegal under international law. The Kellog-Briand Peace Pact in 1928 outlawed war, and that treaty has never been repealed. The Nuremberg trials after World War II made it plain that resort to war was illegal under international law.

International law is actually quite subtle on this issue. If a state of war in fact exists, then the Geneva Conventions operate to protect prisoners of war, the wounded, the Red Cross, civilians (in certain

---

3. *See* Mallison & Mallison, "The Israeli Aerial Attack of June 7, 1981, Upon the Iraqi Nuclear Reactor: Aggression or Self Defense?" 15 *Vand. J. Transnat'l L.* 417 (1982). At the time of the attack, I took the position that the Israeli action was legal under international law, but that Israel owed monetary compensation to Iraq for the actual damage to the nuclear facility and for the four lives that were lost. *The Israeli Air Strike: Hearings Before the Senate Comm. on Foreign Relations*, 97th Cong., 1st Sess. (1981) 85, 88.

circumstances), and other attributes of war. But the triggering of those conventions does not in turn legitimize the war. Similarly, counsel for Israel cannot legitimately deduce any military right from its war with Iraq, since the illegality under international law of the war itself cannot be used to justify continuation of war—even though it may trigger the Geneva Conventions.

A second argument that counsel for Israel might adduce would be that the two-minute "surgical strike" against the Iraqi nuclear facility was for Israel's self-defense. Israel is entitled to act forcefully in self-defense under Article 51 of the Charter of the U.N. Such an argument would invoke the same provisions that attorneys for the United States Department of State used to justify the blockade of Cuba in 1962 during the Cuban missile crisis. However, the argument now is no better than it was then. The self-defense provision of Article 51 comes into effect only "if an armed attack occurs," and there was no armed attack on the United States in 1962 any more than there was on Israel in 1981.[4]

Perhaps counsel for Israel might try to salvage the self-defense argument by quoting the Israeli deputy defense minister, Mordechai Zipori, who said on June 11, "What constitutes the defense of state of Israel shall be determined only by the government of Israel, and not by any other state, not even the most friendly one." The argument is like former President Nixon's self-definition of "national security" as a reason for not turning over the Watergate tapes to the special prosecutors. And it is equally unpersuasive. No court (even our imaginary international tribunal in the case of Iraq vs. Israel) will allow unbounded auto-interpretation to decide legally contested issues. Israel simply has no right under international law to take any military action outside its national boundary in the name of self-defense as it chooses to define that term. If self-defense is to have any meaning in international law, its meaning must have a degree of objectivity and cannot be wholly auto-interpreted.

---

4. The Mallisons, *supra* note 3 at 423-24, do not convincingly distinguish the Cuban missile crisis from the Israeli aerial strike of 1981. Previously, Professor Mallison had written that the American position in 1962 was justified as self-defense under Article 51. *See* Mallison, "Limited Naval Blockade or Quarantine Interdiction: National or Collective Defense Claims Valid Under International Law," 31 *Geo. Wash. L. Rev.* 335 (1962). President Kennedy himself carefully refrained from invoking Article 51 in support of the American quarantine, but he did use the language "in support of our own security" in his address of Oct. 22, 1962, 47 *U.S. Dept. of State Bull.* 716 (1962), and "to defend the security of the United States" in his Proclamation No. 3504 of Oct. 23, 1962, id. at 717, 27 Fed. Reg. 10,401 (1962). *See also* Wright, "The Cuban Quarantine," 57 *A.J.I.L.* 546, 560 n. 53 (1963); MacChesney, "The Quarantine Against Cuba: Legal or Illegal?" id. at 588, 589-90.

Even worse is Israel's claim that its raid constituted permissible "anticipatory self-defense." The idea of "anticipatory" self-defense is almost self-contradictory. One engages in self-defense when attacked; to *begin* the attack is to give the other side, not you, the right to self-defense. Self-defense in the *absence* of an armed attack by the other side is, according to Professor Henkin, "unfounded, its reasoning is fallacious, its doctrine pernicious."[5] In the present-day nuclear balance of terror, the time between the launching of a missile and the destruction of a major city in the Soviet Union or the United States is a mere six minutes for the missiles emplaced closest to the two superpowers. Does the existence of this six-minute time mean that either superpower may, at any time, launch all its missiles on the ground of "anticipatory self-defense?" If so, the doctrine of anticipatory self-defense is a recipe for global disaster, not international law.

So far, then, Israel has not justified its action under international law. But its counsel may still say that unless Iraq can show that the Israeli attack was illegal under international law, it is permissible. Indeed this was the first pre-emptive strike against a nuclear facility in history so one could not reasonably expect international law to contain an actual rule affirmatively permitting such an act. But the absence of an explicit international rule *prescribing* a certain action does not mean that the action is *proscribed*.

Let us hear then from counsel for Iraq. First, the Iraqi attorneys might argue that Israel violated Article 2(4) of the United Nations Charter, using force "against the territorial integrity or political independence of another state." But the long history of these particular quoted phrases, examined in the preceding chapter, suggests that Israel might be able to refute the allegation that it violated Article 2(4).[6] In its pre-emptive strike that lasted all of two minutes, Israel sought no annexation of any of Iraq's territory. Nor did Israel interfere with the Iraqi government or its legal standing vis-a-vis other nations. Thus, although Israel's strike was certainly a use of force, it arguably was not directed against Iraq's territorial integrity or political independence.

Of course, if Israel's attack had been preliminary to a military

---

5. L. Henkin, *How Nations Behave*, 141 (2d ed. 1979).
6. *See* J. Stone, *Aggression and World Order*, 95, 97-100 (1958). *See* also Franck, "Who Killed Article 2(4)?" 64 *A.J.I.L.* 809 (1970); Henkin, "The Reports of the Death of Article 2(4) Are Greatly Exaggerated," 65 *A.J.I.L.* 544 (1971).

campaign directed against Iraq's territorial integrity or political independence, a purposive interpretation of Article 2(4) would result in a finding of illegality of the initial strike against the nuclear reactor. But there has been no evidence of any Israeli purpose beyond the limited one of destroying the nuclear reactor itself. In this respect, Israel's action was analogous to a limited "humanitarian intervention," such as the Entebbe raid,[7] which can be justified along similar lines as not violative of 2(4).[8]

But there is another component to Article 2(4)—that the use of force must not be "inconsistent with the Purposes of the United Nations." Here a purposive, or teleological, inquiry is explicitly mandated. McDougal and Feliciano, although addressing themselves to self-defense under the Charter, suggest three relevant factors for determining the objectives of the claimant (here, Israel): extension or conservation, degree of consequentiality, and exclusivity or inclusivity.[9] Let us examine briefly the relevant questions under these categorical factors, as they might be argued by counsel for Israel.

According to the analysis of McDougal and Feliciano, the question of extension or conservation of values is whether Israel intended to conserve its own values rather than extend them "through acquiring or destroying values held by the opposing participant [Iraq]."[10] In one sense, Israel's action was profoundly conservative: to check possible nuclear proliferation to a regime perceived as unstable or irresponsible. However, having its own nuclear reactor was clearly a value for Iraq. Was Israel's action "therapeutic" in McDougal's view[11]—to remove an enemy's potential for aggression? The difficulty of answering this question leads to McDougal's qualification that a "therapeutic" attack should be "exercisable only by, or under an unambiguous authorization from, the entire community."[12] Yet this qualification is clearly too strong; it swamps McDougal's own factor for analytical purposes. For it is often politically expedient for the community to condemn a forceful initiative in explicit terms, yet to

---

7. *See* Boyle, "International Law in Time of Crisis: From the Entebbe Raid to the Hostages Convention," 75 *Nw. L. Rev.* 769 (1980).

8. *See, e.g.*, Lillich, "Humanitarian Intervention: A Reply to Ian Brownlie and a Plea for Constructive Alternatives," in *Law and Civil War in the Modern World*, 229 (Moore ed. 1974). Contra, Brownlie, "Humanitarian Intervention," in id., 217.

9. M. McDougal & F. Feliciano, *Law and Minimum World Public Order*, 222 (1961).

10. Ibid.

11. Id., 223.

12. Id., 224.

approve of it in fact by stopping short of reprisals against the initiator. There is a subtle interplay of politics and acquiescence that renders any demand for "unambiguous authorization" unrealistic. The very resolution of the Security Council condemning Israel's aerial strike, as we have seen, fell noticeably short of imposing any penalty or sanction against Israel.[13]

With respect to the degree of consequentiality of the values asserted by Israel, there is hardly a more fundamentally important value than the preservation of the lives of the inhabitants of the claimant state. If Iraq were to develop a nuclear weapon capability, the existence of a small state such as Israel would be in jeopardy. In other words, Israel may have been justified in attacking a nuclear reactor in Iraq, where it would not have been justified in attacking a plant that manufactured tanks or conventional artillery, because of the enormous destructive potential of nuclear weapons. Does not any consequentialist perspective require drawing a qualitative line between conventional and nuclear capabilities insofar as an interpretation of Article 2(4) is concerned?

The third factor suggested by McDougal and Feliciano is the exclusivity or inclusivity of Israel's objectives. Professor Thomas Mallison and Ms. Sally Mallison cite the following statement by Prime Minister Begin of Israel in support of their contention that Israel appeared to have acted solely for its own perceived values: "I don't care about the Arab world. I care about our lives."[14] Yet can Begin's statement fairly be read as ruling out any other motivation? Even if it could, is it not possible that a state acting for its own interests could still be carrying out inclusive community interests? If so, what are those interests, and how do they relate to the purposes of the United Nations?

One of the purposes of the United Nations, stated to be a proper concern of the General Assembly, is "disarmament and the regulation of armaments" (Article 11). Armaments are again mentioned in the responsibilities of the Security Council: to "promote the establishment and maintenance of international peace and security with the

---

13. *Supra* note 1. The lack of imposition of a sanction, penalty, or reprisal of any kind, whether from the United Nations or any individual nation, tends to support a claim that the act complained of was in fact legal. *See* discussion in Chapter 5, and also *see* Reisman, "Sanctions and Enforcement," in *The Future of the International Legal Order* 275 (Black & Falk, eds. 1971).

14. Mallison & Mallison, *supra* note 3, 426 (quoting *Washington Post*, June 9, 1981, at A11, col. 1).

least diversion for armaments" (Article 26). Apart from the Charter itself, it is clear that the proliferation of nuclear weapons constitutes one of the gravest threats that has ever faced mankind. Given the fact that nuclear weapons cannot be dis-invented, international stability is compromised each time a new government acquires them. The confusion and chaos that would inevitably accompany any aggressive use of nuclear weapons might rapidly escalate into an unintended war of human extinction. Although Israel's unilateral, military aerial attack on the Iraqi reactor is hardly a peaceful or desirable precedent for the purposes of nonproliferation, it is possible to surmise that the community of nations breathed a little easier after the deed was done. At the time of the attack, Iraq was engaged in a premeditated war of aggression against its neighbor Iran.[15] Counsel for Israel may therefore conclude at this point in the argument that Israel was acting in the furtherance of inclusive community values in frustrating Iraq's desire for its own nuclear capability.

However, Iraq would certainly counter with two arguments against Israel's claim of furtherance of inclusive interests. First, Iraq might argue that Israel acted simply to preserve its own nuclear hegemony in the Middle East, and thus retain its aggressive posture against its Arab neighbors. However, this argument, even if true, simply restates the position that Israel acted out of self-interest; it does not defeat the claim that such action served to promote inclusive interests.

Second, Iraq is a party to the Non-Proliferation Treaty[16] and has had its nuclear installations inspected on a regular basis by the International Atomic Energy Agency, whereas Israel has refused to place its own nuclear facilities under I.A.E.A. safeguards.[17] May we conclude that Iraq's nuclear reactor was in compliance with Iraq's "inalienable right . . . to develop research, production and use of nuclear energy for peaceful purposes," as stated in Article IV of the N.P.T.? The question, of course, is whether I.A.E.A. inspection of the facility will continue to be frequent and thorough enough to

---

15. *See* Falk, "Some Thoughts on the Decline of International Law and Future Prospects," 9 *Hofstra L. Rev.* 399 (1981). Compare Iraq's claim, *supra* p. 65.

16. Treaty on the Non-Proliferation of Nuclear Weapons, 21 *U.S.T.* 483, *T.I.A.S.* no. 6839, 729 *U.N.T.S.* 161 (July 1, 1968), reprinted in 7 *I.L.M.* 811 (1968).

17. Mallison & Mallison, *supra* note 3, 440-41. The Mallisons argue that by joining the N.P.T. and opening its own nuclear installations to I.A.E.A. inspection, Israel would gain leverage over the adequacy of I.A.E.A. supervision: "It would have at least been difficult, and probably impossible, for Iraq to refuse additional international inspection had Israel agreed to the same inspection for itself." Id., 428. How can it be "impossible" for a nation to refuse something?

prevent diversion of fissionable material produced by the reactor to military uses.

Israeli counsel surely would reply that the I.A.E.A. is incapable over time of preventing diversion to military uses. Surely Iraq at some point could simply bar the I.A.E.A. inspection team and announce to the world that it has successfully transferred its fissionable material to its weapons program.

Clearly, Israel was not convinced. Indeed, is it unreasonable to think that Iraq, or any nation building a nuclear reactor under I.A.E.A. safeguards, may at some point bar the inspection team and announce to the world that it has successfully transferred its fissionable material to its weapons program? What is to prevent clandestine transfer at times when the I.A.E.A. inspection team is not present or its attention is diverted? Finally, the building of an indigenous nuclear reactor is of inestimable educational value to government scientists who may be sharpening their expertise for the purpose of developing nuclear weaponry. These considerations suggest that the "right" to develop nuclear energy "for peaceful purposes" may be self-defeating, and that Israel's action may be the precursor of a wholesale reevaluation of the N.P.T. and the I.A.E.A. program. But even if no such reevaluation takes place, is it not clear that there is at least a substantial basis for Israel's frontal challenge to the N.P.T.–I.A.E.A. system?

Since we are imagining a hypothetical case occurring in an international court, we might at this point interpose a question from the bench. Suppose a judge asks, "Should Israel have to pay compensation to Iraq for the destruction of the physical facilities?"

Counsel for Israel might say that, unless the aerial strike were illegal under international law, there should be no ground for assessing damages. Iraqi counsel, of course, would claim both illegality and the right of compensation.

But the judge might then reply, "What if I were to hold that Israel's attack was justifiable so long as Israel paid compensation, but illegal if Israel withholds compensation?" Such a question would indicate an analogy to the United States law of eminent domain: the government is entitled to take private property, but only for a public purpose, and only if fair compensation is paid.

International law has not yet evolved to the point of justifying forcible actions so long as compensation is paid, but it is clear that such a norm would introduce a desirable level of flexibility in international law. If we look closely at the Israel–Iraq case, we can see many reasons why such a rule would be desirable. Israel's preemptive strike of the Iraqi nuclear reactor was that of a peacetime reactor; its fissionable product had not been diverted to military uses. Iraq suffered a severe monetary set-back by the bombing. Yet Israel would only claim justification on the basis of a probability that there would be a diversion to military use of the reactor. In such a situation, arguably if Israel had a right to violate Iraq's airspace and destroy its installation, Israel should also compensate Iraq for the injury. (Interestingly, although I made this very argument at the time of the Senate's hearings on the legality of the Israeli raid, in the summer of 1981,[18] neither Iraq nor Israel picked up the point, and as far as I know, no one else has reacted favorably to it either. It's an argument that neither side liked. Maybe this is its biggest drawback. Or maybe its biggest asset—as in a labor settlement where both sides walk away from the bargaining table disappointed.)

Where do we come out in the case as presented so far? Iraq may have the slightly better argument, because its territory and airspace were violated, its own facilities destroyed by bombing, and all this in an era where war is illegal and the use of transboundary military force, except in self-defense, carries with it a severe burden of persuasion. But now let us examine a broader argument that Israel could make, one that centers upon a really unique feature of the present case; namely, that it involves a nuclear installation and not just an ordinary military target.

To begin, we step back and look at international law from a broad perspective. That law does not simply consist of rules which states either obey or disobey like the rules of a game. Instead international law has evolved over thousands of years as a system for stabilizing the interactions of states and governments by defining presumptions of legality arising out of the customary acts of the states themselves. The purpose of international law is to create the precondition for peace and human rights. This purpose does more than animate the rules of international law; it shapes and defines them.

The Kellogg–Briand Peace Pact and the U.N. Charter were drafted in the pre-atomic age. War was outlawed because a nation's rightful claim to security could be guaranteed on a collective basis by the community of nations. If nation A attacked nation B, all the other

---

18. *Hearings Before the Senate Comm.*, *supra* note 3.

nations would (so the theory went) go to the aid of *B* and repel the aggression. It is indeed no accident that, as we saw in the last chapter, the key words of Article 2(4) originated in treaties of guaranty and collective security pacts. In the absence of nuclear weapons, the collective security system made perfect sense according to the overall purpose of international law.

But in the post-atomic age, the fact of instantaneous nuclear destruction has outrun the old legal rules. Those rules have to be reinterpreted in light of present realities. Israel's predicament is a rather clear illustrative case. A few thermonuclear explosions and Israel would cease to exist in less than the two minutes it took Israeli conventional bombs to destroy the Iraqi installation.

Because of this potential for immediate annihilation, the old safeguard of collective security becomes irrelevant. There is simply no reaction time in the system. As soon as other nations learn that Israel has been attacked with nuclear weapons, Israel will have been destroyed. Indeed, as soon as Israel itself learns of the attack, it will be too late for Israel to protect itself.

Under this view, Israel's last clear chance to protect itself against thermonuclear destruction at the hands of Iraq was to destroy the nuclear installation near Baghdad. Perhaps Israel should be required to compensate Iraq for the property lost, but when one considers that the alternative might have been the thermonuclear death of millions of people in Israel, it would be highly artificial to conclude that Israel violated international law. Indeed, international law would have to be the technical, academic set of rules that many people caricature it to be if it would protect and ensure Iraq's capacity to destroy millions of people.

But now we are at a very difficult stage of analysis. If international law in fact justifies what Israel did, how can we ever hope to draw a line against a forthcoming series of preemptive strikes against nuclear facilities all over the world?

If counsel for Israel were asked this question in the case we are imagining, the standard lawyer's answer would be something like this: It is not up to us to draw the line for all future cases. Our purpose is accomplished if we justify our own case. Future lines can be drawn by the court itself if and when future cases arise.

19. *See* Mallison & Mallison, *supra* note 3 at 435-37.

And the standard judicial response to this contention would be as follows: All right, then, justify your own case. Show that it is potentially different from other possible existing cases, such as the case that would arise if India and Pakistan were to bomb a Chinese installation, or the United States were to bomb a Brazilian reactor.

Israel's answer to the judge's inquiry would probably proceed along the following lines:

First, Iraq is an unstable state that is currently in violation of international law for its war of aggression against Iran and its treatment of its Assyrian minorities in northern Iraq.

Second, Iraq has publicly called for the annihilation of Israel.

Third, Iraq is in a state of declared war against Israel and has resisted Israel's call for an armistice. This point, by the way, is raised not to justify Israel's attack, since as we have seen earlier, two wrongs do not make a right (the state of war is itself illegal; it does not justify military actions in pursuit thereof). But instead, the point is raised to indicate the state of mind of the Iraqi government—one of total hostility toward Israel.

Fourth, it is clear from the absence of concurrent development in Iraq of a nuclear power program that Iraq is not interested in electricity. Thus the nuclear facility was intended to produce nuclear weapons, which in turn were intended to be used aggressively against Israel.

If future cases arise similar to Israel's attack upon the Iraqi reactor, there will be idiosyncracies in the new factual settings. The real question at issue is whether the fact that the target was a *nuclear* reactor goes part of the way to justify the attack, assuming that other facts are needed either to fulfill the burden of proof or to outweigh the nuclear factor and find the attack to be illegal.

In my view, the destructive potential of nuclear weapons is so enormous as to call into question any and all received rules of international law regarding the transboundary use of force. There is something eminently *sane* about Israel's action from the point of view of global survival. Nuclear weapons in the hands of Iraq, which launched an aggressive war against its neighbor Iran, might not only be used by Iraq and cause immense destruction, but might act as a catalyst for the launching of other nuclear missiles leading to a general global nuclear war. I concede that this same reasoning can apply to any nation which achieves nuclear weapons, whether they divert fissionable material from peaceful plants, or steal the weapons, or buy them abroad or whatever. I don't know what international law can do about nuclear proliferation. But when something *is* done, as in the Israeli raid, maybe international law should not be ready to condemn it on the basis of rules prohibiting transboundary military force that were fashioned in the pre-nuclear age.[20]

On our imagined case, if I were judge I'd award the decision to Israel provided that Israel pay Iraq damages for the destroyed plant and for the loss of three lives.

---

20. *See* Henkin, "The United Nations and Its Supporters: A Self Examination," 78 *Pol. Sci. Q.* 504, 532 33 (1963).

5

HUMAN RIGHTS AS ENTITLEMENTS

The idea of international human rights is so explosive, so revolutionary, that even as an idea it has yet to be assimilated into the collective consciousness. For, ultimately, human rights in international law means that the state is *not* the sole entity that possesses rights, it is not the alpha and omega of international law. Instead, individual persons have direct claims under international law. And more revolutionary than that, individuals under international law may have direct claims against their own states.

No publicist of positivist persuasion in the nineteenth or early twentieth century would even have admitted the logical possibility of individuals having claims against their own governments. International law to publicists such as Oppenheim, Hall, Westlake, Wheaton, and Vattel, meant law *among* states. That law might—if pushed to the extreme—bear upon the relation between a citizen of one state and the government of another state (e.g., in a concession agreement), but it could hardly have anything to say about the relation between a citizen and his *own* state. Such a relationship was invisible to international law as then conceived.

But the holocaust put an end to all of that. The "crimes against humanity" at the Nuremberg trials opened the way to recognition of the crime of genocide that a state can commit against its own citizens. We have come a long way from the 1930s when Stalin's massacres of over ten million farmers hardly merited a paragraph on page 19 of *The New York Times*; we have begun to accept the notion that what a state does to its own citizens concerns us.

This is not to say that genocides are a thing of the past. The vast genocide in Cambodia (now Kampuchea) occurred in the 1970s, and as I write these words the gentle Ba'hai people of Iran are being slaughtered. I am not suggesting that we be complacent when I assert that the first step toward combatting genocide has now been taken—to recognize that it is not a matter of exclusive concern to a foreign nation and its own citizens.

But if protection against genocide is a human right, some writers nevertheless assert that it cannot be a matter of international law because genocides still occur today. Professors J. S. Watson and Eric Lane have accused their older colleagues in the field of international law of seriously overstating the international legal status of human rights.[1] The "old school," they charge, has confused a vision of what international law ought to be with an examination of what it really is.[2] To some extent these writers believe, at bottom, that even international law itself is not really "law." In that respect, the best answer I can give to such an assertion has been given in Chapter 1. But to a different extent, these writers assert that the norms of international human rights have not become part of the body of regular norms of international law. To such a claim, I offer the present chapter.

My purpose, then, is to show how human rights norms fit into the general concept of international entitlements which, as I argued in Chapter 1, are what define "states" and account for the enforcement of international law through reciprocal entitlement-violations.

In this chapter, I will be more rigorous and detailed about international entitlements than I was in Chapter 1. There will be a little bit of overlap with that chapter, however, and for that I ask the reader's indulgence.

My argument in this chapter reduces to several distinct propositions about international law: that a nation is defined by its interests and its entitlements; that all nations have the same set of entitlements;

---

1. See Lane, "Demanding Human Rights: A Change in the World Legal Order," 6 *Hofstra L. Rev.* 269 (1978) [hereinafter cited as Lane, "Demanding Human Rights"]; Lane, "Mass Killing by Governments: Lawful in the World Legal Order?" 12 *N.Y.U.J. Int'l L. & Pol.* 239 (1979) [hereinafter cited as Lane, "Mass Killing by Governments"]; Watson, "Autointerpretation, Competence and the Continuing Validity of Article 2(7) of the U.N. Charter," 71 *A.J.I.L.* 60 (1977) [hereinafter cited as Watson, "Autointerpretation"]; Watson, "Legal Theory, Efficacy and Validity in the Development of Human Rights Norms in International Law," 1979 *U. Ill. L.F.* 609 [hereinafter cited as Watson, "Legal Theory"]. See also Watson, "A Realistic Jurisprudence of International Law," 1980 *Y.B. World Affairs* 265.

2. Lane, "Mass Killing by Governments," *supra* note 1 at 279-80; Watson, "Legal Theory," *supra* note 1 at 611-12.

each entitlement has equal legal standing vis-à-vis other entitlements; that international law strives to preserve the equilibrium that equal entitlements create by permitting retaliation by nations whose entitlements have been violated; and that if human rights norms are part of international law, they take the form of universally held entitlements.

I. A "Nation" Is a Collection of Interests and Entitlements

The term "international law" suggests a law of, by, and for nations; they are the "creator-subjects" of international law.[3] Although nations as a whole have the power to shape international law any way they collectively desire,[4] that law itself nevertheless defines what a "nation" is. From the point of view of a given individual nation, whether or not it is a "nation" internationally depends not on what it desires but on whether the "constitutive" rules of international law define it as a "nation." An individual nation in this manner is no different from the "sovereign" described by Professor H. L. A. Hart.[5] A sovereign may be able to make or annul the laws in his own territory, but he cannot regulate the laws that define who the sovereign is or who will succeed to the sovereignty upon his demise.[6] For these "constitutive" laws are the conditions of his own sovereign power. He may influence them, for example, by appeals to the citizenry or by displays of force, but somehow the constitutive laws are larger than the sovereign. The international situation is an a fortiori case. An individual aggregation of people in a territory may try to influence outside groups to label it as a "nation,"[7] but this labeling will or will not occur depending upon the international rules of recognition of nations and whether it comes within those rules.

Thus, at its moment of creation, a "nation" is faced with external rules that have defined it as a "nation." It is already plugged into an international system of rules—by definition. And it finds, upon in-

---

3. A. D'Amato, *The Concept of Custom in International Law*, 33 (1971).
4. There is no international law external to the international collectivity; but any individual nation may only influence the collective consensus as to what the law is. If a single nation could determine what the law is, there would be no possibility of a violation of international law.
5. H. Hart, *The Concept of Law*, 51-60 (1961).
6. Id., 74-76.
7. The Palestinian Arabs on the West Bank are a good example.

vestigation, that there are many other rules that define nationhood and the nation's standing vis-à-vis other nations—rules that it cannot unilaterally change, although it has an equal influence in working with other nations to bring about systemic change acceptable to all.

Our hypothetical new nation might not want to accept any of these rules as obligatory upon itself. For this reason, I will avoid the usual phraseology of "rights" and "obligations" under international law, and instead employ the more objective term of "legal entitlements," or simply entitlements.[8] Thus, although our new nation may want to deny that it has any "obligations" under international law—even if the other nations have chosen to recognize it as a "nation"—it cannot deny that other nations claim for *themselves* certain entitlements. Indeed, our new nation will want to discover what these entitlements are so that it may be more fully aware of its international environment, for the expectations of its neighbors will be of great practical importance to it in its relations with them.

Upon investigation, it will find a rather awesome and fully developed set of entitlements. We are familiar with these as the usual rules of customary international law. For example, it will find that other nations claim exclusive sovereignty over their airspaces, that they do not claim exclusive sovereignty over the high seas, that they claim that their boundaries are fixed and not subject to forcible change by the military aggression of others, and that treaty entitlements survive changes of government. They also claim, among many other things, that their own nationals traveling in foreign countries must be accorded a minimal standard of international protection against the governmental or police action of those countries.[9] Our new nation, looking at this list, will probably conclude that these entitlements are not on the whole a bad lot. Although they serve to restrict the activities of our new nation (for instance, it will not be able to have free use of the world's airspace for its new commercial airline but will rather have to engage in negotiations and reciprocal contracts for international flight), they also present it with an important set of entitlements. If our new nation wants to assert these entitlements, it will derive international legal protection for its own boundaries, its own airspace, its own citizens traveling abroad, and so forth. But the crucial

---

8. *See generally* Calabresi & Melamed, "Property Rules, Liability Rules, and Inalienability: One View of the Cathedral," 85 *Harv. L. Rev.* 1089 (1972).

9. *See* Root, "The Basis of Protection of Citizens Residing Abroad," 4 *A.J.I.L.* 517, 521-22 (1910).

point is that even if it does not want to assert these entitlements, it nevertheless will be looking outward at all the other nations that have been asserting and continue to assert these entitlements against it. Our new nation is faced with the fact that other nations have claimed and are claiming these entitlements as a matter of right and expect to continue to claim them, even against our new nation, even if it does not like any or all of them.

In addition to, and conceptually distinct from, entitlements, our new nation and every nation has its own particular "interests."[10] These are the things that the nation wants, and can include wants that are quite illegal—for instance, rapid territorial expansion at the expense of its neighbors. The set of interests may overlap with the set of entitlements. For example, our new nation's interest in the sanctity of its borders overlaps with an entitlement to the same effect. It may have an interest, as it certainly has an entitlement, to the safety of its diplomatic personnel abroad. On the other hand, our new nation may have a very deep interest in something that has not attained the status of an entitlement (and might never attain that status). For instance, the United States might have a deep interest in breaking up international oil cartels. In domestic law, the United States has such an antitrust power. But internationally an oil cartel is not as of the present writing a violation of any American international entitlement.[11] The American legal interest in breaking up an international oil cartel might be many orders of magnitude greater than the American interest in some of its international entitlements, but to confuse the magnitude of a nation's interests with international entitlements, as these examples suggest, makes no sense.[12] The reverse is also true: a nation may have an entitlement but absolutely no interest in it. Switzerland has an entitlement to jurisdiction over its territorial sea. Lacking a territorial sea and any near-term prospects of obtaining one, Switzerland may be assumed to have a near-zero interest in this particular entitlement. Nevertheless, as a nation, it still "has" the entitlement. A nation may unilaterally control its own interests; it has no unilateral control over its (and every other nation's) entitlements.

---

10. *See, e.g.*, M. Kaplan & N. Katzenbach, *The Political Foundations of International Law*, 240-43 (1961).

11. *Cf. International Association of Machinists and Aerospace Workers v. Organization of Petroleum Exporting Countries*, 477 F. Supp. 553 (C.D. Cal. 1979) (discussing legality of international resource cartels), aff'd on other grounds, 649 F. 2d 1354 (9th Cir. 1981), cert. denied, 102 S. Ct. 1036 (1982).

12. For a critique of the "interests approach" of Kaplan and Katzenbach, *see* D'Amato, *supra* note 3, 145-47.

Thus, when Professor Watson, at a crucial point in his argument, asserts that "it is an inescapable fact that one state's treatment of its citizens is of little interest to other states,"[13] it is clear that he is not making a legal argument, for he is speaking only of interests, not entitlements. And he may be quite wrong even as to interests: consider Israel's interest in the treatment of Soviet Jews, or the interest of African nations in the treatment of South African blacks. Nevertheless, the degree of interest that a nation has in the affairs of another nation has no direct connection to its legal entitlements.[14] Of course, if every state had no interest whatsoever in what other states do to their own citizens, then it would be *unlikely* that there would have arisen an entitlement to protect oppressed citizens in other states. I say "unlikely" because international law, after all, reflects the aggregate interests of states over time. But there is no theoretical, or necessary, linkage between no-interest and no-entitlement. And certainly, as my previous examples have suggested, if Watson is roughly correct that one state's treatment of its citizens is of "little" interest to other states, that fact certainly would neither prevent an entitlement from arising nor defeat one that had already arisen.

II. All Nations Have the Same Set of Entitlements

In sharp contrast to interests that, as we have seen, can vary greatly, each nation's set of entitlements is the same as every other nation's. Occasionally, some writers such as DeVisscher, Kaplan, Katzenbach, and McDougal have made highly curious assertions to the contrary.[15]

---

13. Watson, "Legal Theory," *supra* note 1, at 619.

14. States' interests in such questions, after all, may change over time. Different states may have different degrees of interest (consider, for example, a majority in one state having ethnic or religious ties to a persecuted minority in another state). Indeed, there are signs that people are becoming more empathetic to the plight of other human beings even absent the "old" sorts of ties of religious or ethnic similarity.

15. *See* C. DeVisscher, *Theory and Reality in Public International Law*, 149 (Corbett trans. 1957); M. Kaplan & N. Katzenbach, *supra* note 10; M. McDougal et al., *Studies in World Public Order*, 773-843 (1960). I have previously commented upon these assertions that some states are more important than others in terms of rights under international law. *See* D'Amato, *supra* note 3, 64-65 (DeVisscher), 144-47 (Kaplan and Katzenbach), 218-22 (McDougal). *See also The Antelope*, 23 U.S. (10 Wheat.) 66, 122 (1825) ("perfect equality of nations"). It should be noted that when DeVisscher and other writers talk about special custom, regional custom, or local customs it is clear that the rights appertaining thereto are not shared by the community of nations—any more than all nations share the bilateral treaty rights of two contracting states. The statement in the text that all entitlements are the same refers only, of course, to general rules of international law.

But those arguments have not been taken seriously. Law, in fact, has an internal dynamism that promotes, if not requires, equality; its prescriptions, in nearly every legal system including the international, apply to all its addressees equally.[16] It is indeed hard to imagine rules and norms of general application that do not apply equally to their addressees. To be sure, within organizations entitlements sometimes are different. In the United Nations, for example, the permanent members of the Security Council have more entitlements regarding the practices of the United Nations than have the other members of the Council, and the Council members as a whole have more entitlements than do the members of the United Nations who are not seated on the Security Council. In any treaty regime, the contracting parties may have differentiable entitlements vis-a-vis each other or as against noncontracting parties (e.g. exclusive trade arrangements). But general customary international law, including the entitlements regarding the entering into and validity of treaties, knows no such differentiations.

III. Each Entitlement Has Equal Standing

Each separate entitlement in a national set of entitlements is legally the equivalent of every other entitlement. None has more legal weight or standing than any other. An entitlement either exists or does not exist, but once it exists, it is the equivalent of any other entitlement. This point is by no means obvious, since normally we think of some entitlements as more important than others— for example, the inviolability of national boundaries seems much more important than equal access to the mineral wealth of the ocean floor. But this "importance" is upon analysis simply a matter of what I have defined as national "interests." To an expansionist nation, for example, the inviolability of national boundaries might be an impediment; such a nation would have a very low interest in maintaining that entitlement. Stripped of its "interest" dimension, the system of entitlements appears as an unidimensional set of legal norms legally indistinguishable from each other. Entitlements are like Ronald Dworkin's

---

16. *See* L. Fuller, *The Morality of Law*, 46-49 (rev. ed. 1969); *see also* A. Gewirth, *Reason and Morality*, 129-89 (1978) (incoherent to assert rights yet deny similar assertions by others).

rules—you have one or you don't, one applies or it doesn't.[17] Even international rules of *jus cogens*, or peremptory norms,[18] are no more important than other rules, for these are simply rules that deny the validity of certain substantive provisions that might be included in treaties.[19] As such they are not on a higher plane than, for example, the customary rule of *pacta sunt servanda*; in fact, they may be thought of as conditional specifications of the rule of *pacta sunt servanda*.

That entitlements are mutually equivalent in terms of importance or weight is not a necessary feature of international law. Rather, it reflects the current international legal system. Nations might have evolved a different kind of system. But at least so far they have not. Indeed, it is the present deep divergence in interests among nations that accounts for the equal standing of entitlements. For while nations have been able to agree to a common set of entitlements, their differential interests with respect to any particular entitlement almost ensures the lack of any communal consensus as to relative importance among entitlements. (Of course, some entitlements are trivial—for example, the finer points of diplomatic protocol—and these surely are not equivalent to general norms of customary international law. But among the latter material norms, there is no consensus as to relative importance.)

IV. The Legal System Will Strive to Preserve Entitlement Equilibrium

Given a common set of entitlements of equal weight, which as a whole defines the international legal system,[20] the legal system itself will act to preserve the equilibrium engendered by that set. This

---

17. *See* R. Dworkin, *Taking Rights Seriously*, 26 (1977). Dworkin contrasts "rules" with "principles," the latter having weight that helps impel a decision a certain way without requiring such a decision.

18. *See* D'Amato, *supra* note 3, 132 n. 73 (claim-oriented perspective on peremptory norms).

19. *See* Vienna Convention on the Law of Treaties, opened for signature May 23, 1969, art. 53, 8 *I.L.M.* 679, 698-99 [hereinafter cited without cross references as Vienna Convention on the Law of Treaties].

20. The entitlements as a whole contain primary rules regarding the conduct of states, and secondary rules that "specify the ways in which the primary rules may be conclusively ascertained, introduced, eliminated, varied, and the fact of their violation conclusively determined." H. Hart, *supra* note 5, 92. *See* D'Amato, *supra* note 3, 41-44; D'Amato, "The Neo-Positivist Concept of International Law," 59 *A.J.I.L.* 321 (1965).

equilibrium or stable balance of legal entitlements is, after all, the result of centuries of international interaction and expresses principles by which nations on the whole have consented[21] to accommodate each other. A disruption in the set may be viewed as a tendency toward imbalance, toward disequilibrium. The legal system may be expected to respond homeostatically—to restore the balance by exacting a legal penalty upon the entitlement violator. The entitlements as a set, worked out by nations over the centuries, represent a coherent system such that the violation of any one of them gives rise on the international level to what Festinger has called "cognitive dissonance" on the level of personal psychology.[22] Other nations will react to remove this dissonance by taking legal action against the violator (which, as we shall see, involves retaliatory entitlement-violation). Additionally, the violating nation itself, having introduced dissonance into the system, will expect retaliation, but will not know what kind of entitlement will be involved in the retaliation. Its inability to predict the retaliation serves to dissuade it from committing the initial entitlement violation (the delict); thus the system as a whole tends toward self-preservation of its set of entitlements. This systemic homeostatic mechanism is enhanced by the nature of rule-formation in the international legal system. General rules of international law now are changeable only by the process of custom or consensus. The latter by definition raises no disruptive problem; nations simply agree as a whole to a new rule.[23] But customary law formation, except when accomplished by the effect of treaties upon nonparties, can be disruptive indeed. Like the Hegelian-Marxist struggle of thesis and antithesis, an entitlement (thesis) is met with a violation (antithesis), which violation, if it "catches hold," may give rise to a new rule (synthesis). The violation of the entitlement may thus contain the seeds of a new rule, but the critical question is what the other nations will do about it. If they accept the violation, a new customary rule is on its way toward being formed. But if they isolate the violation, label it a violation, and punish the transgressor, then instead of the seed of a new rule taking hold, the seed is trampled upon and the

---

21. *See* L. Jaffe, *Judicial Aspects of Foreign Relations,* 90 (1933).
22. *See* L. Festinger, *A Theory of Cognitive Dissonance* (1957); cf. D'Amato, "Psychological Constructs in Foreign Policy Prediction," 11 *J. Confl. Res.* 294, 306-09 (1967) (proposing that an individual reacts to the foreign policy environment according to certain behavioral structures and that these "constructs" can be used to predict an individual policy-maker's decision in a given foreign policy situation).
23. *See* D'Amato, "On Consensus," 8 *Can. Y.B. Int'l L.* 104 (1971).

original customary rule is reinforced. What might have been an impediment to the formation of a customary rule instead becomes another instance of its confirmation.

Unless the international legal system is psychologically ready for a new rule (in which case there is already an implicit consensus), it will react to the violation of a customary rule with all the means at its disposal to ensure that the violation does not replace the old rule with its opposite. These means, as we shall see in the discussion of the next principle, are all that the legal system qua legal system can do—namely, to treat the violator as an "outlaw" for the purpose of its transgression, and to respond by a retaliatory deprivation of one or more of the violator's entitlements.

V. A Nation that Violates Another Nation's Entitlement May Expect Retaliation that Preserves Entitlement Equilibrium

The entitlements that define any legal system require a mechanism for self-protection. This is simply a consequence of the nature of systems that have survived and become stable.[24] Domestic legal systems have such mechanisms in legislatures, in courts of comprehensive jurisdiction, and in police enforcement. If *A* steals *B*'s car, the state recognizes that *B* retains ownership of the car even though it is now in *A*'s possession, and furthermore will prosecute *A* criminally, repossess the car, and deliver it over to *B*. Thus *B*'s property entitlement in the car is preserved and vindicated. There is no suggestion that the entitlement itself is in jeopardy of being changed by *A*'s action. In other words, there is no process of customary law formation in this example or in domestic examples similar to it. In contrast, if customary international law were involved in such an example, *A*'s theft from *B* would contain the seeds of a new customary rule (for example, that anyone who forcibly takes possession of another person's property becomes the legitimate owner of such property).[25] Depending on how many previous cases there were of the old rule (protecting ownership in private property against forcible takeover),

---

24. *See* L. von Bertalanffy, *General System Theory*, 78, 161-63 (1968); N. Wiener, *Cybernetics* (1948).

25. In years past, the forcible conquest of another nation's territory conferred title upon the conqueror. *See* J. Brierly, *The Law of Nations*, 171-72 (6th ed. Waldock 1963).

on subsequent reaction to the *A-B* case, and possibly on cases subsequent to the *A-B* case, a new rule of custom may have been presumptively formed, initiated, or defeated.[26] To be sure, in the earliest days of the domestic legal system, before courts knew very much of what was expected of them and before legislatures or monarchs realized that they could create new laws out of thin air, there was a process of customary-law formation akin to that of the international legal system today.[27] But in any modern municipal-law system, the existence of legislatures, which can change any rule the public wants changed, and courts, which preserve existing rules, is sufficient to give the system of entitlements stability through time.

Of course, the international legal system is not devoid of courts, although the courts as a whole certainly do not enjoy comprehensive jurisdiction over all international legal transactions. The present International Court of Justice at the Hague has very limited, consensual jurisdiction, and it has not acted resolutely in recent cases even where jurisdiction was arguably established.[28] The Security Council of the United Nations in principle has central enforcement power to protect against threats to or breaches of the peace, but due to dissension on the Council, it has not yet mobilized an army. There are many regional organizations, arbitral tribunals, bilateral commissions, and so forth in the international legal panoply, but Professor Watson is correct in arguing that there is a "lack of enforcement mechanisms of the hierarchical type."[29] What Watson fails to see, however, is that the international legal system protects its entitlements by processes different from the domestic model.

26. *See* D'Amato, *supra* note 3, 91-102.
27. *See generally* H. S. Maine, *Ancient Law: Its Connection with the Early History of Society and Its Relation to Modern Ideas* (1861). *See also* L. Fuller, *Anatomy of the Law*, 76-91 (1968).
To take a speculative example parallel to that given in the text, suppose that in the early days of a legal system *A* stole *B*'s money, purchased some goods from *C*, and then left the country. *B* applies to a court to get his stolen money back from *C*. The notion of theft and of stolen property might very well have given *B* a prima facie claim to his money. However, the usefulness of money as a mechanism for exchange would be compromised by allowing persons to trace stolen money. By not allowing *B*'s claim, the early court would be developing the law in a fashion analogous to custom in international law. (A later court would then hold, as we know, that if *B* could prove that *C* was not a holder in due course *B* could get the money back.)
28. *See* Dugard, "The Nuclear Tests Cases and the South West Africa Cases: Some Realism About the International Judicial Decision," 16 *Va. J. Int'l L.* 463, 465-68 (1976).
29. Watson, "A Realistic Jurisprudence of International Law," 1980 *Y.B. World Affairs* 265, 267. Even so, there are many kinds of "sanctions" other than force, and the more attenuated the concept becomes the harder it is for positivists, such as Lane and Watson, to accommodate it within their theory of law. *See* D'Amato, "What 'Counts' as Law?" in *Law-making in the Global Community*, 831-88 (N. Onuf ed. 1982).

The way the international legal system protects its entitlements is in effect to declare the nation that violates an entitlement a temporary outlaw and to allow the nation or nations whose entitlements were violated, or even third parties, to retaliate against the outlaw by in turn disregarding one or more of the outlaw nation's entitlements. The criteria as to which entitlements may be violated in retaliation are, in the present stage of international law, quite controversial. There is a strong consensus that the *same* entitlement may be violated, at the very least. For instance, when the Iranian militants held American embassy personnel hostage, there was some talk in the United States of retaliating by arresting Iranian diplomats, consular officials, and students in this country. However, this was widely perceived to be ineffective; the new Iranian revolutionary government might not care about Iranians in the United States who might very well be sympathizers with the old regime of the Shah. Indeed, it is often the case that when state *A* violates state *B*'s entitlement, state *A* has already calculated that retaliation in kind would not be too costly to it. Of course, when it is perceived that retaliation in kind *would* be too costly, the initial violation is probably deterred—and this may be true of the vast majority of cases that never move beyond the planning stage.

As to retaliation by violating a different entitlement, there is a sense in which the retaliation chosen must not be out of proportion to the initial violation.[30] It would not do to punish the Iranians for taking the American hostages by dropping a nuclear bomb on an Iranian city. However, less drastic, but still forceful, military measures were indeed contemplated by the United States during the period the hostages were held captive. A further restriction on the choice of a different entitlement for retaliatory purposes might be some sense that the method of retaliation should be related to the initial delict in time, place, or subject matter. However, all of the foregoing are extremely vague restrictions under present international law. Indeed, it is difficult to imagine how rules could be formulated that deal

---

30. *See* R. Fisher, *International Conflict for Beginners*, 148-49 (1969). Professor Fisher does not purport to be discussing international law in this book, but rather is addressing the broader issue of international conflict resolution. To the extent that he is not talking about "law" itself, he may be correct that it is better strategically to retaliate in proportion, time, place, and manner, to the original delict. But *cf.* J. Gaddis, *Strategies of Containment* (1982) (discussion of usefulness of "asymmetric containment" in United States foreign policy). *See also* R. Fisher, *Improving Compliance with International Law*, 72 (1981) (credibility of sanction a function of relation to the offense) [hereinafter cited as R. Fisher, *Improving Compliance*].

specifically and usefully with questions of proportionality and relatedness when there is such an enormous variety of possible thrusts and counterthrusts in international relations.

The difficulty, or indeed near-impossibility, of formulating rules constricting the choice of retaliations is itself a deterrent to the initial delict. If nation A decides to violate an entitlement of nation B, it risks retaliation along a fairly wide and rather undefined front. The risk is, in most cases, not worth taking. The result is a general condition of systemic stability in which, to use a phrase of Professor Henkin, "almost all nations observe almost all principles of international law and almost all of their obligations almost all of the time."[31]

In the Appendix to this chapter, I try to present some examples of the contemplation or use of retaliation against entitlements as illustrative of the "enforcement and compliance" mechanism in international law. The mechanism may appear less mysterious if we note here that international law explicitly provides for the kind of entitlement retaliation I have described in the area of breach of treaty. If nations X and Y have entered into a treaty, then no matter how long the treaty is and how many articles it contains, if X commits a material breach of the treaty then Y may legally retaliate by disregarding any or all of its treaty obligations to X.[32] Another way of putting this is that a treaty sets up contractual entitlements between the parties. If X violates one of Y's treaty entitlements, Y may legally retaliate by disregarding any or all of its obligations to X in the particular treaty that was violated by X. As in international customary law, there is no differentiation among entitlements in a treaty as to their relative importance or weight. The only restriction upon Y's power of retaliation is that X must have committed a breach of a material entitle-

---

31. L. Henkin, *How Nations Behave*, 47 (2d ed. 1979).
32. *See* Vienna Convention on the Law of Treaties, *supra* note 19, art. 60(3). The retaliatory mechanism I have discussed in the text applies to the international legal system as a system in any given time period. I have attempted to describe the structure of entitlement retaliation as a mechanism for preserving entitlements. Of course, at any given historical time there may be rules that disallow certain kinds of retaliation. At present, article 2(4) is simply a very important entitlement that nations invoke to protect themselves. Conceivably that entitlement might be violated, however, if a nation commits an egregious act that falls short of armed attack upon another nation. For example, if a white minority government began systematically to kill its black nationals, I think that such a blatant example of genocide would trigger military invasion by other nations upon the genocidal state's territory, and article 2(4) would be viewed as simply having been overridden. In sum, I suggest that the entitlement-retaliatory mechanism I have described, while primitive, is the ultimate sanction in international law, more basic even than article 2(4).

ment. In the analogous customary-law situation, the violating nation must have committed a breach of a nontrivial customary-law entitlement.

International law is replete with examples of reprisals, retortions, and other forms of self-help, and the (sometimes) accompanying rules of relatedness and proportionality.[33] Only some of these situations have involved entitlement retaliation (which is not circumscribed by rules of relatedness and proportionality). There have been two recent events, however, that provide an outstanding example of the entitlement-retaliation system: the Iranian hostage crisis and Iraqi war, and the Namibian independence movement. The relevance of both of these is explored in depth in the Appendix to this chapter.

Retaliation for entitlement violation is a constant possibility in the international legal system, and this fact helps ensure the stability of the entire set of entitlements. However, like the old notion of a "just war" in retaliation for what in those days were considered grave entitlement violations,[34] the entitlement-retaliation system I have described could erupt in runaway escalation, given the vagueness of the previously mentioned "restrictions" of relatedness and proportionality. Its escalatory potential constitutes an ever-present threat to world peace. Clearly entitlement retaliation is not the most desirable form of "compliance and implementation," and fortunately it is not the only one. The international legal system contains many of the sanctions that are more typically used in domestic legal systems to secure compliance with norms.[35] For example, when the International Court of Justice has compulsory jurisdiction, its judgments may be implemented by the United Nations under article 94. In addition, the machinery of the United Nations itself, especially the peacekeeping provisions of the Security Council, which have yet to be implemented, allows for international sanctions against lawbreakers. Many treaties set up treaty mechanisms for enforcement. Also there are regional courts, such as the European Court of Human Rights, which have certain powers of enforcement. Finally, international

---

33. *See, e.g.*, I. Brownlie, *International Law and the Use of Force by States* (1963); J. Starke, *An Introduction to International Law*, 548-51 (8th ed. 1977); Bowett, "Reprisals Involving Recourse to Armed Force," 66 *A.J.I.L.* 1 (1972); Paust, "The Seizure and Recovery of the Mayaguez," 85 *Yale L.J.* 774 (1976); and Chapter 2, *supra*.

34. *See* D'Amato, Book Review, 72 *Am Pol. Sci. Rev.* 804 (1978) (reviewing E. B. F. Midgley, *The Natural Law Tradition and the Theory of International Relations* (1975)); M. Walzer, *Just and Unjust Wars* (1977).

35. *See generally* R. Fisher, *Improving Compliance, supra* note 30, 39-72.

legal questions arise very often in municipal courts, and depending on the kind of case, enforcement can at times be extremely effective.[36] All of these procedures offer traditional "sanctions"—namely, direct punishment of the lawbreaker that is designed to deter similar instances of such conduct. This traditional type of "sanction" is conceptually distinct from the system of retaliation by entitlement violation that I have described in this chapter.

However, although the traditional sanctions system works for many cases, at the present stage of international legal development it falls significantly short of universality. The international system has no pervasive judicial jurisdiction over all cases that may arise, and the United Nations is hobbled by its discretionary veto system.[37]

As a result, the system of retaliatory entitlement violation that I have described is the only truly universal mechanism allowed by the international legal system to secure implementation and compliance in the real sense required by Professors Lane and Watson. Realistically, we have to acknowledge it as such, even as we recognize its potential for runaway destructive escalation and even as we work to expand the traditional sanctions system.

VI. If Human-Rights Norms Are Part of International Law, They Are Entitlements

The preceding analysis of entitlement suggests that the international legal system does allow for sanctions for noncompliance with its norms, the sanctions being the threat or actuality of reciprocal entitlement violation that is generally understood and accepted as restorative of entitlement equilibrium. But now the questions arise: when a nation violates an individual's human rights, has that nation violated an entitlement? If so, is that entitlement a part of the international-law set of entitlements? I want to reserve this last question for the discussion in chapter six, and deal here only with the structural

---

36. See *Filartiga v. Peña-Irala*, 630 F.2d 876 (2d Cir. 1980); Gordon, "Current Legal Developments," 15 *Int'l Law*. 265, 280-85 (1981); Comment, "Torture as a Tort in Violation of International Law: *Filartiga v. Peña-Irala*," 33 *Stan. L. Rev.* 353 (1981) (loose discussion of international "consensus").

37. If the permanent members of the Security Council were able to cast vetoes only in certain legally prescribed instances, we might have a universal system of law enforcement; however, the totally discretionary veto has ensured so far in the United Nations history that no principled system of universal sanctions could come into existence.

contention that a nation that violates a human-rights norm can violate what we have defined as an entitlement. While reserving the question of whether or not human rights entitlements actually *do* exist, this section will deal with the more fundamental question of whether or not they *can* exist—that is, whether or not they can fit into the international system of legal entitlements.

Imagine that a soapbox orator begins to make a political speech in state X. Among the small group of people listening to him are A, a national of X, and B, who was born in X but became a naturalized citizen of Y and is now on a vacation in X. The X police suddenly descend upon the scene, and arrest the orator and the twenty or so persons who had gathered around to listen. A and B are jailed without any formal arraignment processes; they are subjected to inhuman and degrading treatment and finally are tortured for supporting (by virtue of their listening to) the subversive orator. Let us further stipulate that both A and B were simply passers-by, and neither was connected in any way with any anti-government political activities in X.

On these facts, Lane and Watson would have no difficulty in concluding that nation X has incurred international responsibility to nation Y for its maltreatment of B.[38] That maltreatment fell below the international minimal standard for a state's responsibility to aliens, and thus clearly violated Y's entitlement that its nationals traveling abroad should not be subjected to such maltreatment by the officials of X.[39] There is no difficulty with this conclusion in present-day international law or even in the international law of the nineteenth century. A classicist might say that state Y is itself "harmed" by virtue of the harm to one of its nationals, and is thus entitled to redress from state X.[40] Since state Y is injured, Y might want to engage in a reciprocal violation of one of X's entitlements in the event that X does not compensate Y for the injury.

But what is it, if anything, that sets B apart from A? Is it the fact that B is holding a passport from state Y? B may not have the passport (he may have lost it), or it may be outdated or invalid for some other reason. Without the passport or some other set of papers, B is, in appearance, the same as A. Both are, say, men in their forties, apolitical, perhaps of the same religious and ethnic group, and were even

---

38. *See, e.g.,* Watson, "Legal Theory," *supra* note 1, at 620.
39. *See* L. Sohn & T. Buergenthal, *International Protection of Human Rights*, 23-136 (1973).
40. *See* McDougal & Bebr, "Human Rights in the United Nations," 58 *A.J.I.L.* 603, 609-10 (1964).

born in the same town in *X*. Why should Watson and Lane have no difficulty with *B*'s case, which they acknowledge is part of international law in the realistic sense of compliance and sanctions,[41] and yet have enormous difficulty with *A*'s case, which they say is outside the realm of international law? Why do they feel that what state *X* does to its own citizen, *A*, within its own borders, is purely a matter of *X*'s "domestic jurisdiction" protected as such by article 2(7) of the United Nations Charter?[42] A possible answer is that *B* is a "national" of *Y*, and that fact "internationalizes" his situation, whereas *A* is a national of *X*, and thus the *A-X* relation is one of domestic law only. Yet, this begs the question. "Nationality" is only an artificial relationship pertaining to international law. It is merely another way of stating that state *Y* has an entitlement in *B*'s protection from *X*. For if *Y* were the only state in the world, there would not have arisen a concept of nationality. (There might have arisen a concept of citizenship, which has to do with voting or other kinds of political eligibility, but not "nationality.") It is the existence of other states in the world that has given rise to a special relationship between *Y* and certain of "its" people, including those who become its people through naturalization, namely, the relationship of nationality. This special relationship would not have arisen had not other states recognized it (and they recognized it, perhaps, because they saw in it reciprocal advantages to themselves in claims of their own "nationality").[43] Once recognized and accepted, it became an entitlement.

Thus, Watson and Lane's theses come down to this: They agree that what *X* does to *B* is a matter of international law in the fullest sense of the word—namely, that *X*'s duties toward *B* are subject to implementation and compliance to the extent that international law can and does ensure such compliance with its norms. And they also agree that what *X* does to *A* is a matter of domestic jurisdiction wholly outside the realm of international law. Thus Lane and Watson (and their followers in the Reagan administration) are *not* saying that in-

---

41. Watson indeed criticizes Lauterpacht and McDougal for their "lack of understanding as to why there is such a difference in the legal status of aliens and citizens." Watson, "Legal Theory, *supra* note 1, at 620.

42. Watson is more strident on this point than Lane. *See* Watson, "Autointerpretation," *supra* note 1. Lane, "Mass Killing by Governments," *supra* note 1, focuses more upon the failure to enforce human rights.

43. International law might have developed quite differently—perhaps that anyone physically within a state is totally subject to that state's laws and that there is no concept of an alien, a non-national, or a stateless person.

dividuals cannot be the subject of international law, or that international law does not exist, or that international law is ineffective, or any of the other discredited positions that from time to time have been asserted by self-styled "realists." Rather, they are saying *only* that international law obtains in the case of B, because B is a national of Y, and does not obtain in the case of A, because A is not an alien within X but rather a national of X who is stuck with whatever maltreatment his own country metes out to him within its boundaries. Finally, as we have seen, the only thing that differentiates A and B is the intangible and indeed question-begging concept of "nationality."

VII. If Human Rights Norms Are Entitlements, Then They Are Universal Entitlements

Our next step is therefore apparent. We must try to discover whether Y has an entitlement to protect A along with its acknowledged entitlement to protect B. We have to decide, in other words, whether there is a "human rights" entitlement in Y that enables Y legally to violate one or more of X's international-law entitlements if X maltreats A, its own national, in the same sense that Y has a "nationality" entitlement that enables Y legally to violate one or more of X's international-law entitlements if X maltreats B, Y's national. Or, to coin a phrase, we must find A to be an "international" of state Y just as B is a "national" of state Y.

To writers such as Lane and Watson, what state X does to its own national, A, within its own borders seems quintessentially a matter of X's domestic jurisdiction. Yet, as Professor Henkin has demonstrated, a matter is exclusively within X's domestic jurisdiction only when it is not a matter of international law.[44] Domestic jurisdiction is a residual concept; it is simply another way of saying that international law does not apply. To be sure, how state X treats individuals within its borders seems to be something within state X's exclusive province. Yet we only have to recall our previous hypothetical example to dispel this illusion. State X maltreats A and B, who are individuals within its borders. B, we assume, carries no papers or

---

44. *See* Henkin, "Human Rights and 'Domestic Jurisdiction'," in *Human Rights, International Law and the Helsinki Accord*, 21-40 (T. Buergenthal ed. 1977).

other identification, and appears to be no different from *A*. Yet *B* is a national of state *Y*. Every international lawyer believes that what state *X* does to *B* is not within *X*'s domestic jurisdiction. The reason given for singling out *B* is that there is some international law link between *B* and another state, a link defined and approved by international law and labeled "nationality." Appearances do not tell us about this; rather, the link is entirely a juridical construct. In short, Henkin and before him Kelsen must be correct in arguing that characterizing a matter as one within *X*'s domestic jurisdiction is simply another way of saying that the matter is not cognizable under international law, and no more than that.[45]

So let us now focus upon *X*'s maltreatment of its own national *A*. Is *X*'s action cognizable under international law? A more precise way of asking this question is to ask if one or more other states can have an entitlement that *A* not be tortured by *X*? If so, which other states? I would suggest that the other states that may claim such an entitlement are *all* the other states, a notion which after all is suggested by the very term "human rights."

The human rights violator is, like the pirate, *hostis humani generis*, an enemy of all mankind, and jurisdiction to punish his violations is universal.[46] In years past, although pirates were theoretically subject to the criminal jurisdiction of any state that captured them, many nations "winked" at the practice so long as the pirates were known

---

45. *See* H. Kelsen, *Principles of International Law*, 290-91 (rev. ed. R. Tucker 1966); Henkin, *supra* note 44.

There are, however, two alternative views of domestic jurisdiction," both suggested by Professor Oscar Schachter, that should be noted. *See* Schacter, Book Review, 17 *Colum. J. Transnat'l L* 531 (1978) (reviewing *Human Rights, International Law and the Helsinki Accord* (T. Buergenthal ed. 1977)). The first might view the concept as something of a shield or barrier to international cognizance of minor human rights violations that occur within a state's territory. For example, the issue of preferential admission to Blacks in American professional schools, if argued to be racial discrimination against Whites, may be too minor an issue to rise to the level of international human-rights concern. Perhaps international law should concern itself only with "consistent patterns or gross abuses," id. at 534. Schachter makes the interesting suggestion that over time the concept of "domestic jurisdiction" might aid the development of standards for determining the nature or frequency of violations that do rise to the international level, which may be preferable to "leaving the drawing of a line entirely to the political judgment of interested States." Id. (Of course, it might be pointed out, the existence of a domestic-jurisdiction line does not mean that its violation will automatically be sanctioned; the political judgment of interested states will still have an impact.) A second possibility is that the concept of domestic jurisdiction can act as a sort of "exhaustion of local remedies" requirement, so that if a state recognizes a domestic human-rights violation and takes steps to remedy it, the international community would not have jurisdiction unless there is a failure to remedy that amounts to a denial of justice.

46. *Cf. Filartiga v. Peña-Irala*, 630 F. 2d 876 (2d Cir. 1980) (discussion of the torturer as *hostis humani generis*).

to carry out their depredations against other states. For instance, pirate vessels known to focus their attentions upon Spanish galleons might have been allowed a certain freedom of action by England, even though England theoretically had jurisdiction. The state immediately affected, Spain, certainly had every incentive to combat piracy, but other nations often did nothing about it even though they were entitled to act. Similarly, with human rights most nations might not care whether state *X* tortures its own national. Perhaps a particular nation might feel specially affected—for instance, if *A*'s religious or ethnic background is the same as that of a majority of the citizens of *Y*, *Y* might feel some special calling to complain about *X*'s treatment of *A*. Certainly many nations in Africa having black majorities feel a special interest in the plight of blacks in South Africa. But like piracy, human rights may allow for a "universal" entitlement without necessarily guaranteeing that any one nation or group of nations will feel motivated, or have the interest, to do something about it.

For Lane and Watson to contend that the often appalling statistics of human-rights violations by governments vis-à-vis their own nationals are evidence that what those governments are doing is legal under international law would be very much like a seventeenth-century legal scholar stating that piracy must be legal because it is flourishing. Rather, the critical legal question for the seventeenth-century scholar was not whether nations in fact combatted piracy but whether they were legally entitled to do so if they chose. Similarly, if *X*'s maltreatment of *A* is a violation of *Y*'s entitlement, what is important is *Y*'s *potential* enforceability (through reciprocal entitlement-violation) of its entitlement.

VIII. Conclusion

It is important not to overstate what this chapter has attempted to do. It has not established that there *are* actual substantive human-rights norms that are part of international law. *That* question is one of the content of customary international law. What I have tried to show in this chapter is that human-rights norms are just like any other international law norms in that they are enforceable through the typical way that all norms are enforced—through reciprocal entitlement-violations. If I have succeeded in demonstrating this much at least, then human-rights norms can be assimilated to general international law without begging the very question that is asked.

Here is how the question can be begged: one can argue that we don't need states to enforce human-rights norms, because the concept of human rights norms has revolutionized our very conception of international law. Human beings are paramount, not states; hence the question is not whether states will or will not enforce international human rights, but rather whether states are legitimate entities at all. Perhaps they are legitimate, but only if they recognize their dependence upon, and derivative status in regard to, individual human beings.

Such an argument—appealing as it might be—begs the question. It is nothing other than a redefinition of international law. By redefining the concept, human rights can be assured a paramount position.

That sort of argument, however, will not prevail against a person who asks, as Professors Watson and Lane asked, whether human rights have any legal status under international law as they conceive it. To argue that their conception is wrong is not to persuade them. Rather, *given* their conception of international law (the classical conception of law created by and applied to states), this chapter has attempted to show that human-rights norms fit *that* conception. The argument I've made is a conservative one. If someday the entire conception of international law changes so that the Watson-Lane question no longer is asked, then the new human-rights concept will win the day even without argument.

APPENDIX TO CHAPTER 5

THE ENTITLEMENT-RETALIATION SYSTEM AT WORK

A. The Iranian Example

The events surrounding the taking of hostages at the United States Embassy in Tehran in 1979 offer several illustrations of different aspects of the workings of entitlement-retaliation in international law. Although multilateral and bilateral treaties signed by Iran and the

United States required Iran to protect American diplomatic and consular personnel against such an attack, and although a similar requirement could be made out under general international law, the Iranian government did nothing by way of protection or intervention.[47] Thus an American entitlement against Iran, requiring the latter to protect American Embassy personnel in Iran, was violated. A second American entitlement was violated when Iran officially endorsed the action of the militants, enabling them to hold the hostages for more than a year.[48]

Were Iran's actions a retaliation for a previous entitlement violation by the United States? Iran took such a position in communications to the International Court of Justice. In a letter of March 16, 1980, the Iranian Minister for Foreign Affairs referred to "more than 25 years of continual interference by the United States in the internal affairs of Iran, the shameless exploitation of our country, and numerous crimes perpetrated against the Iranian people, contrary to and in conflict with all international and humanitarian norms."[49] As far as the court itself was concerned, these vague charges were not specified because Iran refused to participate in the proceedings.[50] The court, as one might have expected, viewed Iran's allegations as part of the "political context" in which the specific dispute (namely, the taking of American hostages) arose. For our own analytical purposes, the labeling of something as "political" is another way of saying that it has not attained the status of a legal entitlement.

This conclusion would follow, under present international law, even if we were to assume that the Iranian charges could be fully specified and proved. The fact is that the customary international law of human rights has not yet reached the level of implicating foreign governments in such situations. Every government's foreign affairs business consists of encouraging or discouraging the actions of other governments, and it is far too soon in the evolution of international law to expect legal responsibility to attach to any such actions of encouragement or discouragement. However, we should not too readily dismiss the Iranian claim. Perhaps Iran has articulated a norm that now needs, for customary corroboration, supporting instances

---

47. *See United States Diplomatic and Consular Staff in Tehran* (U.S. v. Iran), 1980 I.C.J. 3, 6-7, 13-14 (Judgment of May 24) [hereinafter cited as *Tehran Hostages Case*].
48. *See* id. at 33-34.
49. Id. at 8.
50. Id. at 20.

of international behavior that would generate a new customary rule of international law, to the effect that if a government aids and abets another government that is engaged in human-rights violations, the first government has violated an international norm. However, it is clear that although Iran may have articulated such a norm, the articulation has fallen upon deaf ears. The argument made no impression upon the court or the dissenting Soviet judge.[51] At the present time, the proposed Iranian entitlement is clearly rejected by the world community; hence the international legal system, acting to preserve its present set of entitlements, has responded almost uniformly with outrage at the Iranian endorsement of the militants' seizure of American embassy personnel. This seizure was therefore seen to be not in retaliation for a previous entitlement violation, but rather itself an illegal violation of an American entitlement.

Given Iran's violation of the American entitlement of the safety and protection of its diplomatic personnel abroad, let us now consider the posture of the American responses to the Iranian action. Perhaps the most obvious reciprocal entitlement-violation would have been for the United States to seize and hold hostage the approximately 220 Iranian embassy personnel within the United States. Such a move would have satisfied Professor Fisher's criterion of relatedness—the seizure would have been similar in time, place, and manner to the original delict.[52] However, the United States rejected this possibility, reportedly on the ground that it did not want to be accused of following Iran's lead.[53] Instead, the State Department gave Iran five days to reduce the diplomatic staff from about sixty to fifteen and the consulate staffs from a total of 160 to twenty. In light of other alternatives for the United States, to be discussed below, it is interesting to speculate further on why the United States did not do the "obvious" thing and hold Iranian embassy personnel hostage in retaliation for the actions in Teheran. Such an action, I submit, might not be as effective in upholding the entire set of international entitlements as would selecting a different entitlement violation. Instead, what it

---

51. *Tehran Hostages Case, supra* note 47, at 30 (Judgment of May 24). Compare the discussion by Hermann Kahn about "retortions" and "legal harassment," quoted in B. Weston, R. Falk, & A. D'Amato, *International Law and World Order*, 137-38 (1980).
52. *See* R. Fisher, *International Conflict for Beginners*, 148-50.
53. "From the start of the crisis, American officials had considered various ways of retaliating against Iranian diplomats. The possibility of holding them hostage was rejected. The United States did not want to be accused of following Iran's lead." *N.Y. Times*, Dec. 13, 1979, A1, col. 5.

might do is simply help erode the particular entitlement at issue. The international legal system might lose one of its entitlements instead of protecting it. Crucially, the entitlement would not have been lost through the process of custom, since a change in custom requires both an initial deviating act and an acceptance of that deviation by the affected state.[54] But a "spreading" entitlement violation of the sort I have just described, though it would lead to a loss of the general rule of diplomatic immunity, would not have been effected by acquiescence on the part of the affected states but rather by their attempt—futile in the premises—to secure the original norm. Hence, there is some theoretical support for taking a position contrary to the strategic suggestion of Professor Fisher—namely, for the international system to secure its entitlements by allowing the affected nation to retaliate against a *different* entitlement.[55]

Accordingly, the United States considered several other violations of Iran's entitlements when it became clear that the government of Iran was not immediately going to return the hostages.[56] The options considered ranged from a naval blockade of the Kharg Islands[57] to precision strikes against other oil installations.[58] Although the threats certainly served a purpose, helping to ensure the safety of the hostages, the United States made it clear on numerous occasions that military action would be taken if the hostages were harmed.[59] Anyone reading the media accounts cannot fail to be impressed with the fact that practically no objection was raised to the legality of such possible actions. The discussion instead focused upon possible Iranian retaliation against the hostages and the possible adverse reaction of public opinion in other Middle Eastern nations.[60] Although not strong evidence, it is at least some evidence of an underlying acceptance of the international systemic mechanism I have described that would

---

54. *See* A. D'Amato, *supra* note 3, 87-98.

55. The slow refinement of customary laws through the centuries indicates that the international system protects its customary entitlements, allowing them to change by custom (since that is the process by which they were created) but is careful lest they change by the destructive process of spreading entitlement violations. For a discussion of the factors supporting and reinforcing custom, *see* id, 169-229.

56. *See* Halloran, "A Five-Foot Shelf of Iran 'Contingencies'," *N.Y. Times*, Nov. 18, 1979, E4, cols. 3-5.

57. *See N.Y. Times*, Nov. 22, 1979, A10, col. 4.

58. Id., A10, col. 5.

59. *See N.Y. Times*, Nov. 24, 1979, A8, col. 1; *N.Y. Times*, Nov. 25, 1979, A14, col. 6; *N.Y. Times*, Nov. 28, 1979, A10, col. 3.

60. There was, of course, loose discussion in the media about article 51 of the United Nations Charter, but it is farfetched to say that an armed attack occurred against the United States within the meaning of that article.

allow an entitlement violation (i.e., attacking the territory of Iran) in retaliation for an initial entitlement violation (the taking of the hostages).

Better evidence in support of that mechanism can be found in the reaction to the American military initiative that was taken—the aborted rescue mission of April 24-25, 1980. Iran appears not to have asked for an American apology for the violation of its airspace and territory, and certainly the United States tendered no apology. International reaction in general focused upon criticism of strategy and tactics and seemed to say little if anything about legality.[61] The International Court of Justice stated in its judgment that it "cannot fail to express its concern in regard to the United States' incursion into Iran."[62] However, the court then made it clear that its concern was that the incursion could "undermine respect for the judicial process," since it took place while the court was deliberating and writing its judgment in the case.[63] Other than that, the court pointed out that the question of the legality of the incursion was not before it, and that in any event the operation of April 24th could have "no bearing on the evaluation of the conduct of the Iranian Government over six months earlier."[64]

Here, as is often true of legal analysis, it is more important to consider what the court did rather than what it said. For the court held not only that Iran violated the American diplomatic and consular entitlements, but also that Iran must make reparation to the United States (the form and amount of such reparation to be settled by the court in a future proceeding).[65] Surely the American incursion was relevant to the question of reparation. And the court had direct notice of its relevance, because the Soviet judge, in dissent, made the precise point. Judge Morozov, referring to economic actions by the United States against Iran that "culminated in a military attack on the territory" of Iran,[66] argued that the United States "has forfeited the legal right as well as the moral right to expect the Court to uphold any claim for reparation."[67] Under article 53 of the Statute of the Inter-

---

61. *Keesing's Contemporary Archives*, Oct. 24, 1980, 30,534, cols. 1-2.
62. *Tehran Hostages Case*, supra note 47, at 43.
63. Id.
64. Id. at 43-44.
65. The vote on reparations was 12 to 3, and the vote deciding that the form and amount of reparation shall be settled in the future by the court was 14 to 1. Id. at 45.
66. Id. at 54 (Morozov J., dissenting).
67. Id. at 53.

national Court of Justice, the court is required to satisfy itself that an uncontested claim "is well founded in fact and law."[68] Hence there is no doubt that the military incursion was part of the case.

Thus we have an apparent contradiction. The court in its judgment said that the question of the legality of the incursion was not before it. Yet, as we have seen, the incursion's legality was implicated in the court's holding. We can only conclude, given the court's holding that reparations were owing, that the court necessarily had to find as a logical condition to its holding that the American incursion was legal. In other words, the American incursion was a retaliatory entitlement violation permitted by the international legal system in the face of Iran's initial clear violation of the American diplomatic and consular entitlements.

A further indication that this is what the court actually had in mind is its disposition of the issue whether the United States could rely on its Treaty of Amity, Economic Relations, and Consular Rights of 1955 with Iran.[69] Judge Morozov, dissenting, said that the United States could not rely on this treaty because it had engaged in "military invasion of the territory of Iran, a series of economic sanctions and other coercive measures which are, to say the least, incompatible with notions such as amity."[70] But in the court's opinion:

> However, all the measures in question were taken by the United States after the seizure of its Embassy by an armed group and subsequent detention of its diplomatic and consular staff as hostages. They were measures taken in response to what the United States believed to be grave and manifest violations of international law by Iran, including violations of the 1955 Treaty itself.[71]

---

68. Statute of the International Court of Justice, June 26, 1945, art. 53, 59 Stat. 1055, 1062, T.S. No. 993 at 32, 1976 *U.N.Y.B.* 1052, 1066. Professor Stein contended that the only analytical issue in the case regarding the incursion was not whether it was lawful but whether it amounted to a type of contempt of court. Stein, "Contempt, Crisis, and the Court: The World Court and the Hostage Rescue Attempt," 76 *A.J.I.L.* 499 (1982). However, he seemed to conclude both that there was and was not contempt of court. The court, he wrote, gave a "sharp rebuke" to the United States but did not penalize it, which according to Stein "seems a proper exercise of discretion." Id. at 530. In any event, contrary to Stein's argument, the damage inflicted by the United States was not only upon the court and the integrity of its proceedings, but also upon the territory of Iran. The court, in awarding reparations to the United States, could easily have provided for a set-off in favor of Iran for the actual dollar amount of the damages sustained by Iran as a result of the unlawful incursion. That the court did not do so indicates that it implicitly held the rescue attempt to be lawful.
69. August 15, 1955, United States–Iran, 8 *U.S.T.* 899, 284 *U.N.T.S.* 93.
70. *Tehran Hostages Case, supra* note 47, at 52 (Morozov, J., dissenting).
71. Id. at 28.

Thus the court explicitly acknowledged what I have called retaliatory entitlement violation. Its use of the word "including" in the last sentence above quoted indicates that apart from the 1955 treaty the actions by the United States were justifiable. And, interestingly, even with respect to the treaty itself the United States was not limited to the remedy of being able in turn to disobey its provisions (referred to loosely by Judge Morozov as "amity"), but could continue to invoke the treaty against Iran even in the face of such departures from the treaty. Thus the measures taken by the United States must be interpreted as supporting the treaty and enforcing Iran's obligations under the treaty, rather than simply rendering the treaty void. In effect the court has treated the Treaty of Amity as an entitlement of the United States, which the latter may uphold by retaliatory entitlement violations against Iran's entitlements under the same treaty.

Most prominent of all the American responses to the hostage crisis was, of course, the freezing of approximately $13 billion of Iranian assets in American banks, American corporations, and American-controlled bank deposits abroad.[72] Whether the freeze was in violation of Iran's international entitlement to use of its own property abroad, and hence an entitlement violation by retaliation in the sense I have been describing, or whether the freeze was legal, remains a difficult question. I will argue that the freeze's legality is a mixed question, and hence to the extent that it was illegal, it was a partial entitlement retaliation.

The legal position of the United States in regard to the freeze was stated by Roberts B. Owen, Legal Adviser to the Department of State, in oral argument to the International Court of Justice on March 20, 1980, in direct response to a question posed by Judge Morozov requesting explanation of the freeze. First, Mr. Owen argued that the freeze was a direct response to the Iranian threat suddenly to withdraw all Iranian funds from United States banks. The threat "constituted nothing less than an attack on the stability of the world economy and the international monetary system." Legally, this is perhaps an explanation, but hardly a justification. It constitutes a political statement designed to elicit sympathy for the United States in international banking circles, but clearly if Iran had a right to withdraw its money

---

72. Although the exact figure has been disputed, the $13 billion amount is generally used as a rough measure. See Nickel, "Battling for Iran's Frozen Billions," *Fortune*, Dec. 15, 1980, 117.

the consequences of the stability of the international monetary system would simply be a price that the system would have to pay for allowing Iran to build up such significant reserve assets. Second, Mr. Owen referred to the Iranian threat to repudiate obligations owed to the United States and its nationals:

> In response to Iran's efforts to harm the U.S. economy and the dollar, and having in mind Iran's unlawful detention of American hostages, the President of the United States simply froze all Iranian assets in U.S. control for the time being, in part simply to make it possible for U.S. claimants to be made whole if the Government of Iran carried through with its threats to repudiate all of its obligations to such claimants.[73]

The freezing of assets to guard against repudiation of obligations by Iran is akin to an attachment proceeding in a judicial action, and thus if we regard the entire Iranian situation as a "case," perhaps the United States acted legally to secure its legitimate expectations. Even if one were to object that the totality of claims that could be asserted against Iran would fall short of $13 billion—and thus the United States blocked more than was necessary—a rejoinder to that contention could be made to the effect that the hostages themselves might have significant claims for false imprisonment and even maltreatment if that were later revealed. But even with Mr. Owen's argument, as augmented, we still find his phrase "having in mind Iran's unlawful detention of American hostages," which indicates a retaliatory motivation for the freeze. Additionally, nothing was mentioned about interest on the $13 billion that was frozen. Since the money was blocked for more than a year and prevailing interest rates were approximately fifteen percent, there is perhaps as much as $2 billion of interest unaccounted for in the legal arguments before the court. Was the United States threatening to confiscate the "interest" on the frozen assets? If so, that would amount to a violation of an Iranian entitlement (What happened in the end was that, with the return of the hostages, the United States remitted to Iran, as part of the agreed settlement, an initial interest payment of $800 million.[74] But this was clearly ex post the legal question.)

---

73. *Dep't. St. Bull.*, May 1980, at 56.
74. *N.Y. Times*, Jan 21, 1981, A9, col. 1.

As matters turned out, the United States "unfroze" the assets in return for the safe delivery of the hostages. The judicial question of whether the freezing of the assets was in whole or in part a violation of an Iranian entitlement thus became moot. Nevertheless, to the extent that my claim that the freeze was a partial violation of an Iranian entitlement is convincing, the fact that it occasioned such little comment from the rest of the world or the International Court of Justice tends to support the legitimacy of the concept of entitlement retaliation.

A much more dramatic, but equally more controversial, entitlement violation that may have been causally connected with the initial Iranian delict was Iraq's military invasion of Iran in early September 1980. In the first place, and relevant though not critical for my present analysis, the Iraqi invasion in fact helped wind up the hostage problem. According to Lloyd N. Cutler, who was a participant at the highest level in the ultimate negotiations for the release of the hostages, "[i]t took the Iraqi invasion to sharpen Iran's need for arms, spare parts, and money."[75] This linkage between the invasion and Iran's need for the return of its $13 billion in banks controlled by the United States may be taken as a response by two members of the international community (the United States and Iraq, acting of course separately) which had the effect of upholding the international norm of diplomatic and consular inviolability. For the effect of their separate efforts was to secure the release of the hostages, quite apart from any motivation on the part of Iraq to help the United States in this particular way. Indeed, any such motive was probably farthest from the minds of the Iraqi leaders, as far as we can know such things. But the international legal system is not explainable on the basis of crude psychological guesses about the motivation of national leaders; objective reality is the only criterion for law-determination.[76] Putting speculations about motive aside, the fact remains that the Iraqi invasion contributed to the relief that the United States sought from Iran for Iran's initial delict.

My second point will be far more controversial. I contend that if we can step back and take a broad historical perspective, we might well conclude that the Iraqi invasion of Iran was legally related to

---

75. L. Cutler, "Negotiating the Iranian Settlement," 67 *A.B.A.J.* 996, 996 (1981).
76. *See* D'Amato, "The Content of International Law as Psychological Data," 10 *Colum. J. Transn'l L.* 66, 72-77 (1971).

the Iranian violation of the American diplomatic and consular entitlement. Indeed, we might conclude that it was an example of retaliatory entitlement violation. If we can sort out large international movements from the small zigs and zags that preoccupy most present observers, I believe we can recognize that the international legal system itself (acting of course through the states) has attempted to preserve entitlement equilibrium and has done so by allowing the Iraqi invasion as an example of retaliatory entitlement violation.

In support of this proposition, I contend that the initial delict by Iran was universally regarded as an outrageous attack upon a key international entitlement.[77] More importantly, Iraq's invasion of Iran for purposes of territorial aggrandizement, flying in the face of every international prohibition from the Kellogg-Briand Pact[78] to article 2(4) of the United Nations Charter, actually seemed acceptable to the world community. In Professor Falk's words:

> In September 1980, we witnessed for the first time since World War I an example of one country attacking another—Iraq attacking Iran—while the world looked on with indifference. Both superpowers have suggested that this is a context where noninvolvement is the appropriate response. Nor has a dissident voice of any significance been raised in the United Nations or elsewhere in international society. To me, this represents a monumental, unacknowledged retreat from the post-World War I notion that aggression is the most severe form of disruption of international life. . . .[79]

Falk goes on to give some "opportunistic reasons" for the indifference of the world community, but he hardly finds these persuasive.[80] Thus, under Falk's theory, we might have in the Iraq invasion something that is unexplained, unexplainable, totally illegal, and hence a "gap" in the theory of international relations and international law. On the other hand, the theory I have been suggesting in this chapter constitutes, I contend, a full explanation. The "wound" inflicted by Iran

---

77. See Dep't. St. Bull., May 1980, at 46. Iran's official endorsement of the seizure of the diplomats, supra note 47, seems to be the first such official endorsement in modern history, an historical factor contributing to the outrage of the international community.
78. Pact of Paris, Aug. 27, 1928, 46 Stat. 2343, T.S. No. 796, 94 L.N.T.S. 57. Though eclipsed by the United Nations Charter, the Kellogg-Briand Pact retains its validity.
79. Falk, "Some Thoughts on the Decline of International Law and Future Prospects," 9 Hofstra L. Rev. 399, 399 (1981).
80. Id. at 400-03.

Human Rights As Entitlements

upon a critical international entitlement was so deep, so much in need of redress, and so shocking—no nation had ever before ratified the imprisonment of foreign diplomats—that the international community mentally branded Iran an "outlaw" and was willing to tolerate a severe violation of one of Iran's basic entitlements in retaliation therefor, no matter who inflicted it. Iran, in the international systemic sense, got what it deserved.

Admittedly, any political realist might object to my theory on the ground that "international law" is not as important as I make it out to be and that certainly Iraq of all countries was not interested in making Iran respect international law. My reply, briefly, is that no one knows exactly how important international law is, but we do know that it has persisted through the centuries and further, that while Iraq may not have had anything in mind about international law and may have attacked Iran simply for irredentist or expansionist purposes, the important point is the reaction of the world community to that attack. If my theory is correct, Iraq's attack would have been condemned by the world community in no uncertain terms but for Iran's seizure of the hostages. But given that seizure, Iraq's attack was viewed as permissible under international law (just as the possible American military retaliations upon Iranian territory, which I discussed previously, might have been viewed with equal indifference by the world community although they were not carried out by the United States because of its fear for the lives and safety of the hostages).

Even though the reader might find it difficult to accept naked aggression by Iraq as permissible under international law, I would suggest that my theory actually upholds article 2(4) and the general prohibition against aggression, whereas Professor Falk's view would undermine that same prohibition. For those who share Falk's view, Iraq's invasion is a direct violation of an international norm, and the fact that the world community has greeted it with indifference means that the international norm against aggression is on its way to being replaced, via the processes of customary-law formation resulting from state practice accepted by the international community, with a contrary norm—that such aggression is no longer illegal. Indeed, Professor Falk seems to draw such a conclusion and goes on to view the future with great apprehension—and has dire forebodings as well for the role of international law itself.[81] Quite to the contrary, I argue that the Iraqi invasion occasions no such violation of the international norm against aggression, but rather is a function of the "implementation and compliance" problem we have been addressing that the international legal system, in looking out for its own preservation, allows in the name of restoring entitlement equilibrium. Hence, although my theory encompasses the Iraqi invasion in legal terms (personally I deplore the aggression), the consequence of my theory is to preserve intact the international entitlement of every nation against external military invasion of its territory. If this consequence did not follow, I suggest that the world community would not have been indifferent to the Iraqi invasion.

B. The Namibian Example

Our investigation of the Iranian situation in entitlement terms has revealed several aspects of the entitlement-retaliation system, and there is no need to multiply examples for their own sake. However, the gradual emergence of Namibia toward independent statehood deserves brief comment because, absent the international entitlements system, it would be inexplicable.[82]

When South West Africa was given over as a class C mandate to South Africa in 1920, South Africa proceeded to administer the territory as a fifth province and practically to ignore the admittedly vague provisions of the mandate.[83] The mandate provided only the

---

81. *See* Falk, "The American Society of International Law: 75 Years and Beyond," 1981 *Proc. Am. Soc. Int'l L.* 278; D'Amato, Comment on Professor Falk's Remarks, id. at 279. The argument I give in the text may be supported by the following additional consideration by way of analogy. In the event of a violation of article 2(4), the United Nations, acting through the Security Council, has the right to send in an international army to maintain and restore international peace and security (article 42). Such an action by the United Nations army, of course, would not violate 2(4). I suggest that, in the absence of such Security Council procedure, the world community considered Iraq's military action against Iran as privileged in the same sense that the Security Council's action might be. Naturally, the reader is free to reject this analysis, in which case I rest my argument concerning reciprocal entitlement violation on the other examples given in this section.

82. As of the present writing, Namibia is certainly not independent. But neither is it a mere "fifth province" of South Africa. Apartheid has been legally removed, a multiracial coalition controls the National Assembly, and a one-person/one-vote election process has at least been authorized even though there is no short-term hope of democratic elections (at present the stumbling block is supervision and control over such elections).

83. *See The South West Africa/Namibia Dispute*, 75-88 (J. Dugard ed. 1973); Rovine & D'Amato, "Written Statement of the International League for the Rights of Man Filed with the International Court of Justice in the Namibia Question," 4 *N.Y.U.J. Int'l L. & Pol.* 335, 343-49 (1971).

Human Rights As Entitlements

loosest "internationalization" of South West Africa, a frail juridical link to the international legal system. Nations other than South Africa had an entitlement, through the mandate, only to the effect that South Africa itself was required to act for the best interests of the inhabitants of the territory. After the Second World War, South Africa refused to turn the mandate over to the new trusteeship system of the United Nations, and when the League of Nations was formally dissolved in 1946 the juridical link between South West Africa and the world community became even more attenuated. South Africa, through the Odendaal Report, began to plan for *Bantustans*, or homelands, in South West Africa, though the plan upon analysis was sufficiently discriminatory as arguably to violate South Africa's mandatory obligations to the native inhabitants of the territory.[84] Other nations, fearful that South Africa would formally annex the territory, kept up the pressure by a series of United Nations General Assembly resolutions, requests to the International Court of Justice for advisory opinions, and in 1966, a compulsory-jurisdiction proceeding in that court (which proceeding, however, ended in a procedural victory for South Africa).[85] Disappointing as these initiatives were individually, their total effect was to keep underlining the tenuous link between the world community and South West Africa. Perhaps a few hundred years ago such a link would have been ignored by a nation like South Africa for the juridical construct it undoubtedly was, yet such a course of action was not realistically possible for South Africa in recent decades. It was not possible, I contend, because formal incorporations or annexation of the territory by South Africa would have opened up South Africa to retaliatory entitlement violation by other nations.

The entitlement retaliation I have in mind is not the application of "sanctions" against South Africa. For the latter, in the form of economic boycotts, have been in recent years a constant. They would have been applied against South Africa for its apartheid policies whether or not South West Africa was a mandate, or an independent nation, or an integral part of the South African Republic. Despite the occasional talk that the sanctions policy has been the factor in keeping

---

84. *See infra* Chapter 8.
85. *See* D'Amato, "Legal and Political Strategies of the South West Africa Litigation," 4 *L. Trans. Q.* 8, 20-22 (1967), reprinted in segments in *The South West Africa/Namibia Dispute, supra* note 83, at 220-21, 279-80, 281-90.

South West Africa independent,[86] clearly when it is analyzed as a constant, no such power can be attributed to it.[87]

Rather, the gradual emergence of Namibia as an independent state must be attributed to South Africa's self-perceived stake in the entire set of international entitlements. Without those entitlements that enable it to proclaim sovereignty within its own boundaries, that proclaim it as an equal member among nations with equal claims to territorial integrity and political independence, South Africa would be jeopardizing its very existence. It would be vulnerable to the same sort of international indifference that greeted Iraq's invasion of Iran. Hence, South Africa has maintained a careful regard for international entitlements, argued its cases thoroughly and well before the International Court of Justice, objected to all U.N. resolutions directed against it (the objections, as I have argued elsewhere, were of crucial importance in defeating a consensus claim[88]), and refrained from incorporating South West Africa. Instead, it has let the weak mandate entitlement gradually sever the territory administratively from the Union—an underlying corroboration, I maintain, for the efficacy of international law's "implementation and compliance" of its set of entitlements.

---

86. *See, e.g.*, Burns, "South-West Africa, an Orphan Pretoria Can No Longer Keep," *N.Y. Times*, Aug. 15, 1976, §4, at 3, cols. 1-3.
87. *See* R. Fisher, *Improving Compliance*, 67.
88. *See* D'Amato, *supra* note 23, at 117-21.

6

HUMAN RIGHTS AS NORMS OF CUSTOMARY INTERNATIONAL LAW

In Chapter 5, we dealt with the proposition that human-rights norms can logically fit within the set of entitlements that make up the rights and enforceable duties of states. Here, let us take up the substantive question whether there are at least some human-rights norms that in fact are part of customary international law binding upon every state.

I deal with the least controversial human-rights norms: the prohibitions against genocide, torture, and slavery. If I can prove the case for these, the same method of analysis could be extended to other norms at some other time.

The problem with these, and most other, human-rights norms is that they have been articulated in bilateral and multilateral treaties. They are harder to find in the pure "practice of states" except, of course, insofar as the conclusion of a treaty is itself state practice. Thus, to move from a prohibition against slavery in a treaty to a general prohibition against torture even in the absence of treaty is a step that goes to the heart of what is meant by customary international law.

Many writers, who view treaties as a form of contract, say that if a contract between two parties has no external effects on other persons, how can a treaty between two states become part of *general* international law? This is a question I took up at length in my book *The Concept of Custom in International Law*; my arguments were met with initial resistance and yet surprisingly increasing acceptance in the fifteen years since the book came out. Except for some introductory remarks, I will not repeat the arguments in the book, but rather shall focus primarily on objections to my thesis generated by the book, and in particular the objections of Dr. Michael Akehurst.

1. *The Effect of Treaties Upon Custom.* My argument is simply that the multilateral conventions containing prohibitions against genocide, torture, and slavery constitute evidence of customary law binding upon all states and not just the parties thereto. I do not claim that this evidence can be found subsequent to, or apart from, the conventions, but rather that the conventions themselves constitute or generate customary rules of law. To prove this argument it will be necessary to depart from our concentration on human rights—since the argument relates to all generalizable treaty provisions, including human rights provisions—and discuss in detail the theory of customary law formation. The present section will describe my argument. The next section will deal with specific criticisms of my theory that have been made by Dr. Michael Akehurst.[1]

Customary international law is a set of entitlements that have developed through centuries of the "practice" of states. By "practice" I mean not what states do in isolation, but how states interact with each other on any issue; absent *all* interactions, a state is simply acting domestically.[2] Some customary entitlements owe their origin to the following model: state X acts, state Y reacts, and either X's action or Y's reaction or some other resolution of the issue is accepted or becomes operative between X and Y. For example, a courier of state X delivers an unwelcome message to the king of state Y. The king imprisons the messenger. State X responds by sending another courier (obviously a reluctant one) who delivers the message that

---

1. Akehurst, "Custom as a Source of International Law," 47 *Brit. Y.B. Int'l L.* 1 (1974-75).
2. In *IIT v. Vencap, Ltd.*, 519 F. 2d 1001,1015 (2d Cir. 1975), Judge Friendly noted that the fact that every nation's municipal law might prohibit theft does not incorporate into international law the Eighth Commandment's prohibition against stealing. As Judge Kaufman wrote in *Filartiga v. Peña-Irala*, 630 F. 2d 876,880 (2d Cir. 1980), "It is only where the nations of the world have demonstrated that the wrong is of mutual, and not merely several, concern, by means of express international accords, that a wrong generally recognized becomes an international law violation within the meaning of the [Alien Tort Statute, 28 U.S.C. 1350 (1976)]." In other words, if two or more nations commit themselves in a treaty not to allow certain domestic acts—for example, torture, or even in Judge Friendly's hypothetical, theft—that treaty provision internationalizes the issue and takes it out of the purely domestic realm of a state's acts. *See* D'Amato, *The Concept of Custom in International Law*, 79-80 (1971) (Genocide Convention moves domestic genocide into the domain of international relations).

Human Rights as Norms of Customary International Law

unless Y returns the first courier safe and sound X will sack and destroy the towns of Y. If Y releases the first courier with an apology and perhaps a payment of gold, a resolution of the issue in this manner will lead to a rule that official couriers are entitled to immunity against imprisonment. However, if Y were to imprison the second messenger as well, and X was unable for any reason to do anything about it or get Y to change its mind, a different rule would arise to the effect that official couriers have no immunity. We cannot say a priori which of these two results must occur; all we have is the history of state behavior to tell us which rules of international law have become manifest in their customary interactions. In fact, we know that, due either to the perceived need to communicate, or the injustice of ill-treatment of couriers, an early rule of diplomatic immunity became well established as an entitlement of any nation against all other nations. This is the classic kind of example of a practice ripening into a rule of law. But many rules of international law—the vast majority of them, in fact—did not originate along the lines of this model. Rather, most rules began as provisions in treaties. State X and Y agreed in writing to honor the personal safety of their respective diplomats, either because of an earlier incident between them involving the ill-treatment of a messenger, or because they perceived the need to coexist peacefully and avoid problems arising out of the exchange of message-bearing personnel. Early treaties and agreements of friendship, commerce, and/or navigation typically provided for the immunity of diplomatic personnel, a rule that became part of customary law. The treaty in effect replaced the model I have just suggested. Instead of imprisoning a courier and then letting him go to establish a customary rule, the two affected nations committed themselves to that rule in advance by virtue of a binding instrument. (The binding nature of a "treaty" had itself already been established by virtue of customary law.)[3]

Some years ago when I read the classic works of the "positivist" writers of international law, such as Zouche, Wolff, Moser, Vattel, and especially Bynkershoek, I was struck by the fact that nearly everything they claimed to be a rule of international law was in fact a provision of a treaty. The earlier "naturalist" writers, such as Grotius, Suarez, and Gentili, had unabashedly included treaty provisions

---

3. Interestingly, the rule that treaties are binding might itself have resulted from provisions in early treaties containing solemn vows that treaties were binding.

as sources of customary law. The "positivists" were more of a surprise; though they claimed that international law was based upon consent, they were able to find such consent generally in the system on the basis of treaty provisions concluded by only a subset of the nations in the system. In my book, *The Concept of Custom in International Law*, I tried to give a detailed account of the rules we now accept as part of customary law that originated in treaties. My impression is that if we were to remove all the rules of international law that originated as provisions in treaties, we would be left with very few rules indeed—the rare rules that were actually the result of clashing acts and claims and the resolutions of these controversies.

To say this is not to assert that all provisions in treaties become part of the general customary international law. Many treaty provisions are simply not generalizable into rules of law without destroying their content—they are not "norm-creating" treaties. For instance, a "most-favored-nation" clause loses its meaning if it is generalized to give most-favored-nation treatment to everyone without exception.[4] The classic writers on international law, including those previously mentioned, were well aware of these limitations, and regarded the sorting out and identification of generalizable provisions in treaties as their scholarly mission.[5]

At about the turn of the twentieth century, however, several English publicists, including Oppenheim and Hall,[6] put forth the view that treaties simply laid down contractual obligations for the parties and could have no legal effect outside the parties. This view was repeated as dicta by Lord Alverstone in the much-cited case of *West Rand*

---

4. Additionally, there are many treaties that affect a barter or exchange (*e.g.* the "destroyers-for-bases" deal between England and the United States prior to World War II), and these too cannot be generalized. Moreover, many treaties and treaty provisions refer to particular places or organizations and thus cannot state a general rule: for example, treaties affecting the title or rights of passage of particular lands or waterways, demilitarization treaties for particular territories, mandates and trusteeships, boundaries, treaties setting up international organizations, and so forth. *See generally* the list of categories provided by Waldock in 2 *Y.B. Int'l L. Comm'n* 27, U.N. Doc. A/CN.4/SER, A/1964/Add. 1. Finally, if some treaties state one rule and other treaties state the opposite rule, the clash between the two, just like a clash of customary practice, cannot give rise to any one customary rule.

5. The classic writers' approach to international law was no different from Lord Mansfield's approach to developing the "law merchant" rules of the common law in England at roughly the same time. Lord Mansfield found many provisions in contracts which were generalizable, and he applied them to other unrelated contracts when the latter lacked specificity. He had no difficulty accepting as the "practices" of the mercantile class the written agreements concluded among merchants. *See generally* B. Shientag, *Moulders of Legal Thought*, 108-11, 123-50 (1943).

6. W. Hall, *International Law*, 7-8 (A. P. Higgins 8th ed. 1924); 1 L. Oppenheim, *International Law*, 28 (H. Laupterpacht 8th ed. 1955).

Central Gold Mining Co. v. The King,[7] a case now, however, generally acknowledged to have been wrongly decided.[8] I have not been able to find any support for the Oppenheim position apart from the assertion by Oppenheim and Hall that provisions in treaties can either be declaratory or in derogation of the underlying customary law, but do not affect the underlying law.[9] This is more a statement of a conclusion than a reason, a conclusion that follows from equating treaties with contracts and then taking a restrictive view of contracts. Yet, a long line of British and American authors, from Oppenheim to my former teacher, the late Professor (and Judge) Richard R. Baxter, have reiterated this "restrictive-contract" view of treaties.[10]

Several arguments can be made against the restrictive-contract view. First, as Lord McNair and Professor Sohn, among others, have persuasively demonstrated, treaties differ in many fundamental respects from domestic contracts.[11] Second, and much more significantly, the writers who have asserted, with Oppenheim, that provisions in treaties do not affect the underlying customary law have uniformly failed to adduce a single instance of a generalizable treaty provision that has *not* been transmuted into customary law. Third, even these writers accept that provisions in treaties may eventually "pass" into customary international law or "harden" into law. But they have never indicated how or when this "passage" or "hardening" takes place, and they have failed to indicate what evidence we might look for to ascertain that a treaty provision has undergone the rites of passage into customary law. Their inability to give theoretical or practical support to the notions they have invented of "passing" or "hardening," after all these years, suggests that perhaps something is wrong with their initial premise.

An example from Oppenheim's own text indicates the level of

---

7. [1905] 2 K.B. 391, 398.

8. *See, e.g.*, E. Feilchenfeld, *Public Debts and State Succession* 380-96 (1931) (eventual diplomatic settlement by England more liberal than the theories advanced in the case would indicate); 1 D. O'Connell, *State Succession in Municipal Law and International Law* 244, 321, 378 (1967).

9. W. Hall, *supra* note 6, 7-8; 1 L. Oppenheim, *supra* note 6, 27.

10. *See* C. Parry, *The Sources and Evidences of International Law*, 29-32 (1965); Baxter, "Multilateral Treaties as Evidence of Customary International Law," 41 *Brit. Y.B. Int'l L.* 275, 285 (1965-66); Baxter, "Treaties and Custom," 129 *Recueil des Cours* 31 (1960); Waldock, "General Course on Public International Law," 106 *Recueil des Cours* 3, 84 (1962).

In contrast, many continental authors have retained the classical view that generalizable provisions in treaties constitute evidence of customary international law. *See* references in D'Amato, *supra* note 2, 138-40.

11. *See* McNair, "The Functions and Differing Legal Character of Treaties," 11 *Brit. Y.B. Int'l L.* 100 (1930); Sohn, "The Many Faces of International Law," 57 *A.J.I.L.* 868 (1963).

unreality to which insistence upon a theory of "hardening" can lead. As late as the final edition of Lauterpacht's *Oppenheim*, published in 1955, the author still found it "difficult to say" whether a customary international law contains a prohibition against the international traffic in slaves.[12] The author cited numerous international treaties condemning slave traffic, but because of the commitment to the theory that treaty provisions can either be in derogation of or declaratory of customary law, no conclusion as to the latter could be reached. But not long thereafter, the International Law Commission, commenting upon the *jus cogens* provision of the new Vienna Convention on Treaties, found not only that customary international law prohibited international slave trade but that this prohibition was "one of the most obvious and best settled rules of *jus cogens*" in that even new treaties could not derogate from it.[13] Unlike Lauterpacht's *Oppenheim*, the I.L.C. did not miss the forest for the trees.

If we press this example a bit further, we might inquire what evidence Oppenheim or Lauterpacht would desire in order to substantiate a customary international law rule prohibiting traffic in slaves. Certainly one more or a dozen more treaties would not do the trick, because Lauterpacht already cited numerous international treaties prohibiting slave traffic. Thus his prescription in practical terms might be inferred to be as follows: let one nation that is not a party to any conventions on slavery actually encourage the taking of a group of humans as slaves, allow or require one of its vessels to transport these slaves to another nation, hope that other nations will intercede forcibly to halt the transportation, and then have the first nation "back down" and agree to free the slaves and punish the ship's captain. This procedure, or something like it, would then substantiate the prior treaty provisions outlawing the international slave traffic, and presumably would allow Lauterpacht in the next edition to write that, finally, the treaty law has indeed "hardened" into customary law. Similarly, if a writer were to contend that "it is difficult to say" whether the Genocide Convention has passed into customary international law, presumably a nation would actually have to engage in genocide and then desist after a few hundred or a few thousand people have been massacred in order to substantiate the antigenocide

---

12. 1 L. Oppenheim, *supra* note 6, 733-34.
13. Report of the International Law Commission to the General Assembly, 18 *U.N.G.A.O.R.* Supp. (No. 9) at 1 U.N. Doc. A/CN.4/SER. A/1963/Add. 1, reprinted in [1963] 2 *Y.B. Int'l L. Comm'n* 187, U.N. Doc. A/CN.4/SER. A/1963/Add. 1.

rule. If Oppenheim's "theory" is accepted, it would appear that nations would have to engage in such post-treaty "practice" in the slavery and genocide cases—as well as in all other human-rights cases—in order to test whether the treaty rule has hardened into customary law. My position, on the other hand, is that nations have not painted themselves into any such theoretical corner, but rather have manifested by virtue of their behavior over the centuries that generalizable provisions in treaties become part of customary law directly without need for such subsequent "practice."

Finally, the incoherence of the "hardening" theory can be demonstrated theoretically even if we accept the previously described gruesome example of deliberately enslaving human beings as necessary to test whether the treaty rule has become a customary rule. Suppose nation X (not a party to any antislavery treaty) enslaves some people and transports them on one of its ships, and nations Y and Z notify X that X should cease and desist immediately. By what *law* do nations Y and Z object to X's acts? The only prior law on the subject, by definition, is the law in the treaties. Yet, if it is by *this* law that Y and Z object to X's acts, then the law, for international law purposes, is already established prior to X's compliance. In this event, the Oppenheim thesis is redundant. Or to put the point differently, there is no coherent means to establish "hardening" of the sort envisaged by Oppenheim, since its very proof involves invocation of the theory that Oppenheim attacks, namely the theory that provisions in treaties generate customary law immediately and without any such process of "hardening."

To be sure, the subsequent evidence needed to substantiate the "passage" of a treaty provision into customary law might be something other than the action-reaction-resolution model I suggested at the outset. But what might this something else be? The late Professor Baxter in a carefully reasoned lecture argued that this subsequent element must be acquiescence in the rule by the nonparty states.[14] Baxter gave no suggestion, however, as to how this acquiescence might be manifested or proved. And he himself recognized a logical paradox implicit in the idea of acquiescence: the more states that sign a multilateral convention, the fewer nonparties remain and hence the more difficult it becomes to find a consistent attitude of these

---

14. Baxter, "Treaties and Custom," *supra* note 10, at 71-73.

nonparties to the rule in the treaty.[15] Indeed, suppose all the states in the world that are at all interested in the subject matter of the treaty sign it; we might wait in vain for the nonsignatories to express any attitude toward the rules of the treaty.

Nevertheless, a critic may attempt to support the Oppenheim approach by the argument that since the parties to a treaty intend that the treaty shall be binding only upon themselves—which is, after all, why they enter into the treaty—the provisions cannot therefore have any third-party effect. This argument in a sense restates the restrictive-contract notion of treaties. But it is also answerable on its own terms. In the first place, we cannot be sure that the parties to a treaty intend exclusivity of its provisions. Of course, a treaty involving commercial trade or one delimiting boundaries would seem to be of particular and even exclusive interest to the parties, but I have previously ruled out such treaties as norm-creating because they are not generalizable. But taking those provisions that are generalizable, it is not clear that the parties intend them to be exclusive to themselves. Indeed, a generalizable provision would almost by its very nature be one to which the parties would welcome adherence on the part of other states. Moreover, multilateral conventions, which these days are becoming especially numerous and prominent, nearly always contain provisions to which the parties would want other states to subscribe. Multilateral conventions open to all nations seem to manifest an intent to universal inclusivity.[16] At the very least, we might conclude that parties to treaties do not necessarily intend generalizable treaty provisions to be limited to the signatories.

Second, and more importantly, I would argue that whether the parties' intent is resolved on the side of exclusivity or inclusivity, intent is ultimately irrelevant. What the *parties* to a treaty intend its

---

15. Id. at 64. Professor Baxter based much of his reasoning upon the decision of the International Court of Justice in the *North Sea Continental Shelf Cases* (W. Ger. v. Den., W. Ger. v. Neth.), 1969 I.C.J. 3 (Judgment of Feb. 20). For reasons that I give in the next section of the present chapter, the *Continental Shelf Cases* are better construed as delineating the requirements of "special custom" and not "general custom." Under this approach, reliance on that decision is misplaced. But even if the reader does not want to accept my analysis of the *Continental Shelf Cases* as turning on the requirements of special custom, one looks in vain at the opinion of the court to find what the court itself would accept as evidence of "acquiescence" under Baxter's theory.

16. *See* D'Amato, "Manifest Intent and the Generation by Treaty of Customary Rules of International Law," 64 *A.J.I.L.* 892 (1970). In a paper that I wrote for a seminar given by Professor Baxter in 1961, published the following year, I argued that parties to a treaty usually hope that "the general rules they adopt in treaties" are "extended to all nations; a rule is essentially a reciprocal accommodation." D'Amato, "Treaties as a Source of General Rules of International Law," *Harv. Int'l L. Club Bull.*, Apr. 1962, at 1, 29.

effect to be has nothing to do with the use to which the international community of states may desire to put the treaty. Take as an analogy a case in domestic law. The judicial system will give the case precedential effect irrespective of the intent of the parties. Indeed, if both plaintiff and defendant were to stipulate that the decision in their case be confined to themselves, I believe that any court would disregard their wishes and reply simply that the use to which the judicial system wants to put the decision in this particular case has nothing to do with the desire or intent of the parties but rather is a question of the jurisprudence of the legal system. In international law, nations have through history incorporated the provisions of treaties into customary law without regard to the intent of the parties—even if such an intent could be determined, and even if it were determined to express a desire for exclusivity.

2. *Dr. Akehurst's Critique.* In a leading article devoted largely to a criticism of my book on the concept of customary international law,[17] Dr. Michael Akehurst contends that I was wrong in asserting that treaties may generate customary law.[18] It will be instructive to see how he goes about attempting to prove this proposition.

Since Akehurst recognizes that so many rules of customary international law owe their origin to provisions in treaties, and since (with some misgivings) he accepts the cases I cited to prove this proposi-

---

17. Akehurst, *supra* note 1.
18. Akehurst's criticism is ironic, since he also disputes my position that claims are less important than treaties in generating custom. In the book, I asserted that a claim is only the first step toward a unit of "custom." To complete the unit, what is needed is a reaction by one or more other states and a resolution of the issue. On the other hand, if custom can be generated by a claim only, as Akehurst argues, then all kinds of unilateral desires by nations would become law. For instance, a claim made by one nation that the Soviet Union violates international law by not having more than one political party to give the voters a meaningful choice at election time would, according to Akehurst's reasoning, be evidence of a rule of international customary law of which the Soviet Union's one-party system is in violation. Or, a claim by one or more nations that apartheid violates international law would be evidence of a customary rule to that effect binding upon South Africa. A claim by Switzerland that it owns Antarctica, or by Sweden that it owns the moon, or by Saudi Arabia that it owns the mineral wealth under all the oceans would also be constitutive of custom (for Akehurst indeed cites cases involving claims to specific real estate in support of what I would have thought would be the rather different proposition that claims generate general customary law). Akehurst, *supra* note 1, at 2. In domestic law, if one were to argue that any claim made by any private person or by any lawyer constitutes evidence of what the law is, the argument would be thrown out of court. For clearly there is no conceivable restraint upon what any person—or any nation—might claim. And just as clearly, for every claim there is a potential counterclaim. For these reasons, I find Akehurst's position that a mere claim is enough to constitute evidence of *customary law* to be quite unconvincing.

tion,[19] he must find various mechanisms to account for this international practice. One important mechanism builds upon the early Oppenheim view, as significantly modified by Baxter. Oppenheim, it will be recalled, said that treaties are either declaratory or in derogation of the underlying common law, and hence are irrelevant to it. Many years later Baxter argued that those treaties that are declaratory of customary law, but not those in derogation of it, can be cited as evidence of that customary law.[20] I entered the argument at this point and objected that if we are able to determine whether or not a treaty is declaratory of the underlying customary law, as Baxter suggests, then if our answer is positive we would have no need to cite the treaty as evidence at all, for we will have determined independently of the treaty what the customary law on the point in fact is.[21] Before my book was published, I had communicated my objection on this point to Professor Baxter, and he modified his view in his Hague Lectures in 1970, agreeing that the proof of customary law is not "facilitated" by the method of determining what the customary law is dehors the treaty.[22] However, Baxter retained his previous position that treaties that are declaratory of customary international law may be cited as evidence of that custom. After abandoning the idea that proof of whether the treaty is declaratory requires separate research into the custom, Baxter argued that there are two other methods of determining whether a treaty is declaratory of customary law. The first would be "appropriate language in the preamble or elsewhere" that the treaty "incorporates nothing but customary in-

---

19. Akehurst, *supra* note 1, at 42-43. One of his "contrary" cases is *West Rand Central Gold Mining Co. v. The King*. Akehurst takes issue with me on the matter of treaties articulating a rule of custom (the articulation being what I have claimed as the objective evidence of *opinio juris* in D'Amato, *supra* note 2, 160-162). Akehurst writes in a footnote that the "fatal flaw" in my reasoning "is that treaties do not, in most cases, articulate the norm as one of *customary* law (unless one assumes that laying down a rule in a treaty automatically means articulating the rule as a norm of customary law—but that is to assume without argument the very thing which D'Amato sets out to prove)." Akehurst, *supra* note 1, at 43 n. 7. Quite to the contrary, I have never contended that a treaty must articulate a norm as a norm of *customary* law; there are hardly any treaties which would bother to do so, any more than nations X and Y in settling a conflict would refer to their resolution of that conflict as articulating a norm of customary law. Rather, I would contend that the articulation of the norm in the treaty *constitutes* an articulation of the rule for the purposes of customary law determination. Perhaps Akehurst did not see the initial discussion in my book of custom as a *secondary rule* of law-determination in the precise sense offered by Professor H. L. A. Hart in his discussion of secondary rules. See D'Amato, *supra* note 2, 41-44.
20. Baxter, "Multilateral Treaties as Evidence of Customary International Law," 41 *Brit. Y.B. Int'l L.* 275 (1965-66).
21. D'Amato, *supra* note 2, 115, 153.
22. Baxter, "Treaties and Custom," *supra* note 10, at 42, 75 n. 1.

ternational law."[23] And the second is research into the *travaux préparatoires* to see whether the treaty was intended to be declaratory of international law.[24]

My reply to these latter two methods must now be summarized to set the stage for Akehurst's rejoinder. I argued that the first method—looking for language in the treaty that incorporates customary law—simply would put a high premium upon treaty draftsmanship.[25] And with respect to the *travaux préparatoires*, I argued that any good negotiator on either side would invariably contend that the language that he or she champions is a mere restatement of the customary rule in the absence of a treaty. The reason for so contending would be to convince the other side that the language in question adds nothing to existing law and therefore no "bargaining chips" must be paid in order for the other side to accept the language. One may dip at random into the *travaux préparatoires* of any multilateral draft convention and find any number of instances of experienced negotiators resting their case for the adoption of their own drafts on no argument other than the fact that their own draft accurately reflects existing law on the subject in question.

Upon this dialogue, Akehurst builds his exception to his criticism of my theory that treaties generate custom. He takes Baxter's position one step further by arguing that, irrespective of the real intent of the drafters of the treaty, it is possible for us to conclude that a treaty is declaratory of the underlying customary law if we merely find statements to that effect in the treaty or in the *travaux*.[26] Nor is this method defeated, Akehurst adds, if we were to find that the states making those statements (that the treaty is declaratory of customary law) knew them to be untrue.[27] Thus, Akehurst has objectified Baxter's method of proving subjective intent.

Yet it seems to me that the exception that Akehurst thus carves out of his proposition that treaties do not generate custom is large enough to swallow the entire thesis. There will not be many instances, including human-rights conferences, of *travaux* that manifest any intent other than to declare existing customary law. Nor will there be many

---

23. Id. at 42.
24. Id. at 42-46; Baxter, *supra* note 20, at 291-93.
25. D'Amato, *supra* note 2, 157-58.
26. Akehurst, *supra* note 1, at 45-48. I had previously suggested the importance of objectifying all the constituent elements of custom; see D'Amato, *supra* note 2, 33-41, 74-87.
27. Akehurst, *supra* note 1, at 47.

instances of preambles in treaties stating any intention other than to codify existing law, even if those treaties are the result of conferences originally called into being to engage in the "progressive development" of international law. The more important the treaty, the more likely we are to have language expressly declaring the treaty to be a codification of existing law. An example is the Genocide Convention of 1948 which, in its first article (an article given added significance by virtue of the omission of any preamble), states that "[t]he Contracting Parties confirm that genocide, whether committed in time of peace or in time of war, is a crime under international law which they undertake to prevent and to punish."[28] While I have given my reasons for disagreeing with the entire investigation into whether a treaty is declaratory of customary law, if Akehurst's objective approach leads him to admitting that, say, ninety percent of all multilateral conventions and many bilateral treaties (those containing generalizable provisions) will constitute customary law by virtue of statements that we are sure to find in the *travaux* or in the treaties themselves, I would not object to the practical result that he reaches.

A second important mechanism suggested by Akehurst to show that the provisions in a treaty have become part of customary international law is a subsequent statement made by a state that the provision or the rule it describes has become part of customary law. We might label this mechanism an objective restatement of the old "hardening into law" position. I have previously indicated that no writer has come forth with any mechanism for a treaty provision's "hardening" or "passing" into customary law. But now Akehurst appears to have provided such a mechanism. It occurs, according to Akehurst, when states subsequently make a statement or claim that the legal norm in question has become part of customary law.

Yet if we look more closely at Akehurst's article, we find that he has given no example of this mechanism. Thus we might dismiss this effort by Akehurst with the observation that he is only trying to salvage the old "hardening" test by indicating what would be an objective example of "hardening" even though the real world has apparently failed to provide a single illustration of that objective example. And we might conclude that with Akehurst's prior concession regarding

---

28. Convention on the Prevention and Punishment of the Crime of Genocide, art. 1. By "confirming" the crime of genocide, rather than recognizing its novelty, the parties obviously used draftsmanship to help ensure the status of genocide as a universal prohibition.

the ease with which we may find that a treaty is intended to be declaratory of customary law, all or nearly all treaties are subsumed within that exception, thus making Akehurst de facto a supporter of the theory that treaties generate custom, despite his insistence that, but for these exceptions, they do not.

Yet we cannot dismiss this latter theory too quickly because of the support Akehurst claims for it from the Vienna Convention on the Law of Treaties and the *North Sea Continental Shelf Cases*.[29] Neither of these eminent sources provides an illustration of a "subsequent statement" of the sort envisaged by Akehurst, although on their surface they seem to support his theoretical position.

Article 38 of the Vienna Convention provides that "nothing in Articles 34 to 37 [relating to the effect of treaties on third states] precludes a rule set forth in a treaty from becoming binding upon a third State as a customary rule of law, recognized as such." Akehurst contends that the phrase "recognized as such" indicates an intention on the part of the framers that something must happen subsequent to a treaty in order to warrant the conclusion that a rule in the treaty has become binding as a customary rule of law.[30] An examination of the *travaux préparatoires*, however, indicates no such single-minded intent and no common understanding of what the phrase "recognized as such" means.[31] To the Soviet delegation and its ideological adherents, "recognized as such" apparently did indicate the need for subsequent *consent* to the rule, but we must bear in mind that the Soviet position (at least as it was at the time of the *travaux*) was that customary law itself is only binding upon states that have consented to it.[32] Given that restrictive, antihistorical, and theoretically unsound view of general customary law, it is no surprise that the adherents to the Soviet position would not want to recognize in treaties any mechanism for general generation of customary law; they would not even recognize in custom itself any such mechanism. It is improbable that Akehurst would want to endorse the Soviet position if that were the cost of substantiating his argument, for that would leave him with a restrictive view of custom that would render otiose

---

29. (W. Ger. v. Den., W. Ger. v. Neth.) 1969 I.C.J. 3 (Judgment of Feb. 20).
30. Akehurst, *supra* note 1, at 49.
31. U.N. Conference on the Law of Treaties, *Official Records* (1st sess.) at 197-201, U.N. Doc. A/CONF. 39/11 (1969); id. (2d sess.) at 63-72, U.N. Doc. A/CONF. 39/11/Add. 1 (1970).
32. *See, e.g.*, Tunkin, "Remarks on the Juridical Nature of Customary Norms of International Law," 49 *Calif. L. Rev.* 419 (1961).

his entire preceding argument that treaties found through their *travaux* to be declaratory of customary law have that effect upon non-parties.

But there are at least two other meanings that can be attributed to the phrase "recognized as such" that either were expressed during the treaty negotiations or might conceivably have been considered as a meaning by the states that ultimately ratified the convention. For instance, the phrase might mean "understood as such"; it would thus imply that the process of treaty formation of customary rules of law must be understood to create *custom* and not a *treaty obligation* upon third states. Along this line, the delegate from El Salvador acutely observed that it was not the rules of a treaty that could have the effect of becoming binding via custom on third states, but the content of the treaty provisions.[33] Or, "recognized as such" might refer to recognition within the treaty or in its *travaux* (Akehurst's first objective mechanism, but *not* the mechanism of subsequent statements for which he cited article 38). Clearly, article 38 contains great ambiguity in the phrase "recognized as such," which should not obscure the central fact that the article expressly recognizes the process of customary law creation by treaty that I have been describing in the present section of this chapter.

More significant than the Vienna Convention for Akehurst's purposes is his invocation of the judgment of the International Court of Justice in the *North Sea Continental Shelf Cases* of 1969. He contends that the need for *opinio juris*—that is, in his view, the need for statements in the treaty, in the *travaux*, or in subsequent remarks by states accepting the treaty provisions that those provisions are declaratory of international law—"is clearly stated in the *North Sea Continental Shelf Cases*."[34] The court, commenting upon the contention of Denmark and the Netherlands that a customary rule corresponding to article 6 of the Geneva Convention on the Continental Shelf[35] had

---

33. U.N. *Conference on the Law of Treaties, Official Records* (2d sess.) at 64, U.N. Doc. A/CONF. 39/11/Add. 1 (1970).
34. Akehurst, *supra* note 1, at 44.
35. Convention on the Continental Shelf, opened for signature April 29, 1958, art. 6, 15 *U.S.T.* 471, *T.I.A.S.* No. 5578, 499 *U.N.T.S.* 311. Article 6 reads:
> 1. Where the same continental shelf is adjacent to the territories of two or more States whose coasts are opposite each other, the boundary of the continental shelf appertaining to such States shall be determined by agreement between them. In the absence of agreement, and unless another boundary line is justified by special circumstances, the boundary is the median line, every point of which is equidistant from the nearest points of the baselines from which the breadth of the territorial sea of each State is measured.

"come into being since the Convention, partly because of its [the convention's] own impact, partly on the basis of subsequent State practice," said that there must be some showing of *opinio juris* to demonstrate this subsequent behavior that made the Convention's article 6 into a norm of customary law. The court's precise language on this point, which explicitly recognizes the norm-creating process that I have been describing in the present essay, is as follows:

> In so far as this contention is based on the view that Article 6 of the Convention has had the influence, and has produced the effect, described, it clearly involves treating that Article as a norm-creating provision which has constituted the foundation of, or has generated a rule which, while only conventional or contractual in its origin, has since passed into the general *corpus* of international law, and is now accepted as such by the *opinio juris*, so as to have become binding even for countries which have never, and do not, become parties to the Convention. There is no doubt that this process is a perfectly possible one and does from time to time occur: it constitutes indeed one of the recognized methods by which new rules of customary international law may be formed. At the same time this result is not lightly to be regarded as having been attained.[36]

The court then found that as far as article 6 itself was concerned, there was a need to show subsequent acceptance of its rule by other states (for example, by demonstrating *opinio juris*—although the court fails to indicate how *opinio juris* could be shown), and that the contending parties failed to offer such proof of subsequent acceptance.

The court is saying two things. First, there is no doubt that treaty provisions may generate customary rules. Second, article 6 of the

---

2. Where the same continental shelf is adjacent to the territories of two adjacent States, the boundary of the continental shelf shall be determined by agreement between them. In the absence of agreement, and unless another boundary line is justified by special circumstances, the boundary shall be determined by application of the principle of equidistance from the nearest points of the baselines from which the breadth of the territorial sea of each State is measured.

3. In delimiting the boundaries of the continental shelf, any lines which are drawn in accordance with the principles set out in paragraphs 1 and 2 of this article should be defined with reference to charts and geographical features as they exist at a particular date, and reference should be made to fixed permanent identifiable points on the land.

36. *North Sea Continental Shelf* (W. Ger. v. Den., W. Ger. v. Neth.), 1969 I.C.J. 3, 41 (Judgment of Feb. 20).

Geneva Convention did not do so. At this point in the court's opinion we are left unsure whether the reason given by the court for why this particular provision did not generate the customary rule desired by Denmark and the Netherlands—that there was no subsequent *opinio juris* indicating acceptance of the treaty rule—applies generally to all treaty provisions that generate customary rules, or only to article 6. If it is the former, then the thesis I have been contending for in this chapter becomes unnecessary, since any subsequent showing of *opinio juris* should be enough to demonstrate a rule of customary law quite apart from the prior treaty. Thus we are left with the question whether the court is positing the first of these propositions or the second.

Fortunately, we are not remitted to metaphysical speculation for our decision. The court's opinion as a whole makes it abundantly clear that the rule of article 6 was itself inapplicable to the facts of the case and could not have generated a rule binding upon the Federal Republic of Germany with regard to its continental shelf. By omitting the *facts* of the case, the *contentions* of the parties, and the court's decisive *reasoning* in that regard, Akehurst creates the impression that the court was speaking ex cathedra about custom formation. Unfortunately, Akehurst is not alone in dealing with the *Continental Shelf* opinion as if it were cut loose from the moorings of its own pleadings, facts, and judicial holding.[37] Hence we must examine the case itself with some care.

Denmark and the Netherlands contended that the North Sea continental shelf delimitation line between themselves and the Federal Republic of Germany should be decided upon the basis of the equidistance method as specified in article 6 of the Geneva Convention. Germany countered that the continental shelf should be delimited according to the principle that each coastal state is entitled to a just and equitable share. The court, however, held that neither contention was correct under international law. Instead, it found that a nation's

---

37. A leading casebook on international law suggests that excerpts from the *North Sea Continental Shelf Cases* will "provide the answers to, or at least throw further light on," numerous questions posed by the authors regarding the impact of treaties upon custom. L. Henkin, R. Pugh, O. Schachter, & H. Smit, *International Law Cases and Materials*, 38 (1980). The lengthy excerpts from the *North Sea Continental Shelf Cases* that follow, id., 59-65, 84-85, 366-67, do not indicate the territorial basis upon which the court based its result in the cases or the consequence that the territorial basis entails stricter proof of special custom. These qualifications are also not mentioned in the references to the *North Sea Continental Shelf Cases* in *Restatement (Revised) of the Law: Foreign Relations Law of the United States* 31-34 (Ten. Draft No. 1, 1980).

continental shelf is as much its territory as is its land above sea level, and that fairness, equity, or equidistance has nothing to do with the matter. To summarize the court's reasoning in this regard, let us imagine two nations, X and Y, facing each other across a 500-mile wide sea. Suppose that nation X has a continental shelf appertaining to its land territory, and that the shelf extends across the sea for a distance of 450 miles. At that point, the shelf drops down to the ocean floor depth, and then rises precipitously to form the land mass of nation Y. In other words, X "has" a continental shelf and Y does not "have" one. In this situation, the equidistance principle might draw the line of delimitation at 250 miles from X's coast, giving the remaining 200 miles of continental shelf over to Y. A fair or equitable principle might draw the line in roughly the same place. But according to the court, what is involved in the matter of the continental shelf is not fairness or equidistance, but *title* to territory. "What confers the *ipso jure* title which international law attributes to the coastal State in respect of its continental shelf," the court held, "is the fact that the submarine areas concerned may be deemed to be actually part of the territory over which the coastal State already has dominion—in the sense that, although covered with water, they are a prolongation or continuation of that territory, an extension of it under the sea."[38] Thus, under the court's reasoning, X is entitled to the entire continental shelf of 450 miles.

This, then, is the bedrock upon which the court constructed its judgment in the case. But there are two remaining contentions that Denmark and the Netherlands offered. First, they argued that the equidistance principle of article 6 of the Geneva Convention changed matters, so that, whatever title to the continental shelf Germany might have had prior to that Convention, it now only had so much of the North Sea continental shelf as the equidistance principle would allow (a principle that, as we might expect, sharply reduced the total area of the continental shelf that would be allocated to Germany).

The answer to this first contention might best be illustrated by a hypothetical example. Suppose most of the nations in the world conclude a multilateral treaty on the subjects of international law, and that one of the provisions of this supposed treaty contains the following language:

---

38. 1969 I.C.J. at 32.

A "nation" consists of reasonably contiguous territory. No nation may claim as any of its territory land that is separated from the bulk of its territory by more than 1000 miles of ocean.

Suppose further that the United States signs this treaty, but fails to ratify it because it realizes that ratification would mean that its fiftieth state would be forfeited. Is there any process known to international law whereby other states, by entering into a treaty, may deprive the United States of Hawaii? To be sure, the treaty provision I have invented looks generalizable—as does article 6 of the Geneva Convention regarding the equidistance principle.[39] But the fact that the provision appears to be generalizable into a norm of customary law does not make it in fact so generalizable, because the effect of this particular provision would be to change the title to specific territory. To be sure, the situation would be different if Hawaii were *res nullius* or the continental shelf were *res nullius*. But as I pointed out above, the court explicitly held that the continental shelf was as much part of the territory of a nation as its land above sea level. Thus, no matter how many nations ratified the hypothetical treaty I have suggested, the United States could not be bound thereby unless the United States itself ratified the treaty. A nation cannot be deprived of a portion of its territory (such as its continental shelf) except by its own consent.[40] No matter how innocuous a treaty provision might seem to be, if its effect is to change title to specific territory, it cannot have that effect without the consent of the owner.

Second, Denmark and the Netherlands argued that, although Germany did not ratify the Geneva Convention, international conduct subsequent to the Convention had nevertheless elevated the equidistance principle to a rule of customary law. But now we can see that, given the court's primary holding that title to specific territory is involved in this case, the only way that such title may be transferred other than through the process of explicit consent (and there was no showing at all that Germany consented) would be through the process of special custom, which is indeed a form of implied consent. The

---

39. Convention on the Continental Shelf, art. 6 (continental shelf between adjacent or opposite states to use the equidistant median line from baselines, in absence of agreement or special circumstances).

40. Present customary international law requires this result. Of course, international law could change. A new norm could come into being through multilateral conventions that allowed for loss of national territory without the consent of the national owner.

concept of a special custom may apply to settle specific questions regarding territory, such as whether "an alleged regional or local custom" settled a question of territorial asylum in the *Asylum Case*,[41] whether specific territorial capitulatory rights existed in Morocco in the *Nationals in Morocco Case*,[42] or whether Portugal had a right of passage or easement over specific Indian territory in the *Right of Passage Case*.[43] In all these cases, specific *opinio juris* on the part of the defendant against whom the rights were asserted had to be proved as part of the plaintiff's (complainant's) case. A proof of such specific *opinio juris* would satisfy Blackstone's original distinction between general and special custom in giving the latter the required element of consent.[44] Hence, the idea of subsequent *opinio juris* in the *North Sea Continental Shelf Cases* was required by the court before it would divest Germany of title to any portion of its continental shelf territory. In an earlier writing, I attempted to spell out the requirements of special custom at some length, with more detailed references to the preceding cases as well as to the *Anglo-Norwegian Fisheries Case*.[45] The main point of that article bears summarization here: that general custom is entirely distinct from special custom, and that the stringent requirements of proof of the latter (such as a showing of *opinio juris*) should in no way be confused with proof of the former.

Therefore, given its judgment (which I believe was entirely correct) that the continental shelf question was one of title to territory and not fairness of apportionment, the court turned to article 6 as a possible contention—not stated in so many words—that proof of special custom was needed before any change of title could be assumed. (We would expect and insist on the same result in the hypothetical case I gave of Hawaii.) Inasmuch as the court explicitly acknowledged the process of custom generation by treaty, it held only that article 6 was not an example of the generation of general custom. Given the facts of the case and the court's disposition of the matter of title to the continental shelf, the court's remarks on the need

---

41. *Asylum* (Colombia v. Peru), 1950 I.C.J. 265 (Judgment of Nov. 20).
42. *Rights of Nationals of the United States of America in Morocco* (Fr. v. U.S.), 1952 I.C.J. 176 (Judgment of Aug. 27).
43. *Right of Passage over Indian Territory* (Port. v. India), 1960 I.C.J. 4 (Judgment of Apr. 12).
44. *See* 1 W. Blackstone, *Commentaries* *74-75, *78.
45. *Fisheries Case* (U.K. v. Nor.), 1951 I.C.J. 114 (Judgment of Dec. 18). *See* D'Amato, "The Concept of Special Custom in International Law," 63 *A.J.I.L.* 211 (1969).

for *opinio juris* subsequent to the adoption of the Geneva Convention apply only to this or similar cases of special custom. The use to which Akehurst puts the court's remarks on article 6 is wholly unwarranted.[46]

3. *Treaties Into Custom?* It seems to me that the theory that treaties generate customary law stands, at the present writing, upon the following considerations. First, any student of international law reading the literature of the subject, particularly historical texts or the successive editions of a textbook, should conclude that a great many of the rules we now call customary law had their origin as provisions in treaties. Second, as to human rights in particular, treaty law today is clearly the major repository of the rules that we regard as the rules of customary international law of human rights.[47] The most prominent example is perhaps the prohibition against human slavery, as I have already tried to show in this chapter; the more recent prohibitions against genocide and torture are also generally regarded as part of customary law. Of course, Lane and Watson seem to regard these latter two, at least, as outside the realm of customary international law binding upon all nations generally. But their position, it would appear, would logically require them to discard all the rules of customary law that have had their origin in treaties, and that would mean nearly all the rules.

---

46. To be sure, Akehurst prefaced his remarks about the *Continental Shelf Cases* with the qualification, "Despite some ambiguities, the judgment in the *North Sea Continental Shelf* cases supports this [Akehurst's own] view." Akehurst *supra* note 1, at 50. But since he leaves the term "ambiguities" undefined, there is only the slightest hint that he may have misconstrued the cases. More significant is Akehurst's own shifting throughout his article between a view of *opinio juris* as an element in the establishment of custom quite apart from any use the customary rule is put to against a third state, and *opinio juris* as a showing by the specific third state against which a rule is being asserted; the latter is what I have argued is only an element of special custom. If it were the former, then we would probably have little or no general custom in international law, and we would be reduced to the Soviet conception of consent to each and every rule that is asserted against a state.

47. In any litigated case, counsel will of course cite any and all other possible "sources" of international law in addition to treaties. In *Filartiga v. Peña-Irala*, 630 F. 2d 876 (2d Cir. 1980), for example, the court stated that torture was a violation of international law and cited as support the writing of legal scholars, resolutions of the United Nations General Assembly, the prohibitions against torture contained in the constitutions of various countries, and also, of course, international treaties. But not all of these "sources" are equally persuasive. In particular, resolutions of the General Assembly might on occasion represent political desiderata of a majority of nations but not amount to a statement of "law." *See, e.g.,* "Discussion, Contemporary Views on the Sources of International Law: The Effect of U.N. Resolutions on Emerging Legal Norms," *Proc. A.S.I.L.* 327 (1979). Some writers feel that international law can be shown by an international "consensus." *See, e.g.,* Farer, "International Law and Political Behavior: Toward a Conceptual Liaison," 25 *World Pol.* 430, 446 (1973). The problem consists, however, in establishing that the "consensus" exists. Professors Lane and Watson are properly cynical in saying that a consensus on human rights can easily be formed by authors citing each other until something that looks like a consensus emerges.

Yet, doubts remain that treaties do not of themselves generate custom. Akehurst's position, which I have criticized in the preceding section, probably represents what many, if not most, American and English scholars believe to be the case. The persons sharing Akehurst's stance feel that generalizable provisions in treaties do not give rise instantly, or ipso facto, to customary law binding upon nonparties. I think they feel this way largely because of the "contract" view of treaties that I have previously described, and perhaps in lesser part because they may feel it is unfair in some sense to visit new rules upon states who have not joined (for whatever reason) in the treaty that supposedly creates those new rules. Thus, they might feel that one must view "with caution" the proposition that treaties generate custom, even though they might acknowledge that the process undoubtedly takes place "from time to time."

As much as I acknowledge the reality of these psychological perceptions, the arguments that I have made in the last two decades and continue to make in the present chapter stem solely from a conviction that the cautious view in this case is a chimera. No process of treaties "hardening" or "passing" into custom has even been described, much less recorded. Akehurst's attempt to objectify the hardening process (requiring states subsequently to make a statement that they believe a treaty rule has passed into custom—whether or not, Akehurst adds, they actually believe it) again has no real-world exemplar.

Where, then, do we stand? If I am correct in arguing that nothing subsequent to the treaty can be found, or needs to be found, to prove that its generalizable provisions have passed into custom, and if the reader concurs that treaties have furnished us with many if not nearly all the rules of customary law that we now recognize as such, then we are left with two possibilities. The first is that generalizable treaty provisions ipso facto and instantly give us evidence of custom in the same sense that the classic art-conflict-resolution pattern gives us evidence of custom. The second is that such treaty provisions have this effect, but not immediately; some passage of time is required. But how much time? A day, a month, a century? Are there different time requirements for different rules, and if so, how can we discover what they are? These difficulties seem to me to be insuperable, for absent any material thing or process that we can point to subsequent to a treaty that indicates when the treaty rule becomes customary, the time question becomes arbitrary. A "reasonable" time period, however, should perhaps be required so that if two or more states do not like a rule in a treaty signed by other states they may have a reasonable time to enter into a contrary treaty among themselves. Thus, for example, five nations enter into a human-rights treaty that contains a generalizable, yet controversial, provision. Nations V, W, and X do not like this provision and enter into a treaty among themselves that contains the opposite of that provision (i.e., its contradiction). Perhaps we should give V, W, and X time to do this—a reasonable amount of time. If they do not act, then we might say that the first treaty gives rise to customary law.

It should be noted that if V, W and X enter into such a treaty, not only will they carve out a rule for themselves, but their treaty too will generate customary law—a custom that is directly contrary to the custom generated by the first treaty. This is the same process that would occur if some state practices resolved a dispute one way and others, another way; it is like conflicting precedents in domestic law. What an international court might do if faced with conflicting treaties that are argued to generate customary law for a state that is not a party to any of them is a complex question, one that I have previously tried to answer, though the lack of case law on this particular subject makes such enterprises extremely speculative.[48]

Should this "reasonable time" provision be read into the treaty-into-custom process? Perhaps some such provision is all that many scholars would need to secure their concurrence to the proposition that human-rights treaties (among others) by now have generated customary international law binding on all the states. If that is so, my thesis is for the purpose of the present chapter complete. There is no doubt that by now nations have had ample opportunity to enter into treaties providing that slavery, genocide, or torture are legal (and perhaps, although one would have to argue each case separately, treaties contradicting other human rights as well). Since no nations have entered into any such treaties, we might conclude that the prohibitions against slavery, genocide, and torture have "passed" into customary international law.

This conclusion of course follows a fortiori if no time is needed for such "passage." Because of the indeterminateness of what would

---

48. See D'Amato, supra note 2, 92-98. See also Onuf, "Global Law-Making and Legal Thought," in N. Onuf, Law-Making in the Global Community, 21, 28-29 (critique of D'Amato's theory); D'Amato, "What 'Counts' as Law," in id. at 79-100 (reply to Onuf).

constitute a "reasonable time," and because traditional customary law has no such requirement (the act-conflict-resolution scenario generates custom right away, though of course subsequent contrary practice would modify or change that custom), my own preference would be to acknowledge that generalizable provisions in treaties (especially multilateral treaties) ipso facto generate customary rules.

Conclusion

I have tried to show that, through the time-honored process of the generation of customary law by generalizable treaty provisions, international entitlements have arisen that prohibit any nation from engaging in acts of genocide against its own population, or torturing or enslaving any human being. These "human rights," as well as others, may be found in multilateral conventions, but their effect spreads to nonparty states through the customary process of treaty generation of international law. I attempted to defend the thesis of treaty generation of customary law against various contrary contentions that have recently been advanced.

Thus, in the example I gave in Chapter 5, if A, a national of state X, is tortured by state X, state Y has an international-law entitlement against X that X cease and desist the torture and pay damages to A (the damages may be paid to Y, which in turn pays them to A, following the procedure in the *Lotus Case*). A, as it turns out, is an "international" of state Y just as he is a "national" of state X. If international law provides for "implementation and compliance" for A as X's national, it provides, *the same* sanctions for A as Y's "international" in those areas secured by the customary law of human rights. As a national of X, A has certain rights when he is visiting in states other than X. As an "international" of Y, he has a different set of rights against all states including state X when he is back home. These latter rights are precisely those that have been articulated and protected in the generalizable provisions of treaties, particularly multilateral conventions, dealing with various aspects of human rights. To be sure, these international human rights are defeasible if other conventions are entered into that deny such rights. As of the present writing, I know of no international conventions that contradict the various "human rights" conventions, but we must recognize the possibility that, as far as international entitlements are concerned, those entitlements may be destroyed by conventions just as they have been created. As in all other arguments in this book, I think we must above all recognize that as far as the states of the world are concerned, what they do—and not what we want them to do—constitutes international law. On this point I agree with Lane and Watson, whose theses I have otherwise devoted this and the previous chapter to refuting.

We must also recognize that many powerful sources oppose the concept of a human rights law. The United States lives under a regime of dedication to law and the Constitution. If what nation X is doing to its own citizens in X is contrary to international law, American policy makers (or some of them) will feel a pressure to denounce X or to cut off military or economic aid to X. The President, however, generally likes to have wide discretion to decide politically whether or not to give aid to any foreign nation such as X and thus is likely to be predisposed against any *legal* argument that such aid must be curtailed. Naturally, any President will tend to oppose a policy that weakens his personal power and discretion, and thus we may expect resistance from the executive branch to the universality of human rights entitlements. On the other hand, this may be an area where, in the United States at least, international law is ahead of national interests. If the President has an international legal right to complain about what nation X does to its citizens, a new area for the legitimate exercise of presidential power has opened up and perhaps it will be filled someday. If and when that happens, commentators will undoubtedly say that we are expressing our national interest in how nation X treats its own citizens. This is the long-range power of international law that I alluded to in the Introduction to this book.

But if it is any small comfort to the admirers of executive discretion, I would also reiterate that entitlements and interests are not the same thing. Although we may be entitled to complain about what nation X does to its own citizens in X, we may, for other overriding political reasons, not want to show our "interest" in the matter. From a purely personal point of view, with the luxury of not being saddled with foreign-policy-making responsibility, I would consider it a matter of morality that we should protest vigorously against any denial of human rights in any foreign country and take all steps necessary to influence that country to abandon its illegal practices. But my concern in the present chapter is, I hope, a more objective one: to indicate that even if, for political reasons, we do *not* protest against some violations of human rights in some foreign countries, that does not give any favorable coloring of legality to those foreign practices. Rather, the entitlement remains the same even if the interest is not manifested.

At the present level of academic dialogue on the matter of human rights, it is essential to make sure that despair over the wretched state of human rights around the world does not lead to abandonment of the concept of human rights law. I have tried to demonstrate that the concept remains vital, and that no special change in the relationship of states to one another is needed to implement it. It is true that we cannot legally require the executive to combat human-rights violations in foreign countries. Yet that is only a legal concession—and a relatively small one at that. The most difficult issues in the enforcement of human rights are not issues of law, but of politics and morality.

But there are *two* "oughts" that regulate human action. Morality is one of them, and as to that, each person has to make up his or her own mind. But a second "ought" is prudential: it makes sense, given your own interests, for you to do something. In the next chapter, I will try to make an argument that it makes sense for Americans, and especially American businesspersons, to promote actively the idea and realization of international human rights. It will be an argument from the prudential, and not necessarily from the moral, point of view.

7

THE COMMERCIAL AND POLITICAL DESIRABILITY OF HUMAN RIGHTS

When I take up the Nuremberg cases in my class in International Law, I find it quite difficult to convey to the students how radical those proceedings appeared to be in 1947. At that time, the contention that there should be individual accountability under international law seemed to constitute an unfounded and dangerous precedent. How could political leaders be made personally responsible for acts of state such as instituting a war (even an "aggressive" war) or engaging in wholly internal policies (the "final solution" against Jews and other minorities of their own citizens)? Indeed, the Nuremberg result seemed somewhat unprincipled to my teachers when I went to law school in the late 1950s. But today's students, an entirely new generation, find the Nuremberg decisions unremarkable. Of course, they say, the Nazi leaders were criminally guilty of mass murder and should not have been able to hide behind the instrumentality of the state or government.

As the Nuremberg result settles into commonplace international law, we can appreciate the great change that it wrought in the fabric of that law. The previous state system symbolized in the term *international* law changed to a conception of world law which includes individuals as well as states, and gives those individuals rights as well as duties. In 1947, the Soviet Union, which was by far the most aggressive of the victorious allies in demanding execution of all Nazi Party members, perhaps least realized the radical nature of the precedent they were setting at Nuremberg—that in holding individuals responsible under international law, the concept of collectivity that forms the basis of Soviet Marxism tended to be undermined. Of course Stalin probably did not care; he was himself quite immune from the reach of law, despite his genocidal purges of Soviet citizens in the 1930s. But the precedent he helped create at Nuremberg survived him. Its legacy is in part reflected by the sharp, hostile reactions of Soviet leaders whenever accusations are made against them that they are engaged in human rights violations within the Soviet Union or in satellite nations. The increasing sensitivity of the human rights issue attests to its perceived relevance in international law and international politics.

The shift of emphasis in international law from collectivity to individuality seems to be accelerating. Former President Carter's revealing remark that human rights is the "soul" of American foreign policy, and Pope John Paul II's espousal of the cause of human rights, signify that it is an idea whose time has come. Not surprisingly, the military-industrial complex in the United States has been one of the slowest to absorb the idea. Support for the Shah of Iran, to take a recent example, was urged most vehemently by the Pentagon, major banks, and arms manufacturers, in the teeth of evidence that the Shah's brutal repression of Iranian dissidents and his total mental imperviousness to the concept of human rights was not only morally intolerable but also potentially explosive within Iran. The resulting revolution in that country, taking the military-industrial complex by surprise, resulted in many cases of total loss to American financial and commercial interests that had been doing business with the Shah of Iran.[1]

Yet perhaps multinational investments were attracted to Iran because the Shah's regime seemed strong and stable. Could it be possible that the logic of international commerce is inconsistent with the disruptive ideas associated with the term "human rights?" We need only recall that fascism was the theory of the completely strong and stable state, one in which the government was indeed transformed into a business corporation. But even in today's rhetoric, international business persons might fear the "revolution of rising expectations" suggested by the various human rights conventions as posing a latent

1. *See, e.g.,* "Business losses in Iran may get much worse," *Chi. Tribune,* Feb. 23, 1979, § 5, at 7, col. 2.

threat to multinational corporations. For instance, the Covenant on Economic, Social, and Cultural Rights, signed by President Carter and sent to the Senate for ratification,[2] contains not only the right to work but also the right to fair wages, equal pay for equal work, equal work conditions for women and men, and "rest, leisure and reasonable limitation of working hours and periodic holidays with pay, as well as remuneration for public holidays."[3] Also included is the "right of everyone to an adequate standard of living," including food, clothing, and housing.[4] One of the most articulate, though less well-known, documents expressive of the third-world consensus on economic rights is the Cocoyoc Declaration of October 12, 1974.[5] Consider this passage from that document:

> Our first concern is to redefine the whole purpose of development. This should not be to develop things but to develop man. Human beings have basic needs: food, shelter, clothing, health, education. Any process of growth that does not lead to their fulfillment—or, even worse, disrupts them—is a travesty of the idea of development. We are still in a stage where the most important concern of development is the level of satisfaction of basic needs for the poorest sections of the population in society. The primary purpose of economic growth should be to ensure the improvement of conditions for these groups. A growth process that benefits only the wealthiest

---

2. President Carter signed the Covenant on October 5, 1977. *See* "Remarks on Signing International Covenant on Human Rights," 13 *Weekly Comp. of Pres. Doc.* 1488 (Oct. 5, 1977). He submitted it to the Senate for ratification on February 23, 1978. *See* 14 *Weekly Comp. of Pres. Doc.* 395 (Feb. 23, 1978). Carter urged ratification of this Covenant in a presidential proclamation. *See* Proc. No. 4609, 43 Fed. Reg. 56,009 (1978). However, by 1986 it still has not been ratified by the United States.

3. International Covenant on Economic, Social and Cultural Rights, *entered in force* Jan. 3, 1976, arts. 6 & 7, *G.A. Res.* 2200 (Annex), 21 *U.N. G.A.O.R.*, Supp. (No. 16) 50, U.N. Doc. A/6316 (1967).

4. *Id.* art. 11. Of course, the term "human rights" most prominently includes political and civil rights, such as the right to a fair trial, habeas corpus, prohibition against ex post facto laws, freedom from discrimination, and prohibition against torture and cruel or degrading punishment. *See* Universal Declaration of Human Rights, *G.A. Res.* 217A, U.N. Doc. 810, at 71 (1948); International Covenant on Civil and Political Rights, entered in force Mar. 23, 1976, *G.A. Res.* 2200 (Annex), 21 *U.N.G.A.O.R.* Supp. (No. 16) 59, U.N. Doc. A/6316 (1967). I am stressing here so-called "economic rights," since they give rise to the more difficult arguments in light of business interests. If my argument is correct with respect to "economic rights," it should be an *a fortiori* case with respect to "political rights."

5. For the text of this declaration, *see Beyond Dependency*, 170 (G. Erb and V. Kallab eds. 1975) [hereinafter cited as *Beyond Dependency*]. Although the Cocoyoc Declaration was drafted by a group of individuals speaking only for themselves, included were prominent social scientists, natural scientists, and United Nations officials, chaired by Lady Barbara Ward Jackson, in a symposium organized by the United Nations Environment Program and the United Nations Conference on Trade and Development, in close cooperation with the government of Mexico.

minority and maintains or even increases the disparities between and within countries is not development. It is exploitation.[6]

In the present chapter I shall attempt to examine briefly whether any apparent first blush inconsistency between multinational investment and human rights is tenable. I shall consider four arguments. The first and simplest argument I will raise is one of enlightened self-interest. Second, I will attempt to examine what kinds of "rights" are being discussed in the term "human rights" and consider their implications for business investment. Third, I will take a closer look at the already mentioned conflict between human rights and Marxist collectivism. And finally, perhaps the least perceived but potentially the most important issue, I will attempt to distinguish two strands that have become thoroughly confused in the human-rights rhetoric—the rights of individuals and national claims to self-determination—and the implications of that distinction to multinational business.

I. Self-Interest

Left to itself, business is apolitical and perhaps amoral.[7] The business goal of profit maximization encourages efficiency within the company structure but does not directly address the human needs of suppliers, workers, and consumers. Yet indirectly, as Robert Owen among others argued in the nineteenth century, human needs should figure into profit maximization: the more fully a worker's needs are provided for, the more loyal and efficient the worker becomes.[8] In this sense, increasing the worker's standard of living—and concomitantly the worker's stake in industrial success—should be in the general interest of the business community.

But the human rights issue today is more than a plea for calculation of long-run, self-interested profitability, as Owen might have argued. Rather, the increasing aspiration for human rights, reflected in the previously quoted Cocoyoc Declaration, is one that multinational

---

6. *Id.* at 173.
7. According to Irving Kristol, "It is, in my opinion, as absurd to praise the profit motive—i.e., economic action based on self-interest—as it is to condemn it. The human impulse to such action is, like the sexual impulse, a natural fact." "No Cheers for Profit Motive," *Wall St. J.*, Feb. 20, 1979, at 18, col. 4.
8. *See* R. Owen, *A New View of Society and Other Writings* (G. Cole ed. 1927). Robert Owen (1771-1858) was a very successful businessman as well as a philosopher.

Desirability of Human Rights

business can only ignore at its own peril. For instance, the dictatorial regimes in Cuba, Chile, and Iran seemed eminently stable and businesslike until suddenly they were toppled by international revolutions. Such revolutions seem increasingly likely in a world where the human rights idea has "caught on," in countries where the government ignores the human rights of the citizenry and allows too great an economic disparity between the favored elite and the masses. And when such revolutions occur, investment losses can be total. Indeed it may already have become more prudent for a multinational corporation to open up a new plant in a country that has a reasonable tax on profits and makes sure that the tax benefits the people, than to invest in a country that has an invitingly low tax but ignores the welfare of its citizenry. Although the return on investment in the former case may be less dramatic initially, it might continue for a long time; the latter case, on the other hand, could at any moment explode in revolution and total confiscation.[9] Hence, in terms of self-interest, international business must become increasingly realistic about the implications of what has seemed to many to be a "soft" issue; namely, the issue of human rights.

II. Nature of the "Rights"

Some observers have asserted that "human rights" such as the right to food, clothing, housing, medical care, and education, cannot be taken seriously since, unlike typical rights such as those found in the Bill of Rights, the so-called human rights require positive acts by

---

9. The same calculation should apply to foreign policy. The Dulles-Kissinger approach that emphasized personal friendships and commitments with national leaders, resulting in military alliances with dictatorial and repressive regimes, can result in enormous losses when these regimes are toppled. The new human rights approach, on the contrary, holds the promise of forging longer lasting ties with the peoples of foreign countries. In addition, it tends to create a world environment compatible with American values in which the United States may feel more secure. The Dulles-Kissinger rhetoric that we "need" military alliances with foreign governments has been persuasively advertised and sold within the United States, but apart from some segments of the business community which stand to gain directly from that program (arms manufacturers and bankers, for instance), the rhetoric has not persuaded most upon careful analysis. Our present nuclear stockpile—enough to incinerate the rest of the world several times over—is a more reliable deterrent and safeguard for our national security than nuclear weapons and missiles in the hands of foreign governments who have paper commitments to us.

Nor do we need their territories as "bases" for our missiles. Our nuclear submarines, under our direct control and at any given time dispersed under the oceans of the world, are all the "bases" we need. In addition, missile sites within the United States can reach any target on the planet with incredible accuracy.

others in order to be actualized. For example, the right to food depends upon farmers producing the food and shippers transporting the food to the claimant. The right to medical care requires that doctors be available and willing to provide it. In contrast, rights found in the Bill of Rights, such as freedom of speech and religion, and the right to due process of law, seem to exist as present realizable claims. Thus, Joel Feinberg constrasts human rights with actual rights, and says that

> when manifesto writers speak of them [human rights] as if already actual rights, they are easily forgiven, for this is but a powerful way of expressing the conviction that they ought to be recognized by states here and now as potential rights and consequently as determinants of present aspirations and guides to present policies.[10]

But the contrast suggested by Professor Feinberg tends to be misleading. Every right, whether a human right or a Bill-of-Rights right, only makes sense if there is a corresponding duty.[11] Freedom of speech and religion imposes upon others the duty not to interfere with the exercise of that freedom. The right to due process of law places upon courts and governmental officials the duty to take positive steps to provide due process to the claimant. Similarly, the right to work places upon others the duty to provide the work.

But here is where careful consideration is needed. Just as the right to speak implies the right to remain silent, so too the right to work implies the right not to work and the right to a paid vacation implies the right to skip that vacation. Let us analyze two of the human rights—the right to food and the right to work. If I am a poor farmer (and sixty-five percent of the world's workers are peasant farmers existing in a subsistence economy),[12] I have the right to grow food for myself and my family or not to do so. I have the right to eat or not to eat, to work or not to work. Of course, at the subsistence level, these rights seem rather academic; surely I will work and nat-

---

10. Feinberg, "The Nature and Value of Rights," 4 *J. Value Engineering* 255 (1970).
11. *See* Hohfield, "Some Fundamental Legal Conceptions as Applied in Judicial Reasoning," 23 *Yale L.J.* 16 (1913). Sometimes duties are addressed to particular persons (*e.g.*, to the courts in the due process example) or to an indefinite class (*e.g.*, to all who are required to give food to a starving person). Professor Feinberg notes the latter possibility in a free speech example but does not appear to carry through its general implications. *See* J. Feinberg, *Social Philosophy*, 95 (1973).
12. Ferguson, "International Human Rights," *Harv. L. Sch. Bull.*, Winter 1979, at 16, 18.

urally I will eat the food I produce. But now suppose I am capable of producing more food than I need. And suppose further that there is another person, perhaps in another country, who is starving and asserts a "right to food." If the surplus food that I can produce with my labor is enough to save that other person from starving, he might claim that he has a right to that food. But what, then, of my right not to work? Must I be coerced into working extra hours so that I can produce surplus food to feed someone else? If so, then my right to work is a sham, for in fact I am being forced to work. To be sure, I might recognize a moral right of that other person to some portion of my excess labor, but I would want to know more about that other person—is he simply being lazy, or is he working as hard as he physically can but with poor soil or in a poor climate? If he is simply lazy, I feel a lesser moral obligation to work long extra hours to feed him. And in any event, the extent to which I feel a moral obligation is a matter of my own judgment. I do not want to be coerced by the government into working extra hours so that the product of my extra labor can be distributed free to others. Or I could make a different argument which results in the same conclusion. I could work only the "extra" hours and have all the food I produce be distributed to others, leaving nothing for myself. Then I could claim that I, too, have a right to food, and therefore the food that others produce should be distributed to me.

In short, a *universal* system of human rights results in contradiction if the corresponding duties can only be achieved by coercion. This conclusion has enormous implications for the free enterprise system. For the poor farmer is perfectly willing to produce excess food if he can trade it for other desired goods that he cannot efficiently produce for himself. For example, if in one year I can produce a thousand dollars' worth of surplus wheat, I would do so if I can sell that wheat and—even if the government takes half of the money for taxes—use the after-tax income to buy a television set.[13] The television set makes the extra labor worthwhile, and in turn provides my surplus wheat to the entrepreneurs who designed the television set and the workers who constructed it. In sum, this simple example indicates that only through a free market mechanism can human rights be universalized.

13. What ultimately counts is not the amount of after-tax dollars nor the rate of taxation, but rather whether material incentives (such as TV sets) exist that can be purchased by a certain amount of extra labor.

Any other system so far devised seems to require, to some degree, human slavery. Both political extremes of fascism and communism require forced labor to meet distributive ends fashioned not through individual choice but by the government.

Human rights can therefore only be actualized by a free market system that encourages producers to produce goods and services that they anticipate will be valued enough by other producers so that the latter will sell their surplus labor to get what they want. Thus, for example, the right to work and the right to a paid vacation are not at all impediments to international business. Rather, they call upon governments to provide the incentives to make international business work. If multinational enterprise grows, more jobs will be created, and the right to work will become actualizable.

III. Human Rights vs. Collective Rights

If the argument in the preceding section is correct, we can see that the idea of human rights is a threat to collectivist theories such as Marxism. Under Marxist theory two collectivities—the working class and the capitalists—fight an inevitable war in which the capitalists are ultimately destroyed.[14] In the resulting single-class society, mass freedom can exist because the enemy has been removed. But history diverges from Marxist theory. Marx held that the government withers away, but in fact the state must become increasingly powerful in order to coerce those who are unwilling to do their share of the work. The slogan "from each according to his ability"[15] means that the government must first determine the ability level, and second must enforce a person's labor at that level. Workers may not be given material incentives for greater productivity without the risk that differential wealth patterns will arise that lead to the reemergence of capitalists.

Indeed, communism requires that workers remain a homogeneous group. The logic of collectivism works toward individual *equality in fact*, in contrast to human rights theory which works toward individ-

---

14. See K. Marx, *Das Kapital* (1867), translated in K. Marx, *Capital: A Critique of Political Economy* (S. Moore and E. Aveling trans. 1906).
15. Konstitutsiia (Osnovoi Zakon) Soiuza Sovietskikh Sotsialisticheskikh Respublik (Constitution (Fundamental Law) of the Union of Soviet Socialist Republics) art. 14.

ual *equality under the law*. Equality in legal rights means that the person who chooses to work harder will reap greater material rewards than the person who takes it easy (although the latter is certainly free to regard non-work as a reward in itself). Differences in material wealth constitute the essence of free enterprise. Only in a system of such factual differences are profit-making and profit-retention meaningful.

But history has also shown that when wealth differences are perceived to become intolerably great, a mass revolution will occur that brings about sudden wealth redistribution. The free enterprise system seems incapable of sufficient self-regulation to avoid such extreme differences in wealth; indeed, the internal motor of capitalism seems to accelerate as profits increase, as attested by the "robber baron" legacy of nineteenth century United States. To avoid revolution, capitalist societies have had to enact—often against the bitter opposition of the business sector—wealth transfer payments in the form of progressive taxation. Such redistribution of wealth through taxation saves the free enterprise system against the excesses of its internal logic. In other words, successful participants in the free enterprise system must submit to taxation so that transfer payments may be made to unsuccessful participants, enabling the latter to have some of the material rewards of the system (food, clothing, shelter, etc.). The human rights conventions reach the same conclusion, although the focus is upon the recipients rather than upon saving the free enterprise system. The general duty to provide each person with food, clothing, shelter, etc., necessarily calls for a taxation system that results in transfer payments to the poor.

However, one might well ask what is special about taxation? If taxation becomes too onerous, is it any different from communism? Doesn't taxation involve coercion? My reply is that taxation might very well become onerous if we view it as an end in itself. But if we adopt the perspective of the human rights conventions, we see that what is substantively essential is not taxation per se but rather maximizing transfer payments so that everyone may receive the basic necessities of life and have a stake in the system. Yet as soon as we focus upon maximization of transfer payments—and hence maximization of tax revenues—a limiting mechanism naturally occurs. If the level of taxation is pushed too high, disincentives to produce will result, and tax revenue decreases. To illustrate, an increase in the level of taxation from ten to twenty percent might very well increase tax revenues, but an increase from seventy to eighty percent might decrease total revenues.[16] At the higher levels, non-work becomes marginally preferable to work since it is marginally worth so little in after-tax money to do the extra work. By fine-tuning the taxation rates to maximize revenues over a long period of time, governments will be furthering the cause of human rights and, incidentally, removing the preconditions for socialist revolution.[17] Concomitantly, the government is not coercing labor. A tax on income can be avoided if a person chooses not to work at all. By setting a tax rate such that enough people have an incentive to produce even if their income is taxed at that rate, individual choices whether to work or not to work will in fact determine the tax level. It would be distorting language to call this kind of taxation "coercive;" in fact, it is fully consistent with, if not required by, a theory of universal human rights.

IV. Human Rights vs. National Sovereignty

If there is something antithetical between human rights and collectivism, may there not also be a clash between human rights and national prerogatives? Third-world rhetoric would have us believe that there is no such clash. The language of the previously cited Cocoyoc Declaration shifts ambiguously between rich nations and rich individuals, and between poor nations and poor persons. In talking about "reliance primarily upon one's own resources,"[18] the

---

16. The "Laffer curve" illustrates this phenomenon of taxation. At either extreme—0% or 100% of income—the government will realize no tax revenues. Somewhere in between revenues will be maximized. Of course, governments often take a long time to realize that high tax rates are operating as a disincentive to work and production, since the immediate effect of a tax increase is usually to increase revenue (in the short run) until more people and industries realize that extra work doesn't "pay."

17. Perhaps the twentieth century's most important contribution to the analysis of social justice, J. Rawls' *A Theory of Justice* (1971), reaches the same result through a posited mechanism of disinterested individuals bargaining among themselves for the optimal distribution of societal wealth. In that scheme, Rawls sets up transfer payments from the most advantaged members of society to the most disadvantaged, but only to the point at which the latter do not become marginally worse off because of production disincentives upon those who are taxed leading to an aggregate decline in the benefits received by the disadvantaged. However, the result of the disinterested bargaining is to create a just society, a result coincident with the human rights thesis. Interestingly, before he gets to the redistribution scheme, Rawls requires that a just society foster the maximum liberty of each individual consistent with aggregate liberty. In this manner, his result accords with that reached in the second section of the present chapter, in that coerced labor would violate the "liberty" principle.

18. *Beyond Dependency, supra* note 5, 174.

Desirability of Human Rights

Declaration does not make clear whether "one" is a third-world nation or an individual laborer, although it mentions in the same context the need for "increased national self-reliance."[19] The document calls upon the powerful nations to keep "hands off" third-world countries, to allow them to "find their own road to a fuller life for their citizens."[20] In affirming the idea of national sovereignty over natural resources, the Declaration aligns itself with earlier United Nations resolutions on "permanent sovereignty" over natural resources.[21] In these positions, the Declaration is typical of claims that are heard daily. Industrialized nations are admonished for having "exploited" the natural resources of third-world nations, such as the oil in Iran or the copper in Chile. The United States is blamed for consuming a disproportionate amount per capita of the world's natural resources.

Yet if the industrialized nations feel any "guilt" over such charges, their feelings may be traced to the success of the propaganda in mixing the human rights moral issue with the claims of national sovereignty. For, in the first place, nations such as the United States have paid for the natural resources that they have imported from the third-world. If third-world countries had a better use for them than selling them to the industrialized nations, they should have kept them. But in fact the minerals in the ground were of little use to the developing nations, and therefore the decision was made to sell them at the going market price. If as a result the people of many of those nations remain poor, their poverty is not the fault of the buyers of their mineral wealth, for without such buyers they would be even poorer. Perhaps for this reason the sales of such minerals continue today despite the rhetoric.

Secondly, we might ask by what human right do the people in mineral-rich areas claim ownership of those mineral resources. If we can sort out claims of national sovereignty over natural resources from human rights claims, we find that the two are entirely different from each other. As a matter of human rights, we certainly should give a worker the product of his labor consistent with the claims of

---

19. Id.
20. Id.
21. Resolution on Permanent Sovereignty over Natural Resources, *G.A. Res.* 803, 17 *U.N. G.A.O.R.* Supp. (No. 17) 15, U.N. Doc. A/5217 (1962). *See* Charter of Economic Rights and Duties of States, art. 2, *G.A. Res.* 3281, 29 *U.N. G.A.O.R.* Supp. (No. 31), U.N. Doc. A/9631 (1974).

159

others to some portion of that labor. But why should we assign to any person or group of persons the vast wealth that by an accident of nature happens to be located within the physical territory that they claim is a nation? From a human rights standpoint, it would be far more defensible to allocate all underground mineral wealth to every human being regardless of the location of that wealth. It should be a matter of common ownership available to all, like the high seas in international law. Of course, a person who extracts mineral wealth has commingled her labor with the minerals, and is entitled to some portion of the worth of the extraction. But she should receive no more than the market price for such labor, which would be fixed by open competition for the job. Any proceeds above that amount should be distributed to the people of the world in the priority given by the human right conventions—food first, then clothing, shelter, and so forth.

Yet we await in vain any statement by a mineral-rich third-world nation that its underground wealth should be distributed to poor persons in foreign countries. Instead, we receive rhetoric that subtly blends human rights with national sovereignty claims of right.[22]

Generalizing the proceeding argument, I would contend that a universal system of human rights would tend toward the dissolution of all national claims to special rights or privileges of the citizenry. For a nation, upon analysis, is a collectivity. Its boundaries are artificial, for the purposes of universal human rights. To the extent that human rights makes any inroad at all into national sovereignty claims, the effect will be to protect international business against expropriation or confiscation. In this respect, there is a fundamental affinity between the goals of multinational business enterprise and the goals of human rights.

V. Human Rights vs. Governmental Control of Foreign Policy

The Reagan administration from 1980 to the time that I am writing these words (1986) has been extraordinarily successful with the

---

22. Although certainly not third-world rhetoric, J. Rawls' *A Theory of Justice* (1971) much more subtly involves the same confusion between social rights and the boundaries of nations. Professor Rawls' goal is to work out a justice system for a given society. But there are significant conceptual problems in relating a society patterned on his model with other nations of the world, particularly poor nations. For further analysis of this point, *see* D'Amato, "International Law and Rawls' *Theory of Justice*," 5 *Den. J. Int'l L. & Pol'y* 525 (1975).

American public with regard to at least two huge categories of national interests: promoting American business and commerce, and scaling down the size of the national government. Not often noticed, however, is the fact that as the Reagan administration scales down the size of the government in Washington *in relation to the states*, it is scaling *up* the powers and scope of the national government *in relation to foreign countries*. The Reagan administration wants more, not less, control over American business enterprises doing business abroad, over American citizens travelling abroad (increasingly onerous passport restrictions), and on businesses suing other businesses (for antitrust or unfair competition) when the corporations that are sued are American corporations doing business abroad. The administration has opposed human-rights cases in American courts brought against foreign countries, often filing letters claiming sovereign immunity on behalf of foreign governments or foreign heads of state (It filed such a letter on behalf of President Ferdinand Marcos in a case brought in Seattle in 1982 alleging that Marcos hired assassins to murder two political opponents in a labor union hall; the letter was successful and the judge dismissed Marcos as a defendant).[23] Outside of the human-rights area, the administration opposes antitrust cases by American plaintiffs against foreign governments or foreign corporations. By asserting control over all these matters, the administration perhaps gains bargaining chips vis-à-vis foreign states ("We'll drop this lawsuit if you vote with us in the U.N."), but only at the cost of destroying private rights. By arrogating to itself all these private claims and lawsuits, the United States government seems to be moving toward the Soviet model of control over all aspects of its relations with foreign states.

The Soviet Union is the best example of a nation that disallows any private initiatives abroad. Thus it is able to exercise a monolithic control over its foreign policy. If the Reagan administration aspires to similar power, it undoubtedly can impart an ideological unity to what might otherwise be a market-like cacophony of private international claims that often might annoy foreign governments. But what the administration seems unwilling or unable to appreciate is the degree to which the unregulated approach has worked so far in promoting true American interests abroad. If we look at the world

---

23. See *Estate of Silme G. Domingo v. Republic of the Philippines*, Civ. No. C82-1055V (W. D. Washington, 1982). I am of counsel to the attorneys for the plaintiffs in this case.

as a whole, the forces of capitalism are in the ascendant; we have merely to consider China and Korea as prominent examples. In contrast, socialism is in disarray. The Soviet Union is having an enormously difficult time internally in motivating its labor force, and the historic strike by Polish workers a few years ago represents an historical fissure in the Marxist-Leninist vision.

But in seeking, consciously or unconsciously, to emulate the Soviet approach, the Reagan administration may be committing an historic blunder. Instead of appreciating how well private initiatives have worked for this country in its commercial relations with other nations, the administration seems to believe it can "do it better" if it "takes charge." It is hardly necessary to point out that this runs directly counter to the administration's strictures against "Big Government" and its propaganda in favor of private initiative. It may be that either the administration is simply inconsistent, or that the heavy Washington bureaucracy has compensated for being scaled down with respect to domestic policies by scaling itself up with respect to foreign policy.

What the Reagan administration seems to need, at the time of this writing, is the courage of its own convictions. If it really believes that private initiatives work best at home, there is no reason to believe that they won't work best abroad. If it really believes that human freedom and dignity are promoted by a free market, then it should embrace that concept vis-à-vis other countries and allow private, pluralistic approaches to Americans doing business abroad. Any ideological monolithism that the government might impart to our foreign policy by controlling contacts that American businesspersons or corporations make with foreign companies or nations is more apt to be a disaster than an advantage.

From a purely pragmatic point of view, a significant reason why private business has been able to work on an international scale is that countries simply distrust investment or technology that comes from the Soviet Union. These countries know that any Soviet business is controlled by the Kremlin, and therefore is liable to interference for political reasons. A country is much more apt to be distrustful of a Soviet investment initiative than it would be of an American investment initiative, simply because it can rely on *business* motivations to keep the American initative viable. If we look at this from a systemic point of view, it is clear that the international economic system thrives when it functions in purely market terms. Political initiatives are dysfunctional and are met with resistance.

If my analysis is correct, then the worst thing that the United States government could do for American business abroad is to attempt to control everything from the State Department. To the extent that such a policy succeeds, foreign countries will perceive the political control behind American business the same way that they now perceive the iron fist behind all Soviet business initiatives. Our government might succeed in imparting a form of "ideological unity" to our foreign policy, but only by weakening and perhaps eventually destroying the one element that made it so strong so far—the element of private business decision-making.

A free market is just what the name implies. It is in the long-range interest of the United States to have a free world market. Private business initiatives go hand-in-hand with the realization of private worth. Human freedom and dignity flourish where the heavy regulatory hand of government is absent. Of course, this is not to say that government has no legitimate role at the margins; a free market does not necessarily work in the best interests of the poor, the homeless, the starving. (The point is of course contentious; it is not clear that socialism works either, if it eventually destroys the initiatives of individual producers and entrepreneurs.) But the theory that a government knows better than private business what is best for private business is a bankrupt theory. To the extent that the Reagan administration supports private business initiatives at home, it should understand that the same policy is best for the position of the United States vis-à-vis the rest of the world—even if it means that burcaucrats in Washington might have to adjust themselves to a lesser regulatory role.

Sometimes I think (well, at least on Mondays, Wednesdays, and Fridays) that the greatest of all evils in the world is creeping bureaucratization. The Soviet Union has become a Giant Bureaucracy. It is the best example in history of the dulling of initiative that comes from bureaucratic rule; it has perfected the art of the cover-up to artistic brilliance; and it has become the victim of its own bureaucracy in the sense that well-meaning people in the Soviet government who might want to change the system find that they simply cannot do so. It is a myth to think that the Secretary of the Communist Party has unlimited power; he has great power in some areas, but not in the area of changing the bureaucracy. For he is a creature of the bureaucracy.

One of the truly exciting facts about the Reagan administration is its commitment to scale down the government bureaucracy. But if it does so in the areas that impact directly upon most citizens (that is, areas that are internal in the United States), it should not by inadvertence or power-lust or sheer inconsistency increase the size of bureaucratic control over matters of foreign policy. It should re-think its attempts, by treaty, to control matters of extradition and to take them away from U.S. courts. It should re-think its desire to take away anti-trust claims from private parties when foreign corporations or subsidiaries are involved. It should reduce, rather than increase, passport control where American citizens are involved. In short, it should take free enterprise seriously.

For bureaucrats, ultimately, are persons who exercise power but have not had to create value. Most people *work*, and their labor results in an increase of goods that are of value to other people. Our lives are improved by the collective labor of all. But bureaucrats really don't work. Of course they "work" in one sense, but they don't really *produce* anything. Rather, they regulate what other people produce. Thus, the more bureaucrats in a society, the less productive the society becomes, until the society is so top-heavy with bureaucrats that they reduce everyone's freedom by commanding people to do this and not to do that. A top-heavy bureaucracy in this sense has gone past the point of reversibility. We have a model for it; it is called the Soviet Union.

And that is why I feel, at least some of the time, that bureaucracy and human rights are inversely proportional. And that is why I feel, most of the time, that private business, human rights, and small government, are mutually reinforcing.

8

TERRITORIAL APARTHEID

If violence in South Africa is to be avoided, some method must be found to reach an accommodation among the different races. Integration, as in the United States model, is the possibility that most observers hope for. The "homelands" approach, partly implemented by South Africa, is entirely different. In theory, separating the races physically would eliminate racial strife. In months to come, South Africa may move more vigorously to implement and enforce a homelands policy, regardless of the preferences of the rest of the world.

Whether a homelands policy—territorial apartheid—will ever succeed is in large part a function of its fairness in terms of conception and implementation. However, the question of fairness is not easy to deal with in respect to South Africa, because the government's policies have not been fully worked out and are not explicit or open to external scrutiny. To develop a thoughtful approach to the question of fairness, then, may require study of a territorial apartheid model *other* than the one that is evolving in South Africa.

Such a model is presented by the Report of the Odendaal Commission (1964) on Namibia, then known as South-West Africa. The analysis in this chapter, which I originally wrote in the mid-1960s, asks three questions of the proposed land allocations of the Odendaal Commission:

(1) Are they fair?
(2) Do they treat groups "equally"?

(3) Would implementation probably eliminate invidious discrimination?

Our examination of these questions using primarily South African sources, particularly the Odendaal Report, may help illuminate issues that could well challenge us with respect to South Africa in the near future.

I. Are the Odendaal Proposals for Land Allocations Fair?

Do the Odendaal proposals for "homelands" or "Bantustans" offer a fair allocation of land to each group in South West Africa? The groups as defined by the Population Census of South West Africa of 8 May 1951 are as follows:

(a) *Whites.* Persons who in appearance obviously are, or who are generally accepted as, white persons, but excluding persons who, although in appearance obviously white, are generally accepted as Coloured persons.
(b) *Natives.* Persons who in fact are generally accepted as members of any aboriginal race or tribe of Africa.
(c) *Asiatics.* Natives of Asia and their descendants.
(d) *Coloreds.* All persons not included in any of the three groups mentioned above.

The Odendaal Commission has recommended 10 separate homelands for the non-European population, nine of which are to be allocated to the Natives and one to the Rehoboth Basters, a Colored population group. In addition, three Colored townships are to be set up within Windhoek, Walvis Bay, and Luderitz for the rest of the Colored population. Table 1 shows, first, the land area allocated to the nine Native Bantustans and the Colored Bantustan townships; this leaves 495,927 square kilometres of land in the rest of South-West Africa. Not all of the remainder, the Government stresses, is allocated to the European population, for it includes 135,447 square kilometres taken up by the "diamond areas," the game reserves, the Namib desert, and large areas of unalienated state lands. However, the latter would be at the disposal of the European central government that remains after the various Bantustans are excised from the territory, and thus it is reasonable to include these lands in the European category.[1]

South Africa stressed at the Hague in the South-West Africa case that roughly equal amounts of land, exclusive of government lands, are allocated to non-Europeans and Europeans. However, the per capita figures, which of course were not given in the Odendaal Report, tell a different story.

If one looks at the actual land available per head within the Bantustans on an individual basis, as in Table 2, the inequities are striking. It may be seen that more than half of the black population is assigned a per capita land area of 0.23 square kilometers, with the average being 0.74. In contrast, the whites have a per capita land allocation varying from 21 to 29 times the *median* black allocation and 7 to 9 times the *mean.*

The foregoing quantitative comparisons tell only part of the story. The quality and desirability of the allocated lands must also be taken into account. South Africa emphasized in the proceedings before the International Court of Justice that, so far as agricultural resources are concerned, in some aspects the Natives are favored. For example, 70 percent of the non-white population, and only 20 percent of the white population, are to be found in the most favorable rainfall region. Moreover, in the Bantustans as a whole the annual rainfall is greater in quantity and superior in its effectiveness (evaporation and variability).[2] However, as we have seen, the Bantustans must support a much higher population density. Thus a figure of annual rainfall per capita, if one could be imagined, would clearly favor the Europeans. In addition, the European farms are already artificially irrigated and operating on a commercially profitable basis; the contrary is true of the Bantustan farms. Furthermore, the soil type generally favors the European farms; it contains the greatest amount of loam,

---

1. Republic of South Africa, *Report of the Commission of Enquiry into South West Africa Affairs 1962-1963* (Pretoria, 1964), p. 29, Table XVIII (hereinafter cited as *Odendaal Report*). "Coloreds" are designated as such and also as "Basters." The latter of "mixed descent" live in the Rehoboth Gebiet. Id. at 33. There is no distinction, except for place of residence, between "Coloreds" and "Basters" in the Odendaal Report. In practice, of course, the determination that any given individual belongs to any of these groups can often be a highly difficult and dissatisfactory procedure. For analogous difficulties encountered in South Africa, *see* Suzman, "Race Classification and Definition in the Legislation of the Union of South Africa, 1910-1960," 1960 *Acta Juridica*, pp. 339 ff.

2. Republic of South Africa, *Rejoinder: South West Africa Cases* (Cape Town, 1964), vol. 1, pp. 310-11.

TABLE 1

Allocations for:	Land Area (sq. km.)	Population in 1960	Sq. km. per capita
Natives	312,433	424,047	0.74
Coloreds	14,785	23,965	0.62
Europeans, excluding Govt. lands	360,480	73,464	4.92
Europeans, including Govt. lands	495,927	73,464	6.76
Totals	823,145	521,476	1.58

TABLE 2

Proposed Bantustan	Land Area (sq.km.)	Population in 1960	Sq. km. per capita
Ovamboland	56,072	239,363	0.23
Tswanaland	1,554	9,992	0.59
Namaland	21,677	34,806	0.62
Eastern Caprivi	11,534	15,840	0.72
Damaraland	47,990	44,353	1.08
Rehoboth Gebiet	13,860	11,257	1.23
Okavangoland	41,701	27,871	1.50
Hereroland	58,997	35,354	1.67
Bushmanland	23,927	11,762	2.03
Kaokoveld	48,982	9,234	5.30
Totals	326,294	439,832	0.74

whereas the sandy soil is located predominantly in the northern Bantustan areas.[3]

South-West Africa is rich in natural resources, but with scarcely any exceptions the copper, zinc, and gold deposits are within the European farm and town areas.[4] The fabulous diamond mines are located without exception in the Woestyn game reservation and the Namib Desert, which will remain as "unallocated government lands." The Blacks will never receive, under the Bantustan proposals, any voice or interest in the central government, which vests in itself ownership of all these mineral rights and unallocated lands.

In terms of industrial development the contrast is, if anything, clearer. The "Police Zone" of southern South-West Africa, most of which will be retained by the Whites after the Bantustans are excised from the territory, contains nearly all the factories, processing plants, mines, transport and communication systems, banks, newspapers, and commercial farms in the country. Nearly all the tarred roads in the territory lace the European area, although several "National Roads" have been planned for the Bantustans by the Odendaal Commission. Similarly, nearly all harbors, railways, and airlines are found in the Police Zone.[5] Water resources also favor the European area, although here the Odenaal Commission has made a far-sighted proposal for costly development of water and hydro-electricity in the Bantustans, known as the Kunene Scheme.

One might at this point object that the Police Zone cannot be compared with the Bantustan areas because the Whites own the industry in their area and there could be no question of taking away from them what they own. This would apply also to the mines and natural resources, the proprietary rights to which reside in a government in which no non-European has suffrage. On the other hand, subsistence-level native labor has contributed to much of the industrial and mining wealth of South-West Africa. On the labor theory of value, this industrial development really "belongs" to the Blacks. Moreover, black tribes were in occupation of the territory before the white settlers trekked into South-West Africa from South Africa at the turn of the century: thus it could be argued that the Blacks own the mineral rights and even the land itself.

3. *Odendaal Report*, p. 16.
4. Id. at 24.
5. Id. at 374-88.

Of course, such arguments, whether based on Marxism and history or capitalism and effective power, will never be fully persuasive in themselves. The point at issue here is that the neutral observer should not a priori exclude any characteristic of the land, such as industrial development, before making a fair division of the remainder. Rather, all the characteristics—natural resources as well as improvements, climate as well as location, rainfall as well as irrigation—must be taken into account in deciding whether the Odendaal locations are fair and reasonable.

No question of the quality or quantity of land can ever be fully settled by objective measurement because land is not fungible (in the legal sense of one unit being replaceable by another). Any partition scheme must necessarily allocate land areas, each of which is unique in its own way. How can a fair division be made, even in theory?

In a comparable instance involving the allocation of unique items, Professor Fuller cited a case where a testator left his valuable paintings to be divided equally between his two heirs.[6] The market value of the paintings would not, it was soon realized, be helpful in making a division, since it could not take into account the sentimental value of individual paintings to the sons. However, the administrator of the estate devised an allocation scheme much like the one children use in dividing a piece of cake. He instructed the elder beneficiary to divide the paintings into two groups, and then gave the choice of groups to the younger beneficiary. To be sure, the functions were not equivalent: one beneficiary had complete freedom to divide the paintings in such a way that he himself would be indifferent as to which group he received, while the other had only the freedom to choose one of the groups. Yet a fairer, simpler, and perhaps more ingenious method of division could hardly be conceived.

One might posit in theory a comparable division of the South-West Africa land. It would not even be material whether the Whites chose to make the initial division or retained the right to choose between the divisions formulated by the Blacks. Either way, absolute fairness could be achieved, within the initial postulate that the Blacks and Whites had equivalent group rights. Of course it is extremely improbable that the Whites would voluntarily agree to such an allocation method, but its theoretical possibility suggests that a fair standard is itself within human capacity.

---

6. Fuller, *The Forms and Limits of Adjudication* (1959, mimeo.), p. 39.

It is furthermore possible to approach theoretical fairness in an undramatic and realistic manner, through the process of negotiation and arbitration. Indeed, bargaining between equals, unresolved points being settled by conciliation or arbitration procedures, has historically been successful when there was a tacit or explicit understanding that both sides would discuss the matter on an equal footing and submit to the arbitration of differences.

Perhaps the Odendaal Commission tried to capture some of the moral authority of negotiation procedures by its practice of conducting numerous well-publicized public hearings throughout the territory in 1962 and 1963. In the course of the South-West Africa litigation at the Hague, the plaintiffs attacked the Odendaal findings in part because the commission had not consulted enough with the Blacks and not held a public referendum on its submissions. But both of these charges seem to miss the essential significance of true negotiation procedure. In the first place, a hearing is entirely different from face-to-face negotiation, for although the public is "heard" it has no bargaining leverage to press its desires upon the commission. A black person technically may have been "consulted," but he leaves the hearing room without knowing whether his listeners had any predisposition to be receptive to his testimony.

In the second place, referenda or other democratic procedures cannot take the place of negotiation. For even on the dubious assumption that a free, knowledgeable plebiscite could be held on the question of accepting or rejecting the Odendaal Commission's findings, an affirmative vote might merely be the expression of public realism that the government would not offer a better deal if the present one were rejected. Moreover, the choice presented to the Natives would not be to pick either side of a division of the territory in a manner analogous to Professor Fuller's example cited previously, but rather to choose between the Odendaal Commission's allocations and the status quo. Thus democratic procedures, even if they were essayed in this case, would not be the equivalent of fairness or reasonableness in the allocations.

Since the South African government in fact has offered neither negotiation, division-and-choice, nor plebiscite in this situation, the only way to evaluate the fairness of the Odendaal proposals is to compare them with what might have been the results of the former procedures. If the Whites had known in advance that the Blacks

171

would be given a choice, would the Whites have been willing to risk a Black choice of the lands that the Whites in fact retained—lands having the overwhelming preponderance of mineral wealth, industrial development, transportation and communication systems, good farming soil and so forth? Would they have been willing to risk changing places with the Blacks in the amount of land per head, taking 0.74 instead of 6.76 square kilometers per capita?

Alternatively, if the Blacks had had a free choice, would they have chosen the land that has been set apart for the Bantustans, even conceding the fact that it has generally better rainfall conditions and even though water, electricity, educational, and hospital facilities would be improved in the years to come? Would they have rejected the Police Zone, which is already well supplied in these respects, and whose farms are already profitable despite the generally less favorable rainfall conditions? Unless the reader's answer to any of these questions is affirmative or even doubtful, it is hard to conclude that the Odendaal allocations have been fair or reasonable to the population as a whole.

The foregoing arguments have assumed that the choice of land is simply a matter between Whites and Blacks, an obvious simplification whose leading advocate is the government of South Africa. Thus, if racial parity is assumed, the Whites in South-West Africa can claim at least an equal share of land with the Blacks, even though they are greatly outnumbered by the latter. As mentioned previously, one of the government's central arguments advanced in explaining the Bantustan proposals to the International Court of Justice was that the total land area allocated to the Europeans is only slightly higher than the total allocated to the non-Europeans, exclusive of government lands. This dualism pervades all the government arguments. It is also noteworthy that the government usually minimizes the complexities introduced by the existence of a third group, the Coloreds, by using the inclusive category of non-Europeans.

However, the very classification of the population into various "races" must be a factor vitally relevant to the fairness of the Odendaal recommendations. Clearly, real or apparent "racial" distinctions are at the heart of the Bantustan scheme itself, just as religious differences have been the cause of some partitions in the past. Like political gerrymandering, classification according to "race" tends to increase the "weight" of individuals associated with some groups at the expense of individuals associated with other groups. Thus, while race classification must be accepted as a premise of the Odendaal plans, it may nevertheless result in unfairness to the population.

Therefore the analogy to the elder and younger beneficiaries of the valuable paintings does not really fit the "European," "Colored," and "Native" classifications in South-West Africa. Nor can negotiation be a fair procedure if the European group is treated on an equal basis with non-Europeans, since their constituents are numerically fewer. However, a modification of these procedures might be proposed. Since the ratio of Natives: Europeans: Coloreds in the territory is approximately 18:3:1, a fair procedure might consist of having the representatives of the Natives divide the territory into 22 parts, and then let the Colored representative choose one part and the European representative choose any three parts. Of course, the Europeans, with their present monopoly of power and in no immediate danger of revolution, would not even listen to so radical a suggestion. Yet this procedure does suggest a model for a fair allocation of land per capita on the basis of group membership. We have seen that the European population has in fact retained a self-selected area amounting to slightly over $13/22$ of the territory (including government lands). If their share of $3/22$ of the total population is compared to this, the discrepancy suggests the degree of unfairness involved in the Odendaal allocations.

II. Are the Groups Treated "Equally"?

The very division of people into groups, as noted above, is artificial as well as superficial. But in the present analysis we are taking South Africa's own definitions and assumptions, for it is always true that the strongest case is made if there are no changes in the proponent's own premises. Therefore, let us proceed to examine the *kinds* of "equality" that may be at issue in the Odendaal Commission's recommendations, and then analyze them against the facts as adduced by that commission. This analysis of the treatment of groups in a single territory is the context within which the particular land allocation of territorial apartheid discussed earlier may be evaluated.

A. Mirror-Image Equality

The laws, practices and policies most basic to "separate development" are those relating to exclusionary residential areas. These have at first glance an obvious mirror-image egalitarianism. For example, while "Natives" cannot live in urban areas in the Police Zone occupied by the white population group, the reciprocal exclusion of residence by white persons in the Native reserves is absolute. Similarly, with respect to farm land, legislation bars "Natives" from alienating land located in the Native reserves while, due to an aggregate of practices and policies, no "European" has ever transferred farm land in the Police Zone to a "Native."[7] A related form of reciprocity is claimed for curfew restrictions applying to the residential areas. "Curfew hours" may be posted applying to "Natives" found in "European" urban areas (the hours are usually between 9 p.m. and 4 a.m.), while any "European" (exclusive of clergymen, medical practitioners, and officials) desiring to enter a "Native" residential area at any time must secure a permit.[8]

However, these mirror images are clouded by factors relating to the size of the lands involved and their comparative economic development. "European" farms and towns in the Police Zone comprise a total of 394,390 square kilometers, while "Colored" and "Native" areas combined within the Police Zone and the Northern Reserves amount to 240,891 square kilometers.[9] The enormous disparity on a per capita basis has already been mentioned. In addition, the Police Zone contains most of the wealth of the territory and a highly developed economy, whereas the reserves provide no more than a subsistence economy. As the government concedes, this is precisely

---

7. *Counter-Memorial, South-West Africa Cases*, vol. 5, p. 11, para. 4. Although there is no statutory impediment, this may be accounted for in part by local real estate practices, the inability of most "Natives" to afford such land, the fact that no "Native" has officially "requested" financial assistance under the land settlement laws for the purchase of such land (id. at 27, para. 13), and the fact that any purchase would give to a "Native" precarious tenure inasmuch as he could at any time be moved from his land "to any place within the mandated Territory" by a government in which he is not represented. *The Laws of South West Africa 1928*, p. 58.

8. *Counter-Memorial*, vol. 6, pp. 128-129, para. 50.

9. The figures are obtained as follows: "European" farms, 389,650 sq. kilometers, *Counter-Memorial*, vol. 5, p. 32, para. 24. "European" towns, 4,740 sq. kilometers, *Odendaal Report*, p. 29, table XI. "Non-European" farms obtained by deducting above area of "European" farms from total farms given in *Odendaal Report*, p. 29, table XI; this amounts to 21,249 sq. kilometers. Other "non-European" areas, 219,642 sq. kilometers, *Odendaal Report*, p. 111, para. 425G (given as 21,607,745 hectares). Unalienated government lands and nature reserves make up the difference of a total 823,145 square kilometers of land in the territory.

why the "Natives" wish to come to the "white" areas in the first place.[10] Moreover, with respect to the curfew restrictions, theatres and other places of amusement are located primarily in the "European" urban areas, whereas there is little reciprocal reason for "Europeans" to want to visit the "Native" residential areas. This situation is aggravated by the fact that there are large numbers of "Natives" who have their real homes in the Northern Reserves working as migratory laborers under two-year contracts in the Police Zone. Separated from their homes and families, these "Natives" would be attracted to off-hour recreational facilities in the towns in the Police Zone, whereas there is no comparable group of "Europeans" working under contract near "Native" residential areas.

The statutory inability to transfer land in "Native" reserves to Whites also operates to the detriment of the black population group. This result is somewhat paradoxical in light of the original motivations for such legislation: that in the absence of restriction, "Native" chiefs might sell all the tribal land to "European" speculators for personal gain.[11] But at the present time, given the subsistence economy of the "Native" reserves, the only way to attempt private capital for development from the "European" banks would be for a black landholder to give the bank a mortgage on his only asset—his land—as collateral. But the statutory restrictions on land alienation mean that in practice the land is not mortgageable since it could not be foreclosed by a "European" bank in the event of default on the mortgage. Such limitations on property rights could ensure the self-perpetuation of subsistence economy, but would, in any event, alter the utility of property ownership to the unreciprocal disadvantage of the less-privileged groups.

B. Strict Equality

One type of claim that is obviously open to proponents of separate but equal policies is the claim of strict, or literal, equality. Some care must be taken, however, in judging whether the claimed equality is more than superficial. For example, in the educational sphere, the

---

10. *Counter-Memorial*, vol. 6, p. 115, para. 5.
11. Id. at 56, 57, paras. 51-54.

policy of "mother-tongue instruction" is central to separate development in South-West Africa. It is the government's "ultimate aim" that the vernacular be used "as the medium of instruction in all standards."[12] It is claimed that no language deserves preference over another, and that strict equality requires that English or Afrikaans be confined to the "European" children and not be forced upon the "Natives."[13] While some progress has been made in developing textbooks and instructing teachers in the "Native" languages—Ndonga, Kuanyama, Kuangali, Herero, Nama and Tswana having thus far achieved the status of school languages—other important languages have not yet achieved school status, including Diriku, Kuambi, Bushman, and Sikololo (Silosi). It would seem that the very difficulty of using such languages in textbooks would argue against their suitability as media for instruction; indeed, the government concedes that the "Native" languages, developed to meet the day-to-day needs of people living in a subsistence environment, "are all poor vehicles of abstract thought."[14] Thus, this particular manifestation of the concept of strict equality could lead to permanent deprivation of great literature, abstract reasoning, and world culture to the "Native" children who are instructed in their "mother tongues," a detriment which is absent from the education of "European" children.

A variant form of strict equality is the policy justification which is itself grounded on the assumption that the consequences of apartheid are fair and equal. For instance, one frequently asserted justification for barring "Natives" from engaging in large-scale business operations,[15] from promotion to senior positions in the civil service,[16] or promotion to authoritative positions in business enterprises[17] is that "Natives" lack the necessary experience which is a strictly equal prerequisite for all persons of any race who wish to attain these positions. Thus, with respect to mining operations, the government has argued in the South-West Africa Cases that

> the Native population has as yet not acquired the experience, and generally do not as yet have the initiative or the means, to undertake

---

12. *Counter-Memorial*, vol. 7, p. 23, para. 18.
13. Id. at 18-23, paras. 10, 19.
14. Id. at 83, para. 15.
15. *See, e.g., Counter-Memorial*, vol. 5, p. 64, para. 42.
16. *See, e.g.,* id. at 180, para. 85 (d).
17. *See, e.g.,* id. at 72, paras. 11, 12.

prospecting and mining operations, which . . . must usually be on a large scale to render them profitable.[18]

Yet it is difficult to see how Blacks may attain experience when only "a European of the age of 18 years or more" may qualify for a prospecting license in the Police Zone,[19] or when all the important technical and responsible posts in existing mining enterprises in South-West Africa are statutorily restricted to "Europeans."[20] It is circular to argue that the inequality of Blacks requires inequality of treatment when those inequalities themselves came about as a result of the social system of apartheid.

C. Substantive Equality

More common than claims of strict equality, yet more difficult to evaluate, are policies which are obviously different in their application to population sub-groups but which are claimed to be fundamentally or substantively fair and reasonable. One instance may be seen in the various statutory provisions relating to old age, disability and blind persons' pensions or grants.[21] This social security legislation explicitly differentiates between "Europeans" and "Colored persons" in setting rate scales, while it excludes "Natives" altogether from the public pension schemes. The minimum income entitling a "European" person to a pension is fixed at a higher rate than it is for "Coloreds," and the maximum pension benefits payable to "Colored persons" are fixed at lower rates than for "Europeans." The justification advanced by the government for these different scales is that the income of the "Europeans" is, on the whole, "substantially more" than the income of the "Colored persons."[22] Although there is no withholding of income to finance social security, the pensions are financed out of the public revenues, to which the contribution of the "Colored people" by way of taxes on incomes

18. Id. at 64, para. 42.
19. *The Laws of South West Africa* 1954, p. 781 (Ordinance No. 26).
20. *See infra* text at fn. 56.
21. *The Laws of South West Africa 1956*, vol. 1, pp. 4-183, 206-207; id. 1960, vol. 1, pp. 10-23; id. 1962, pp. 4-21.
22. *Rejoinder*, vol. 2, p. 307, para. 44.

177

and on persons is "but a fraction of the contribution made by the European population."[23]

This distinction could theoretically be vitiated by a showing that *some* individuals classified in the "Colored persons" group have substantially higher incomes than a corresponding number of "Europeans," and thus to them the general pension scale is discriminatory. But although official figures are unavailable on this point, it is unlikely that a significant number of "Colored persons" exists in this category. Numerous statutes and ordinances bar authoritative positions in the economy and public service to "non-Europeans."[24] Job discrimination exists because of the action of "European" labor unions (there are no "non-European" trade unions in South-West Africa)[25] and the admitted fact that most "Europeans" would refuse to serve in positions where "non-Europeans" might be placed in authority over them.[26] However, a different case can be made against the scale differentiation. It is possible to argue that there exist a number of "Colored" workers who, but for the legislative and social impediments just mentioned, would have been receiving a higher pay on the open market for the work they are doing because of their skills and the quality of their job output. This, of course, would not apply to all the members of the categorized "race," but it is inconceivable that it would not apply to a significant percentage of them. The higher pay that these workers would have been receiving finds its way, instead, into the profits of the employers, where it is then taxed. Thus, this amount of money is an indirect contribution by the "Colored" workers to the public finances, yet no recognition of it appears to be given in the pay scale for "Colored" as opposed to "European" pensioners.

With respect to "Natives," total exclusion from social security is justified on the ground that "a form of communal subsistence is practiced within the family group" of "Natives" living in the reserves.[27] Although the connection is not made, it is implicit in this justification that the black worker will *continue* to receive subsistence when he returns to his family group, just as his wages supplied a

---

23. Ibid. It is assumed that the government is talking about per capita contributions here; otherwise the argument would be trivial.
24. *See, e.g., Counter-Memorial,* vol. 5, p. 59, para. 29; id. at 72, para. 12; id. at 144-145, para. 110.
25. *Rejoinder,* vol. 2, p. 333, para. 39.
26. *Counter-Memorial,* vol. 5, p. 59, para. 30.
27. *Rejoinder,* vol. 2, p. 307, para. 45.

subsistence living. Yet it is also arguable that a significant number of black workers are receiving lower wages than they would command in an open market because of their association with the "Native" group. Or, it could even be argued, citing the labor theory of value, that the entire economic well-being of the area is the result of the labor contributed by the Blacks.

A single case study offers a somewhat dramatic insight into a more specific claim of substantive equality than the social security example just cited. During 1958 and 1959, South-West Africa experienced a very acute drought. Extensive governmental measures were undertaken for the relief of persons affected. Under one governmental program, financial assistance in the amount of R4,900,000 (1 Rand was then equivalent to approximately $1.40) was made available to "European" farmers and R217,000 was made available to "Natives." The plaintiffs in the South-West Africa Cases charged in April 1961, that the disparity in these figures evidenced discriminatory treatment.[28] Replying to this charge in 1963, South Africa pointed out that the amount made available to the "European" farmers was applied solely towards providing loans at approximately four percent, whereas the distribution to the "Native" farmers was primarily in the form of free grants (R170,000 as grants,[29] R47,000 in loans[30]), mostly as subsidies for "mealies" and transport.[31]

In general, it is indisputable that an outright grant is more desirable than a loan, and could be a substantial compensation for a differential in amounts made available. However, a very large loan can often be more economically useful than a very small grant. In particular, in emergency situations when one is faced with total ruin, an adequate loan is almost as desirable as an equivalent grant and infinitely preferable to an inadequate grant. The future can take care of itself. Future interest payments are trivial compared to the necessity of avoiding starvation or bankruptcy. In this light, a simple calculation shows that the *total* amount given to the "Natives" in the form of free grants is less than just one year's simple interest at five percent on the R4,900,000 loaned to "European" farmers. On a per capita basis, the amount loaned to a "European" was R66.7 compared to

28. *Government of Liberia, Memorial: South West Africa Case* (The Hague, 1961), p. 89, para. 33 (v).
29. *Counter-Memorial*, vol. 5, p. 39, para. 36.
30. *Rejoinder*, vol. 2, p. 302, para. 34.
31. *Counter-Memorial*, vol. 5, pp. 36-38, paras. 31-35.

a "Native" per capita grant of R0.4 and a loan of R0.1.[32] Absent such comparisons, the general claim that the financial assistance to the "Natives" was comparable because it was largely in the form of grants might have been a persuasive example of substantive equality.

Some claims of substantive equality, like their "strict equality" counterparts, appear to rely on an assumption that the consequences of apartheid are themselves equitable. An obvious example is found in the field of expenditure for education. In 1920, when the Mandate for South-West Africa was granted, education of "Natives" in the territory was almost nonexistent. On the basis of this fact, South Africa has argued before the International Court of Justice that

> the various factors and conditions which inhibited the introduction and development of education in the case of the Native groups, rendered it almost inevitable that expenditure in the Territory should have begun on a basis of substantial excess on the side of European education over that of Native Education.[33]

Rather, it is clear that the only reason why the precise opposite did not hold true is the reliance on an assumption of the desirability of a system of social apartheid.

This assumption persists in the justifications for present-day disparities in educational expenditures. The figures for 1962-1963 are as follows:[34]

The South African government argued in the South-West Africa Cases that "although there has been differentiation, there has in fact been no unfair discrimination"[35] for the following reasons:

> (a) Educational expenditure "must, in the first place, be considered in the light of the social and economic status and levels of development of each of the groups, and their respective educational needs."[36]

---

32. Using 1960 population figures of Table 2, *supra*.
33. *Counter-Memorial*, vol. 7, p. 213, para. 24.
34. The per capita figures on all children attending school are given by the government in *Counter Memorial*, vol. 7, pp. 128-129, paras. 79, 81, and id., p. 182, para. 35. These figures may be misleading, as only 46.16 percent of "Native" children of school age attended school in 1962 as opposed to 99.66 percent of "European" children. *Odendaal Report*, p. 245, table LXXXII, and id., p. 249, table LXXXIII.
35. *Counter-Memorial*, vol. 7, p. 213, para. 24(a).
36. Id. at 213, para. 24(c).

(b) Although salary scales of "European" teachers are higher, the average "European" primary school teacher generally spends about six years more at training institutions than the average "Native" primary school teacher.[37]

(c) There are many more "European" students in the upper primary and secondary classes than "Native" students, and their expenses run higher because of the better equipment, materials, and better-trained instructors.[38]

Clearly these explanations beg the question, for it is apparent that they rest fundamentally on the assumption of the equitability of the consequences of apartheid which they are trying to justify.

Still another form in the educational field of claimed substantive equality occurs with respect to the sharp contrast between syllabuses offered for black children and for white children. In the lower primary courses, the black children, but not the white children, receive instruction in the following subjects: drawing, cleaning work, weaving and claywork, needlework (girls), scrap work (boys), and gardening.[39] Since these subjects obviously take up school-day time, proportionately less time must be allocated to basic study in academic subjects

TABLE 3

	Per capita expenditure (in Rand) on all children of school age	Per capita expenditure (in Rand) on all children attending school
"Native" Children		
Police Zone	11.92	27.32
Northern territories	3.92	8.19
South-West Africa as a whole	6.59	14.28
"European" Children		
Including net estimated hostel expenditure	156.50	157.02
Excluding hostel expenditures	108.09	108.45

37. Id. at 214, para. 24(d).
38. Id. at 214, para. 24(e). In 1960 in the upper standards VII, X, there were 2,151 "European" students and 111 "Native" students. Ibid.
39. Id. at 119, para. 66.

than the white children receive. In the higher primary courses, subjects given to the black children but not to the white children include gardening, tree planting and soil conservation (boys), wood, leather and scrap work (boys), needlework (girls), and handicrafts.[40] In the secondary schools, the difference lies in the options open to white students to take a strictly academic course or the general or practical courses, while the black children do not have the option to follow the strictly academic course.[41] There is additional differentiation within the "industrial course" programs at some schools. The white children may take highly differentiated courses in these fields, while the black children are confined almost totally to practical courses in woodwork, tailoring and bricklaying.[42] Further technical training is possible on the winning of one of six bursaries open to all students in South-West Africa. However, the South African government testified in the South-West Africa Cases that "thus far no Native student has in any way merited" one of these bursaries.[43]

The claimed justification for this differentiation is that it is derived from the position of the various groups in society and therefore is utilitarian. As explained by Dr. H. F. Verwoerd to the South African House of Assembly, in introducing the Bantu Education bill in 1953:

> What is the use of teaching a Bantu child mathematics, when he cannot use it in practice? That is quite absurd.[44]

Earlier in his presentation he stated:

> Racial relations cannot be improved if the wrong type of education is given to the Natives. They cannot improve if the result of Native education is the creation of frustrated people who, as a result of the education they receive, have expectations in life which circumstances in South Africa do not allow to be fulfilled immediately, when it creates people who are trained for professions not open to them, when there are people who have received a form of cultural training which strengthens their desire for the white-collar occupations to such an extent that there are more such people than openings available.[45]

---

40. Ibid.
41. Id. at 119, para. 67; 176, para. 26.
42. Id. at 137-139, paras. 1, 4; 182, 183, paras. 36, 37.
43. Id. at 150, para. 25.
44. Union of South Africa, *Parliamentary Debates, House of Assembly* (1953), vol. 83, col. 3585.
45. Id. at col. 3576.

Territorial Apartheid

The argument with respect to South-West Africa has remained essentially the same. In 1963 the South African government argued before the International Court of Justice that

> a Bantu who qualifies himself for a profession in which he will, because of the stage of advancement of his own group, have to depend for his livelihood on the services of European employees, or on European patronage, runs a grave risk of total frustration.[46]

Thus, the utilitarian scheme of education designed to train Blacks to take their place in society without "frustration" can be argued to be logically necessary to the social system of apartheid. The argument, of course, supports itself by its own bootstraps: because of the initial racial differentiation, separate educational policies having sharply divergent aims are justified, an effect of which is to *create* differing skills and abilities among the population.

A similar illogic pervades the explanations for sharply lower salary scales for "Native" as opposed to "European" teachers in the territory.[47] One argument is that there are more economic alternatives open to Whites, and thus a greater salary inducement is needed.[48] Second, "the qualifications demanded in the case of European teachers are generally higher. . . ."[49] Finally, a teacher's salary

> should, in [the government's] view, bear a relationship to the normal income of other members of his group, otherwise he might become separated or estranged from them as a result of an artificial financial barrier.[50]

As Dr. Verwoerd explained to the South African Senate in 1954:

> The Bantu teacher must be utilized as an active factor in this process of development of the Bantu community to serve his community and build it up and learn not to feel above his community so that

---

46. *Counter-Memorial*, vol. 7, p. 206, para. 20(e).
47. *See* tables, id., pp. 122-127, 133-136, and cf. tables, id., pp. 178-181. The commencing salary of a married male "European" teacher in the lowest category, including a special allowance, is R1,406, p. 181, para. 34, compared to R696 for a "Native" teacher, id., pp. 125-126, paras. 74-75, with comparable qualifications (Standard X plus a teacher's training course; grade 3: id., p. 125, para. 74; cf. id., p. 54, para. 72).
48. Id., p. 210, para. 22(c).
49. Id., p. 210, para. 22(b).
50. Id., p. 211, para. 22(d).

he wants to become integrated into life of the European community and becomes frustrated and rebellious when this does not happen, and he tries to make his community dissatisfied because of such misdirected and alien ambitions.[51]

As to this last argument, it cannot be denied that assimilation might operate in the short run to deprive the lesser privileged groups of important personalities. Nevertheless, it should be noted that the argument that salaries should not be raised so that assimilation does not start is based solely on the desirability of extending the system of apartheid and for that reason cannot be held to prove that this particular manifestation of apartheid results in substantive equality.

The use of an argument which has historically proved to be invalid as a justification for substantive equality may reveal an unexpressed bootstrap reliance on the system of apartheid. This may be seen with respect to collective bargaining in South-West African industry. There are no "Native" trade unions in the territory, and the relevant ordinances neither recognize nor provide for the registration of such unions.[52] The government contended in the South-West Africa Cases that

> the Native inhabitants of the Territory have, as a whole, not yet reached a sufficiently high level of development to appreciate the true meaning and purposes of trade unionism.[53]

Moreover,

> the interests of Native workers, if left to the protection of trade unions, could be neglected and . . . such workers could be exploited by unscrupulous individuals.[54]

Similar arguments were often advanced in the early days of trade unionism in other countries. Yet, if it is accepted that such arguments have proved erroneous in practice, then they must be all the more dependent in the case of South-West Africa on the assumption of

---

51. Union of South Africa, *Parliamentary Debates, Senate* (1954), 11th Parl., 2nd Sitting, cols. 2606-2607.
52. The Laws of South West Africa 1952, pp. 464 ff. (Ordinance No. 35).
53. *Rejoinder*, vol. 2, p. 334, para. 41.
54. *Counter-Memorial*, vol. 5, p. 99, para. 35.

social apartheid. For if the experience (however fumbling at first) of trade unions is denied to the Blacks, they may never attain a level of development on a plane with the "European" workers who presumably "appreciate the true meaning" of trade unionism.

D. Marginal Inequality

The South African government may claim that observed instances of unequal treatment are relatively insignificant compared to the underlying equality. If the instances are truly insignificant, the argument has merit. Sometimes, however, this justification is used for situations which only appear to be marginal. For example, the Mining Regulations of 1956 provide that only "Europeans" can be employed in the following posts in existing mines in South-West Africa:[56]

The argument of marginal inequality is formulated by the South African government as follows:

> If . . . the assumption is made that there is a sufficient number of Natives competent to fill all the said 190 posts, then the regulations in question would at present prejudicially affect only 190 Natives, i.e., slightly more than two per cent of the Native employees in the industry.[57]

Of course, another way of looking at this is to say that, out of 100 percent of the available posts, Blacks are excluded from 100 percent.

TABLE 4

Designation of Post	Number of Posts in the entire mining industry
Manager	6
Assistant, sectional or underground manager	4
Mine overseer	6
Shift boss	22
Ganger	104
Winding engine driver	20
Banksman and onsetter	28
Total posts	190

55. Id. at 36, para. 30.
56. *Rejoinder*, vol. 2, p. 260, para. 77 ("Departmental Information").
57. Ibid.

E. Transitional Inequality

Another justification for the admittedly discriminatory provisions of the mining regulations just examined is that they are only transitional in nature and do not affect long-run considerations of equality. In the words of the South African government arguing before the International Court of Justice, the mining provisions

> constitute one of the "unpopular control methods" [quoting Prime Minister Verwoerd] which are considered desirable in the phase of transition from guardianship to separate self-realization, and which are destined to fall away when developments in the latter respect remove the reason for them.[58]

The difficulty with transitional inequality is the indeterminate length of the period of transition. Transitional socialism in the Soviet Union, for instance, has demonstrated remarkable longevity. Or, to take an example from the history of South-West Africa itself, the following letter may be cited. It was written by the representative of the Union government to the Permanent Mandates Commission of the League of Nations in 1928:

> Owing, however, to the present low state of civilisation among the natives, no native is at present employed either by the Administration or by the Railway Department on work involving the risk of human life, such as driving a motor-car or working an engine. A certain colour bar is therefore being observed in practice, but it is certainly not a statutory enactment and is purely temporary, that is until such time as the native is sufficiently advanced to be able to undertake this responsible work.[59]

While some "Natives" since 1928 have achieved slightly better jobs on the railways, such as boiler attendant, cook, station porter, stoker, and pumper,[60] it is clear that the general policy remains basically unchanged. As the Minister of Transport announced to the South African House of Assembly in March, 1956:

---

58. Union of South Africa, *Parliamentary Debates, House of Assembly* (1959), vol. 99, col. 64.
59. Permanent Mandates Commission, *Minutes*, vol. 14, p. 278 (letter of Mr. Werth, November 19, 1928).
60. *Counter-Memorial*, vol. 5, p. 73, para. 15.

We only employ Natives to serve their own people where it is practicable, and where it is acceptable to the rest of the staff. But it will certainly not be acceptable to the staff or the public that Natives should be employed, even on Native trains, as firemen, conductors, or guards. That is not my policy, and it will not happen.[61]

III. Can Territorial Apartheid Eliminate Discrimination?

Regardless of the conclusion one may draw as to the fairness of the Odendaal allocations, the question remains whether the very concept of Bantustans can ever result in fairness to the entire population. This question may be treated separately from the allocation question, not only because the allocations might some day be changed, but also because it might be argued that the Odendaal allocations constitute the "last" prejudice, or "final solution," and that after that hurdle is passed all racial prejudice will disappear.

The question of prejudicial discrimination was aired extensively in the South-West Africa case, even though no decision was reached on the merits of the dispute. In the course of the legal arguments at The Hague, South African lawyers conceded that discrimination would be a violation of South Africa's alleged duties as a mandatory power in South-West Africa, but contended that apartheid was not discriminatory. Rather, they argued that apartheid meant "separate development" without inequality or discrimination. Moreover, they described the proposed Bantustan system as the fruition of the policy of separate development, where even the possibility of prejudicial discrimination would cease to exist.

The arguments on this point before the International Court of Justice were inconclusive, and indeed turned out to be irrelevant to the Court's decision. Nevertheless, one must admit that if each Bantustan were to become a politically independent and economically self-sufficient enclave, and if all physical contact between its inhabitants and the Whites outside were to cease, then it would be hard or impossible to support an accusation of on-going and overt discrimination. In order to examine whether these hypotheses are realistic,

---

61. Union of South Africa, *Parliamentary Debates, House of Assembly* (1956), vol. 7, cols. 2135-2136.

we might begin with South Africa's consistent and repeated argument that each Bantustan will have "political independence" coupled with "economic interdependence" with the white areas.

Taking first the notion of "economic interdependence," it is clear that this term can cover a spectrum of situations, ranging from virtual self-sufficiency with moderate trade to the subservience of a manpower pool that can only export its labor. At present, South and South-West Africa depend on Native labor for the mines and industries. It has been clear since the concept of homelands was introduced that the capitalists of Southern Africa have no intention of losing their labor force when the workers take up residence in the homelands. In order to continue to tap the labor market, new factories will be located along the borders of the Bantustans, gradually "phasing out" those farther in the interior of the white areas. They will thus be able to draw upon the huge labor supply within the Bantustans and yet remain on "European" soil to enjoy the security and favorable legislation of the central government. A "commuting" labor force will be added to the migrant labor system. This entire process is developing in South Africa, where factories are being located along the borders of the Transkei.

The fact of the "border industries" is well known, but few have speculated as to its long-term implications, which include the following. First, the up-to-date factories that will be constructed will be so far advanced beyond the fledgling service industries and small shops which might be set up by the Blacks that internal Bantustan factories—even if they could be set up—could not compete in a free market with the border industries. The technological gap would be so great as to preclude efficient competition. Rather, the Blacks within the Bantustans would probably buy all their products from the European factories in which they work.

A second factor favoring the border industries is their ability to continue to trade with sources outside South-West Africa, whereas trade restrictions could easily be placed on any products manufactured inside a Bantustan. None of the Bantustans, it may be noted, has an outlet to the sea. Of the 10, four are isolated from the others, two have a common border with only one other Bantustan, and only four have common borders with as many as two others. Thirdly, the centrally located white areas are laced with modern communications and transport facilities, linking the industries to each other and to their counterparts in South Africa. The increased efficiency resulting from the easy exchange of technology, parts, and services among these industries makes it appear impossible that any Bantustan industry could catch up.

Fourthly, if in spite of all these competitive advantages some European investors wanted to locate their plants within a particular Bantustan, prohibitive legislation could easily be passed by the central government on the principle that the Bantustans should remain "pure" for their inhabitants. Finally, those outside would have no motive to invest in predominantly Native-owned factories in the Bantustans. This follows from the facts that Europeans are not allowed to own land in the Bantustans—which is inherent in the concept of separate areas—and that Blacks, living at a subsistence level, have only their land to offer as security for any loans from outside. This land would be worthless as collateral, due to the inability of the white lenders to take up the title to the land in the event of default on the loan.

These considerations add up to the prediction that even the largest and potentially most viable Bantustans will be economically subservient to the white areas. This in itself constitutes a form of unequal treatment, as it consigns the Bantustans to permanent economic dependence. But, even more important, it means the perpetuation of a system where Blacks work in a territory under laws which will favor the politically represented employer rather than the alien laborer. And of course it means a continuation of the interaction between worker and employer in numerous border industries, making the original notion of physical separation of the "races" inapplicable during the working day. The "races" will not in fact be separate; their points of contact will simply be relocated.

It is moreover clear that Blacks who at present work in the mining and transport industries in the white-controlled areas will continue to be employed there as migrant laborers even after they change their residences from the shanty towns to the Bantustans. These industries, which cannot be moved to the borders of the Bantustans, are fully dependent upon black labor and it would be difficult to see politically how they could be made to give up this source of labor.

If the "economic interdependence" of the Bantustans in fact represents economic subservience, it is even harder to visualize "political independence" for them. For the smaller Bantustans, such as

Tswanaland, Eastern Caprivi, Bushmanland, or Kaokoveld, or for the three Colored townships, political independence seems impossible. Furthermore, it must be remembered that the impetus for setting up the Bantustans comes from the world pressure against South Africa; without outside pressures, South Africa would never have undertaken the trouble and expense necessary to establish Bantustans. It follows from this that South Africa would not tolerate a situation where the Bantustans might become a source of insecurity for the Whites. The United Party fears that there would be "eight or nine Cubas right within the mandated territory of South West Africa";[62] and the government does not need to be reminded of this fear by the Opposition. In 1951, when there was greater opposition to the Nationalist Party, and when the Party leaders were talking more frankly than they do today, Dr. Verwoerd stated with respect to a plan that was one of the precursors of the homelands proposals:

> Now a Senator wants to know whether the series of self-governing areas would be sovereign. The answer is obvious. It stands to reason that White South Africa must remain their guardian. We are spending all the money on these developments. How could small scattered states arise? The areas will be economically dependent on the Union. It stands to reason that when we talk about the Natives' right of self-government in those areas we cannot mean that we intend by that to cut large slices out of South Africa and turn them into independent States.[63]

It is obvious that "political independence," like "economic interdependence," is a slogan that can cover a wide range of meanings. For the most part South Africa has refrained from specifying what the term means; when definitions have been attempted, they have ranged from control over a large segment of internal affairs to equal membership in a free association of states similar to that of a commonwealth.

It would be futile to pursue the kaleidoscopic meanings appended to this obviously politically charged term. A more concrete indication of its meaning can be derived from the *Odendaal Report*, which spells out the amount of political independence proposed for each

---

62. Sir de Villiers Graaf, *Parliamentary Debates: House of Assembly* (1964), col. 5465.
63. *Parliamentary Debates: Senate* (1951), cls. 2893 4.

Territorial Apartheid

Bantustan. With minor individual variations, each Bantustan will have its own "Legislative Council," which will gradually take over from the present South African Department of Bantu Administration all legislative and administrative functions except the following: defense, foreign affairs, internal security, border control, posts, water affairs and power generation, and transport. Moreover, all legislation will be subject to the approval and signature of the State President of the Republic of South Africa. Finally, the highest courts of appeal for the Bantustans will be the Supreme Court of South Africa, South-West Africa Division, and the Appeal Court of the Republic of South Africa. These exceptions speak for themselves.

Of course it is possible for South Africa to argue that eventually these exceptions will wither away and that the homelands will become increasingly independent. In that event the most significant inquiry would be, what is the present intention of the South African Government as to the length of such a transitional period? Dr. Verwoerd told the House of Assembly in 1958 that the "ideal" of total separation could not "be attained within a space of a few years, or even for a long time to come."[64] Mr. Van Der Merwe in the same House referred in 1964 to the "normal evolution of centuries" during which the Bantustans would obtain their independence.[65] In the 1966 election campaign in South Africa, a Nationalist Member of Parliament reportedly told his constituents not to worry because freedom for the Bantustans would not be granted for another 200 years.[66]

64. *Parliamentary Debates: House of Assembly* (1958), col. 3805.
65. *Parliamentary Debates: House of Assembly* (1965), col. 5481.
66. Joseph Lelyveld, "Apartheid Wins New Mandate," *N.Y. Times*, 3 April 1966.

9

THE INDIVIDUAL VERSUS THE STATE

In Chapter 5, reference was made to the profound revolution in international-law theory to accommodate the modern notion that individuals have human rights that are cognizable under international law. This notion has two sides to it: first, that the individual has legal "standing" to make claims, and second, that a state cannot defend itself against such claims by the notion of "sovereignty." In the present chapter, I should like to explore the relation between individual standing and state sovereignty in international law.

In the first section, I turn to the nineteenth century for what in some respects was an anomaly. The nineteenth century was the zenith of state claims to sovereignty under the positivist theory that reigned supreme, and yet claims of individuals had somehow to be heard. To be sure, these were usually claims of businesspersons (where presumably enough money was involved to get their governments interested in backing them up), and the claims themselves were brought by the states and not the individuals. The notion was that the states "espoused" the claims of individuals. Yet the notion was not free from difficulty, and it presaged later human-rights developments.

In the second and third sections of this chapter, I will consider how these international-law questions of individual standing and state sovereignty folded into American law. Section two is a brief analysis of the state sovereignty question as it appeared in 1789, which was the time of passage of the Alien Tort Claims Act by the First Congress of the United States. Section three again deals with that Tort Claims Act, but in the specific context of the *Tel-Oren* Case and Judge Bork's highly restrictive (and, as I shall argue, antihistorical) view of what the Act was intended to do. Finally, section four attempts a theoretical look at the individual versus the state.

I. The "Espousal" of Individual Claims

Against a backdrop of positivist theory and state supremacy, let us look at how a hypothetical, but generically representative, case might have been handled under the international law of the nineteenth century. Let us suppose that Mr. Smith, a national of state *A*, secures an invitation from the government of state *B* to enter into that state and set up a commercial enterprise. Things go well for a time, but then a riot occurs, and the government of state *B*—jealous perhaps of Smith's success and his profits—fails to provide police protection for Smith. The riot results in physical injury to Smith and extensive damage to his business headquarters.

Smith asks his attorneys to look into the question of what recourse he might have against state *B*. Let us consider, then, what international publicists in the nineteenth century might have said about such a case.

International publicists could have opted for any of the following three positions: (1) Smith has no recognizable claim at all; (2) Smith's claim is real but unenforceable; or (3) Smith's claim can be espoused by his nation, nation *A*, making it a legitimate claim under international law. While many present-day texts suggest that (3) is the position selected in the nineteenth century, in fact (1) was chosen. To understand this is to get an insight into the workings of the international legal system as it was visualized by the positivist theorists of the last century and as it still is perceived by some writers today.

Smith had no claim at all under international law because he was neither a proper subject nor object of international legal claims. But in the real world he *did* have a claim. To leave it unenforced would be to create a tension that the system would have to resolve in some manner or other. Thus, what happened in practice was something like the following.

State *A* would make a claim against state *B*. If we want to be inaccurate, we might say that A would "espouse" Smith's claim against state B. This is inaccurate because, as we have seen, Smith had no personal claim at all, and hence there is no claim to be "espoused." What state A was really doing was asserting its *own* claim, under international law, against state B. This comported well with the theory of the day. In theory, state A could be harmed in several ways: directly (as when it is the victim of aggression), indirectly (for example, being barred from navigational use of an international river), or through harm to its detachable components (a vessel on the high seas, or a national travelling abroad such as Mr. Smith). State B, recognizing the harm to A, might pay a sum of money—say, $50,000—to A. This payment may have been *measured* by the actual damages incurred by Mr. Smith, but only coincidentally and not necessarily. For instance, instead of $50,000, A might have demanded and received from B a 21-gun salute. Such a demonstration would have satisfied A's claim against B, while leaving Mr. Smith with aught but cold comfort.

Now Smith would like to get the $50,000, which we have assumed has now been paid over by state B to state A. Could he bring suit against state A? If so, international law would not help, since international law did not recognize Mr. Smith as a claimant. Not only was international law not a help to Mr. Smith, but in fact it worked against him. Perhaps emboldened by the nationalistic basis of nineteenth century international law, state A probably would have a doctrine of sovereign immunity against suits by its own citizens. So Mr. Smith had no claim against state B under international law, and no claim against state A under the domestic-law equivalent called "sovereign immunity." Nineteenth-century international law regarded states as surrounded by hard-shelled boundaries. Whatever went on inside the shell was a matter for the state alone, a matter of domestic jurisdiction. Smith's lawsuit against his government was inside the shell, and thus was invisible to international law. Only when the shells themselves bumped up against each other did international law step in.

But even if state A had decided to *waive* its right of sovereign immunity in Smith's case, state A would still have a conclusive defense on the merits against Smith. Its defense would be that, under international law, Smith could not have sued state B, and hence any monies collected from state B *belonged* to state A and not to Smith.

Indeed, it was state *A* that was *injured*, and state *A* that was compensated, and *not* Smith. So Smith would have lost his lawsuit on the merits!

If matters were left that way, international investment and international tourism would have been over-deterred. Despite the nationalism of the nineteenth century, there was recognition of the importance of international tourism and investment. So, to accommodate persons such as Mr. Smith, states such as state *A* would typically turn over to Smith the $50,000 minus the usual transaction costs.

Nevertheless, the barriers to international investment were substantial. There were risks at every point in the chain: that the host state might fail to give protection to the investor such as Smith, that Smith's home state might decide not to intercede diplomatically against the host state, that the host state might not satisfy the demand for damages, and that even if satisfied the home state might not turn the money over to Smith. As a result of these risks, only investments promising huge rates of return were contemplated, and the entrepreneurs who sought out such investments abroad were gamblers and aggressive capitalists who usually brought along their own mercenaries. When they got into trouble in the host state, they usually had the economic and political clout at home to convince their governments to intercede in their behalf diplomatically or by sending gunboats.

In turn, host states saw their national patrimony being successfully exploited by self-made millionaires from abroad, and became jealous of the success of these enterprises. If the system had been rational (and who can say for certain that today we are any more rational?) the host governments would have made investment easier and resort to courts fairer; they would have encouraged moderate businesspersons from abroad and not just gamblers, and they could have recouped a good portion of their patrimony by taxation. Instead, the system encouraged high-risk, high-reward investments that were a visible source of frustration, when successful, to the host governments. And the host governments then tried to resort to legal innovation to get hold of what they considered their fair share of successful foreign enterprises on their own territory.

I want to mention just two of these legal innovations, associated with the great Argentine jurist Carlos Calvo (1824-1906), because of

The Individual Versus the State

the light they throw upon the theoretical international law system of the nineteenth century and the pitfalls accompanying the all-or-nothing "legal"-type regulation of international transactions. The first was the insertion of a "Calvo clause" in contracts entered into by foreign entrepreneurs and host governments. For example, if Smith Inc. entered into a dredging contract with Mexico, part of the contract might contain a clause that in the event of a dispute between the parties, Smith waives its right of diplomatic protection from the United States, Smith's home country. Assume now that a dispute arose. Smith Co., either out of arrogance or a calculation that Mexican courts would not be fair in a case where the Mexican government was a party, used its political clout back home to get the United States to espouse its claim. I use the term "espouse" advisedly here, because from Mexico's and Calvo's point of view, that is exactly what they thought Smith Inc. was getting the United States to do.

But Mexico (and Calvo) were in for a surprise. The United States might intervene diplomatically, saying that Smith Co. had *no power* to *waive* a right that *belonged* to the United States itself. Or, with greater analytic precision, the position of the United States was that its intervention was necessary to protect its *own* right against a denial of justice by Mexico against one of its nationals. In other words, there was no diplomatic "espousal" of *Smith*'s claim here; Smith had no claim. Rather, under international law the United States was *itself* injured by virtue of the injury to Smith Co., and it was this injury which was the basis of the right to compensation asserted by the United States. Smith Inc. neither itself sustained the injury nor was in any position to waive the right of the United States to compensation. Hence the fact that Smith signed the "Calvo Clause" was legally irrelevant.

The failure of the Calvo clause to do the work expected of it led to a second legal initiative. Calvo and others perceived that at the root of the problem was the concept of *nationality*. It was Smith Inc.'s United States nationality that gave rise to the right of the United States. Absent the nationality connection, the United States would *not be injured at all* if Smith Inc. was injured. Hence, the sure-fire way to avoid diplomatic intervention by the United States was to get rid of the nationality link.

This was accomplished by requiring foreign entrepreneurs to renounce their own citizenship and take up citizenship in the host country. For Smith Inc., it would mean becoming a Mexican corporation. Then, any damage to Smith Inc. would be a matter between Smith and Mexico, and no other nation.

Although the Calvo clause approach had not worked at all, the Calvo Doctrine approach worked all too well. Foreign investors were deterred. To give up one's nationality to do business abroad signified putting one's life in the hands of an alien government. The price was too high for all save the highest-possible rewards (such as oil-drilling concessions where the oil reserves were already proven.) Investors refused to become nationals of the host country; waivers were granted; enterprises were launched; and eventually, in many cases, expropriation of successful enterprises followed. (Today, less intrusive measures, such as requiring foreign corporations to joint venture their deals with corporations or shareholders of the host country, constitute a more sensitive and workable legacy of Calvo's ideas, favoring the accommodation of the competing interests of foreign investment and local patrimony.)

Let us now leap forward a hundred years or so, to the present day. The same structural kind of problem that troubled Calvo troubles us now, but in a different area—that of human rights. It's the same sort of problem because it involves individuals versus the state. Whereas a hundred years ago international law involved state *A* versus state *B* "espousing" (in the inappropriate use of this term, as we have seen) the claims of individuals, today we are increasingly unwilling to concede invisibility for the individual. We are less inclined to allow a government to be the solely aggrieved party when one of its nationals is harmed by a foreign country. We are increasingly skeptical that a government will "espouse" the claims of its nationals because governments are too often part of the problem and not part of the solution. The same risk factors in the chain of legal liability that Mr. Smith faced in the nineteenth century for his business enterprise confronts individuals today in their assertions of basic human rights, but the stakes seem higher today because at issue are rights that are fundamental to human existence and not just to the individual's bank account. Rather than accept the risk factors, the human-rights revolution in international law challenges the existence of the chain altogether; it asserts that the *true* parties in interest are not states, and that the rights asserted belong primarily to individuals and not to their states or governments. (To be sure, the World Court in this respect is still a nineteenth century institution, allowing only states to appear as parties; in such a forum, claimants for human rights can do no better than to obtain, if possible, state "espousal" of their claims. But this observation does not mean that human-rights claims are retarded; it only shows that the World Court is an extremely limited and old-fashioned forum.)

Perhaps I might be permitted a futuristic speculation: if the nineteenth century was characterized by State v. State, and the twentieth by Individual v. State, the twenty-first century might see international law becoming addressed to the claims of Individual v. Individual. Transboundary international legal claims involving individuals only, but invoking public international law, might be the direction in which we are headed, assuming, as usual, species survival.

If we are moving toward a universalist concept of international law where individuals and groups within states can assert legal claims against individuals and groups in other states, today we are only in the formative stages of that concept. As the notion of human rights becomes increasingly perfected, it requires giving standing to individuals and groups to claim entitlements under international law. The perception is all-important, and precedes any implementation. New institutions which are beginning to allow standing to individuals and to groups in human-rights cases, albeit in limited circumstances, are the European Court of Human Rights and the Inter-American Court of Human Rights.

The human-rights breakthrough of the twentieth century is to allow claims of individuals against governments. The issues are more basic today: freedom from torture, genocide, and enslavement; right to a voice in choosing one's government; right to food, shelter, and clothing. These issues of course have had varying receptivity, and any assertion thereof is still regarded as a challenge to the state that would be in a position to "espouse" the claim.

II. The "State" in the Eighteenth and Nineteenth Centuries

In 1789, the year that the Alien Tort Claims Act was enacted as part of the Judiciary Act, the subjects and objects of international law were not well defined. Indeed, the very term "international law" had not yet been invented. But the framers of the Constitution were well acquainted with the "law of nations," referred to in the body of the Constitution as well as in the Alien Tort Claims Act. The content of the law of nations could be found in the great treatises of Grotius, Zouche, Pufendorf, Wolff, Moser, and Vattel. These books explicated the principles of the law of nations that were acknowledged to be applicable anywhere against any person or entity that transgressed them. The law of nations was conceptualized as similar to the *jus gentium* of Roman law—the pervasive principles applicable to foreigners within the Roman Empire. Any court or tribunal was not only empowered, but was in fact required, to apply the law of nations whenever an appropriate case arose—or, as we would say today, whenever there was subject-matter jurisdiction.

There was little distinction in the writings of that era as to the nature of potential defendants, since there were probably more types of political entities at that time than exist today in the era of the nation-state. In 1789, there were not only states, but also principalities, duchys, free cities, armed bands in de facto possession of territory, colonies, protectorates, capitulatory regimes, entities such as the Holy See, and so forth. A writer in 1789 would have boggled at the attempt to define the law of nations in terms of its subjects and objects. Instead, classical writers of that time sensibly confined their treatises to the content of the rules of the law of nations.

For example, writers of that era were concerned with defining the international crime of piracy, but not with the question whether an act of piracy might be "immune" from accountability because the pirates were directly commissioned by a political entity or state. The latter question did come up, however, in the U.S. Supreme Court in 1820, where a person arrested as a pirate interposed in his defense a commission from a foreign power. The Court held that the law of nations did not preclude Congress from defining the act as one of piracy rather than belligerency.[1] The same case also demonstrates the impact of international-law definitions of piracy upon the law of the United States. The Court held that Congress could not constitutionally include "murder" in its definition of "piracy" because the Constitution only empowers Congress to define "Offenses against the Law of Nations" in Article 1 Section 8, and the law of nations itself, according to the Court, confined the definition of piracy to robbery and did not allow an extension to include murder.

---

1. *United States v. Pirates*, 18 U.S. (5 Wheat.) 184, 201–02 (1820).

The Individual Versus the State

Since no writer up to 1789 dealt with the question of torture as a possible violation of the law of nations, we can only speculate as to what the jurisdictional result would have been in 1789 if torture had been prohibited under that universal law. It is clear from the treatises of the day that officials and their political entities had no immunity from violations of the law of nations. Since torture is an official act, the law of nations would have held officials and their political entities liable in 1789. Under the assumption that torture would have been prohibited by the law of nations in 1789, it is clear that jurists of the day would not have recognized a barrier called "sovereign immunity" any more than the Supreme Court would have recognized in 1820 an immunity for an official foreign commission given to a pirate. Rather, the jurists of that era would have written that the perpetrator of a crime under the law of nations is obviously accountable for that crime; otherwise it would not be a crime under the law of nations. However, since torture was not a recognized prohibition in 1789, the question today cannot be settled definitively in retrospect.

At any rate, it is clear that as of 1789 there was no general concept of sovereign immunity in the law of nations. Instead, the law of nations was conceived by the leading jurists of that day as applicable universally, whenever appropriate to the case at hand.

However, the concept of "sovereign immunity" began to emerge in the positivist jurists who wrote in the nineteenth century and who dominated international legal thinking up until the end of the Second World War. These writers included Oppenheim, Westlake, Hall, Phillimore, Lawrence, and Wharton. It is important to note what the concept of "sovereign immunity" meant and what it did not mean. "Sovereign immunity" did not mean that a state was above international law. No matter how oriented toward the philosophical position of positivism a writer of that era might have been, he invariably acknowledged that rules of international law were *binding* upon the states. States are "sovereign" only in their own domains and then only when no rule of international law intrudes. For example, a state is not "sovereign" over an ambassador within its territory who is the representative of a foreign state. Indeed, no one would have used the term "sovereign" in such a case. Rather, it would have been said that an ambassador is subject to the jurisdiction of the territorial state, and is directly protected by the rules of international law that are binding upon that state.

What the positivist writers asserted as the meaning of "sovereign immunity" was that the courts of one state were precluded from imposing liability upon another state. These writers were concerned to exclude what they believed was the mistaken notion of extraterritorial sovereignty. Their theory might work as follows: An American court cannot impose liability upon the Republic of Argentina for the simple reason that the Republic of Argentina is *itself* not within the jurisdiction of an American court. But that is not to say that various properties and assets of Argentina are immune from liability. To the extent that these properties and assets may be found within the United States, a court may find Argentina "liable" up to a fixed dollar amount of these assets. Strictly speaking, this "liability" is exhausted upon whichever of the following two possibilities happens first: an aggrieved plaintiff satisfies a judgment by attaching the assets of Argentina within the United States, or there are no further assets of Argentina to be found within the United States. Upon the expiry of either of these two possibilities, no further "liability" would attach to Argentina. Thus the term "liability" is a convenient shorthand to denote an assertion of jurisdiction over Argentina's *assets* that are within the United States, to satisfy a claim that the plaintiff has proven against Argentina under international law. It is a judgment that the plaintiff has a better entitlement than does Argentina to a fixed dollar amount of assets within the jurisdictional reach of the court.

The positivist conception of sovereign immunity is well illustrated by two leading cases of the era. The first, *The Schooner Exchange v. McFaddon*,[2] involved the libel of a French armed vessel by the alleged former owner. Chief Justice Marshall held that under the law of nations the vessel was clearly within the jurisdiction of the United States. France, as a sovereign nation, clearly enjoyed no extraterritorial immunity within the United States as a matter of principle. However, a particular immunity could be implied. Marshall in fact inferred an immunity for the vessel, but it was one that could easily have been changed by Congress without violating international law. Notably, there was nothing in the case showing a violation by France of international law when it took the vessel in the first place. In that respect, the case is similar to the 1964 case of *Banco Nacional de Cuba v. Sabbatino*,[3] where a later Supreme Court found that a foreign

2. 11 U.S. (7 Cranch) 116 (1812).
3. 376 U.S. 398 (1964).

expropriation of American property was not in violation of international law.

The second leading case is *The Santissima Trinidad*.[4] A privateer vessel was commissioned by the United Provinces of the Río de la Plata, which later became the republic of Argentina. At issue was the ownership of certain property aboard the vessel allegedly captured as prize of war. Justice Story held that the property in question was the fruit of a capture made possible by the illegal refitting and augmentation of the vessel in a United States port in contravention of the international law of neutrality. Justice Story distinguished *Schooner Exchange*:

> It was there shown that it was not founded upon any notion that a foreign sovereign had an absolute right, in virtue of his sovereignty, to an exemption of his property from the local jurisdiction of another sovereign, when it came within his territory; for that would be to give him sovereign power beyond the limits of his own empire. But it stands upon principles of public comity and convenience, and arises from the presumed consent or license of nations, that foreign public ships coming into their ports, and demeaning themselves according to law, and in a friendly manner, shall be exempt from the local jurisdiction. But as such consent and license is implied only from the general usage of nations, it may be withdrawn upon notice at any time, without just offence, and if afterwards such public ships come into our ports, they are amenable to our laws in the same manner as other vessels. . . . [But] whatever may be the exemption of the public ship herself, and of her armament and munitions of war, the prize property which she brings into our ports is liable to the jurisdiction of our Courts, for the purpose of examination and inquiry, and if a proper case can be made out, for restitution to those whose possession has been devested by a violation of our neutrality.[5]

It is clear from this excerpt, and from the case itself, that Justice Story found no defense of sovereign immunity to be applicable when the foreign state itself was alleged to have violated international law. The commission from the United Provinces of the Río de la Plata did not immunize the vessel with regard to prize when the capture was

---

4. 20 U.S. (7 Wheat.) 283 (1822).
5. Id. at 352-54.

in violation of the international laws of neutrality. This case was therefore substantially different from *Schooner Exchange* which, as has been shown, did not involve a finding by the Court that France had violated the law of nations.

In conclusion, the writers of the positivist era asserted strict territorial jurisdiction, and hence "sovereign immunity" meant to them that the courts of one state could not obtain jurisdiction over a foreign state itself. But they did allow the adjudication of claims to property found within the territory of the forum state, only excepting those cases where state practice impliedly gave immunity to the foreign power.

III. The Tel-Oren Case: A Glimpse of the Future?

A human-rights case decided by the United States Court of Appeals in 1984, which was denied certiorari by the Supreme Court, seemed to encapsulate many of the trends discussed in this chapter so far. Yet the case was clearly "too much" for the three-judge panel, which ruled against the plaintiffs in three separate and largely conflicting opinions.

The events at issue in *Tel-Oren v. Libyan Arab Republic*,[6] occurred March 8, 1978, when 13 heavily armed members of the Palestine Liberation Organization left Lebanon for Israel under instructions to seize and hold Israeli civilians in ransom for the release of PLO members incarcerated in Israel. On the main highway between Haifa and Tel Aviv, they stopped and seized a civilian bus, a taxi, a passing car, and later a second civilian bus, taking the passengers hostage. While proceeding toward Tel Aviv with their hostages gathered in the first bus, the terrorists fired on and killed numerous occupants of passing cars as well as some of their own passengers. They also tortured some of their hostages. At a shoot-out with the police at a police barricade, the terrorists shot more of their hostages and then blew up the bus with grenades. As a result of the terrorists' actions, 22 adults and 12 children were killed, and 63 adults and 14 children were seriously wounded.

The plaintiffs in *Tel-Oren* are most of those wounded and the

---

6. 726 F.2d 774 (D.C. Cir. 1984).

survivors of most of those killed, as well as guardians and next friends of the wounded minors. Some of the plaintiffs are citizens of the United States, some of the Netherlands, and some of Israel. They brought suit in the United States against the PLO, the Libyan Arab Republic, the Palestine Information Office, the National Association of Arab Americans and the Palestine Congress of North America. The district court dismissed their action for lack of subject matter jurisdiction and as barred by the applicable statute of limitations. The court of appeals affirmed the dismissal in a brief per curiam opinion, but then appended three separate concurring opinions of Judges Edwards, Bork and Robb, comprising a total of over 50 pages. While there are interesting points in all three opinions, I shall confine my analysis to the opinion of Judge Bork, because it raises in acute form the issue of individual versus state and the future viability of using American courts for human-rights claims against foreign governments.

On a superficial reading, it is quite clear that a terrorist attack perpetrated by the PLO in Israel is not something over which United States courts have or should have jurisdiction. Let the victims seek redress elsewhere, whether in Libya, Israel or some other country having close ties to the incident or to the victims. Why stretch American jurisdiction to cover such a case? Such arguments, I submit, depict a traditional resistance to the very concept of human rights in international law. If human rights means anything in international law, it means that traditional state-based jurisdictional exclusivities must give way to a more fundamental realization that the rights of people count for more than the rights of states. I tried to give this perspective an operational meaning in Chapter 5, in which I argued that the 19th-century notion of nationality as a basis for a state's espousal of a national's claim should be reinterpreted under the human rights law of the 20th century by substituting internationality for nationality. Specifically, the United States itself has a real interest in seeing to it that nationals of other countries are not the victims of terrorism or genocide perpetrated by their own governments or by other entities in foreign lands. The new law of human rights, in short, calls for a change in world view. The interest that a country has in its nationals is expanded, under the law of human rights, to include an interest in non-nationals, especially where basic human rights are threatened.

Let us look at the real basis for the claims by the *Tel-Oren* plaintiffs. Concretely, they were suing in the United States for a sum of money—representing assets owned by the PLO. The action was for money damages against the PLO (for the moment, I omit the other defendants). What the plaintiffs, under my theory, were saying is that the money and other assets owned by the PLO in the United States are *already* under the general jurisdiction of the United States, and yet the *ownership* of these assets more properly belongs to the plaintiffs as compensation for the terrorist attack sponsored by the PLO than it belongs to the PLO. Under this view, if the United States wants to allow the PLO to have bank accounts and assets in the United States, it should condition this allowance on the nonviolation by the PLO anywhere in the world of basic human rights. If plaintiffs such as the ones in *Tel-Oren* can show that they were the victims of a fundamental violation of human rights by the defendant PLO, then the United States should not continue to protect the assets of the PLO in this country against the claims for compensation by such plaintiffs. Or to put the matter a different way, the court of appeals, in dismissing the plaintiffs' claims, was in fact upholding the right of the PLO to ownership of its assets in the United States against the human-rights claims for compensation by the *Tel-Oren* plaintiffs. Looked at in this light, I submit that the dismissal of the plaintiffs' claims was not a neutral act, but rather a recognition that at that time the court of appeals was not willing to accept the consequences of the meaning of international human rights. But it does not mean that the plaintiffs were wrong in asking the court to broaden its perspective. (Of course, the plaintiffs did not argue in these terms; I am simply supplying an after-the-fact theoretical perspective for their general right to claim redress in United States courts.)

Judge Bork's complex opinion turns on the question whether international law gives the plaintiffs a "cause of action." Since the court's disposition of the case was on the pleadings, dismissing the plaintiffs' action, the following findings are either explicit or implicit in Judge Bork's holding:

> (1) The court has jurisdiction over the case, both with respect to the Israeli plaintiffs (28 U.S.C. § 1350) and with respect to the American plaintiffs (28 U.S.C. § 1331).
> (2) The plaintiffs have "standing" to sue; that is, they are the real parties in interest and have allegedly suffered direct injury.

(3) The action is not barred by the "political question" doctrine. (However, Judge Robb, concurring in the result, would have barred the case as a "political question.")

(4) There is no defense of "sovereign immunity" available to the PLO, which is not a "state." (However, one of the defendants, the Libyan Arab Republic, would have been able to assert a sovereign immunity defense had the case proceeded to the merits.)

(5) There is no "act of state doctrine" defense available to the PLO, for the same reason.

However, the missing ingredient from this list is the elusive notion in U.S. law of "cause of action." Let us examine briefly what this notion is and what it is not. The idea of a "cause of action" is not the same as that of "jurisdiction." Let me give a very simple example. Suppose a small-claims court is given jurisdiction over all claims having a value less than $1,000. That mere statutory grant of jurisdiction does not mean that anyone alleging a claim, no matter how fanciful, of less than $1,000 may obtain relief in the small-claims court. If A sued B for $500 for interfering with astrological wave patterns between A and the planet Jupiter, we could simply say that although the small-claims court has "jurisdiction," A has not shown a "cause of action."

What, then, is a "cause of action?" Rather surprisingly, according to the Supreme Court, the phrase became a legal term of art only in 1848, when the New York Code of Procedure used it in abolishing the distinction between actions at law and suits in equity.[7] This rather late arrival of the term upon the legal scene raises at least a question when it is applied to interpret the alien tort statute (28 U.S.C. § 1350), originally passed as part of the Judiciary Act of 1789. Nevertheless, the term under present law appears to carry two different meanings that tend to overlap. In the first place, having a cause of action refers to having "recognized legal rights" that a litigant claims were invaded, which furnishes a basis for a litigant's claim for judicial relief. Second, Judge Bork explains, "to ask whether a particular plaintiff has a cause of action is to ask whether he 'is a member of the class of litigants that may, as a matter of law, appropriately invoke the power of the court.' "[8] Careful readers of Judge Bork's opinion will

---
7. *Davis v. Passman*, 442 U.S. 226, 238 (1979).
8. 726 F.2d at 801.

note that he tends to suppress the first, more traditional, reading of the term; rather, he emphasizes the second meaning, which, as we shall see, is conducive to achieving his desired result of a narrow and restrictive interpretation of international law.

Perhaps even more useful to the goal of achieving a narrow reading of international law are the policy pressures adumbrated by Judge Bork that militate against finding for the plaintiffs. These pressures are summarized by the labels "act of state doctrine" and "political question doctrine," for while these doctrines do not directly apply to the present case, the underlying reasons for them nevertheless exert a steady pressure. The reasons have to do, vaguely, with separation-of-powers concerns under the U.S. Constitution, judicial interference in foreign policy and the less than precise nature of rules of customary international law. (As an example of the latter, Judge Bork cogently asks whether the law against terrorism applies against an organization such as the PLO, which is not a state and whose members are not public officials. I think this question can be answered in the affirmative under existing customary international law, but only after detailed argument and concededly not as a matter of "black letter" rules.) This is not the place to examine whether the underlying rationales of the act of state and political question doctrines, or even the doctrines themselves, are sound; suffice it for present purposes to note that while Judge Bork uses these rationales as a supporting weight for his analysis of cause of action, it is only a weight and not a conclusive or dispository consideration. Therefore, we may turn to the main issue, which in Judge Bork's terms is whether international law gives rise to a cause of action in the present case.

Judge Bork does not require an express grant of a cause of action by the rules of international law; indeed, there can be no such express grant because international law clearly is not addressed to the particular concerns of United States courts or their post-1848 concepts of a cause of action. Rather, it would suffice for Judge Bork to be able to infer a cause of action from the body of international law. Nor does Judge Bork draw a distinction between the Alien Tort Claims Act (28 U.S.C. § 1350) and the general jurisdiction act (28 U.S.C. § 1331) for the purpose of possibly inferring a cause of action from international law, and therefore we need not concern ourselves here with their particular intricacies and differences. However, because the Alien Tort Claims Act is the more specific of the two, providing for federal jurisdiction in "any civil action by an alien for a tort only, committed in violation of the law of nations or a treaty of the United States," Judge Bork's analysis begins with, and focuses largely upon, that Act.

The core of Judge Bork's opinion consists of three arguments: (1) treaties do not provide a cause of action for the plaintiffs; (2) the reasoning applied to treaties carries over to customary international law, which is then seen as similarly not providing a cause of action; and (3) apart from treaties/custom, the law of nations, with very few exceptions, does not provide a cause of action. I will here attempt to summarize Judge Bork's arguments under these three headings, and then, in the next part of this section, I will offer a critique.

(1) The alien tort statute, as we have seen, provides for civil jurisdiction over actions by an alien "for a tort only, committed in violation of the law of nations or a treaty of the United States." The *Tel-Oren* plaintiffs listed 13 alleged treaties as having been violated; of these only 5 are currently binding on the United States.[9] As to those 5, Judge Bork found by examination of their language that they call for implementing legislation by the states parties, or impose obligations upon those parties to fulfill in good faith the purposes of the treaties. Hence the treaties, Judge Bork concludes, are not self-executing. As a result, they do not grant individuals a cause of action to seek damages for violation of their provisions.

(2) Since the alien tort statute mentions the "law of nations" and "a treaty of the United States" without distinguishing between the two, they stand in parity. Hence if a mere violation of the law of nations would itself provide the plaintiffs with a cause of action, a mere violation of a treaty would do the same. But this would mean, according to Judge Bork, "that all existing treaties became, and all future treaties will become, in effect, self-executing when ratified. This conclusion stands in flat opposition to almost two hundred years of our jurisprudence. . . ."[10] Therefore, a mere violation of the law

---

9. The 13 alleged treaties listed by Judge Bork, of which the first 5 are binding, are: the Geneva Convention relative to the Protection of Civilian Persons in Time of War, the Convention with respect to the Laws and Customs of War on Land (both Hague Conventions of 1899 and 1907), the Charter of the United Nations, the Geneva Prisoners of War Convention of 1949, the OAS Convention of 1971 on Terrorism, the Protocols to the Geneva Conventions on Humanitarian Law of 1949, the General Assembly Declaration on the Principles of Friendly Relations, the Universal Declaration of Human Rights, the International Covenant on Civil and Political Rights, the General Assembly Resolution on Protection of Civilian Populations in Armed Conflicts, the Genocide Convention, the General Assembly Declaration on the Rights of the Child and the American Convention on Human Rights. 726 F.2d at 808-09.

Id. at 820.

of nations cannot itself provide a cause of action in United States courts. Only those rules of international law which themselves provide that individuals may sue to enforce them may be used to infer a cause of action in American courts. In other words, under Judge Bork's view, most of the rules of international law are similar to a non-self-executing treaty; they have no impact upon individuals. Only a self-executing treaty, or a rule of international law that itself provides for enforcement by individuals, can give rise to a cause of action in courts of the United States.

(3) Even apart from the analogy between non-self-executing treaties and the rules of customary international law, Judge Bork finds that nearly all rules of international law address states and not individuals. He relies extensively upon Oppenheim for this proposition, quoting from the eighth edition:

> Since the Law of Nations is based on the common consent of individual States, States are the principal subjects of International Law. This means that the Law of Nations is primarily a law for the international conduct of States, and not of their citizens. As a rule, the subjects of the rights and duties arising from the Law of Nations are States solely and exclusively.[11]

Noting that international law is becoming increasingly concerned with individual rights, Judge Bork nevertheless finds that human rights law today remains vague and at a high level of generality, consists more of aspirations and ideals than of legal obligation, and in any event is not intended for judicial enforcement at the behest of individuals. On this latter point, the *Filartiga* case,[12] upholding jurisdiction upon an allegation of official torture abroad of the son of an alien suing in the United States, is of questionable merit "because the court there did not address the question whether international law created a cause of action that the private parties before it could enforce in municipal courts."[13]

The argument that nearly all rules of international law are addressed to states and not individuals is another way of saying that individuals are not members of the class of litigants that may appropriately invoke

---

11. 1 L. Oppenheim, *International Law: A Treatise*, 19 (H. Lauterpacht 8th ed. 1955), quoted in id. at 817.
12. *Filartiga v. Peña-Irala*, 630 F.2d 876 (2d Cir. 1980).
13. 726 F.2d at 820 (Bork, J., concurring).

the power of the court, which, as we have seen, is the second of two meanings that can be applied to the term "cause of action." Judge Bork's position, therefore, is a general one: that while nations are members of the class of litigants designated by the rules of international law, individuals are not; hence, the former may have a "cause of action," but the latter do not. Moreover, Judge Bork's position applies equally to the alien tort statute (28 U.S.C. § 1350) and the general jurisdiction statute (28 U.S.C. § 1331); indeed, it would apply to *any* attempt by an individual to invoke international law in United States courts. There is thus an enormous breadth to Judge Bork's ruling: it would pretty much wipe out the invocation of customary international law in American courts (for the instances in which nations, as opposed to individuals, would bring suit in American courts are extremely rare).

But the breadth of coverage of Judge Bork's principle would include the alien tort statute itself, and this gives rise to a particular difficulty: how would that statute *ever* apply to an alien suing for a tort? Judge Bork asks what kinds of alien tort actions Congress might have had in mind in 1789 in enacting the statute. He finds in Blackstone (who was familiar to the Founding Fathers of the Constitution and the attorneys in the first Congress) three classes of cases: violation of safe conducts, infringement of ambassadorial rights and piracy. Judge Bork concludes that these three classes are possibly the only ones Congress meant to reach, but in any event, the present case of torture clearly does not fall under any of them. Judge Bork admits that this leaves "quite modest" the "current function" of section 1350,[14] but given the policy reasons for not entangling courts in foreign affairs questions, that constricted view of section 1350 is acceptable to Judge Bork.

My specific criticisms of Judge Bork's opinion are as follows:

(1) Judge Bork argues that only self-executing treaties can give rise to a cause of action for individuals. He thus makes an ingenious link between the concept of "cause of action" and treaties that are "self-executing," a link that I believe is unexceptionable, harmless, and yet irrelevant. It is true that a non-self-executing treaty cannot give rise to a cause of action for individual plaintiffs, but for a reason entirely different from what Judge Bork thinks. The reason is not that there is any intrinsic link between "cause of action" and "self-exe-

---

14. Id. at 816 (Bork, J., concurring).

cuting"; rather, it has to do with the unlikelihood that a non-self-executing treaty would be "violated" in a manner that could cause harm to an individual plaintiff.

To see why this is so, let us consider what a non-self-executing treaty is all about. Such a treaty binds the states parties to it to enact legislation that will implement the treaty principles in their own domestic spheres. Hence, a non-self-executing treaty can only be *violated* if a party to it fails to pass the requisite implementing legislation. In the event of such a failure, that party will be in breach of the treaty vis-à-vis the other parties, but the breach will consist solely in that party's failure to enact the requisite legislation. Suppose, for example, that the United States enters into a treaty with Poland containing the provision that Polish ham should be allowed to be sold in American supermarkets without interference by state or local government, and that the United States undertakes to implement this principle by passing the appropriate legislation. If, after the treaty enters into force, the United States fails to enact the legislation, Poland will have a legitimate complaint that the United States has committed a breach of the treaty. Now suppose that an importer asks for a restraining order in court against local officials seeking to bar the sale of Polish ham. The court might say, along with Judge Bork, that the treaty does not give the importer a "cause of action" in this matter. But the court would be more accurate in saying that the local ordinance barring the sale of Polish ham, which the local officials are seeking to enforce, is valid law because the treaty has not been implemented by Congress. The local ordinance, therefore, is not in *violation* of the treaty. In fact, there has been no violation of the treaty that is relevant to the importer's lawsuit. The "violation" of the treaty that has occurred has nothing to do with Polish ham, or the right to import and sell Polish ham. Rather, the "violation" is at an entirely different level, consisting of the failure of Congress to pass implementing legislation.

Technically speaking, the importer of Polish ham would only have a claim, akin to a shareholder's derivative lawsuit, against the United States Congress, charging that as a member of the public he has been deprived of a property interest (profits in the sale of Polish ham) owing to the failure of Congress to live up to its treaty commitments to Poland. Under present United States law, such a lawsuit would have practically no chance of success; it would be barred by lack of standing, the "political question" doctrine and the general constitutional right of Congress to enact or not to enact legislation. But I spell it out here to underline my main point, which is that an individual is not directly "hurt" (except in this attenuated sense of a citizen's derivative lawsuit against Congress) by a "violation" of a non-self-executing treaty.[15]

(2) Given the preceding argument, we now see that Judge Bork's fear, that allowing a cause of action under section 1350 for a mere violation of the law of nations would equate to rendering all treaties self-executing, is misplaced. For a non-self-executing treaty is not "violated" the way a rule of customary international law would be violated. Under section 1350, *only* self-executing treaties are capable of being violated in a way that per se affects individual rights. There is no danger that non-self-executing treaties could ever be included under section 1350; nor could their violation be held parallel to violations of the law of nations, simply because only governments can violate non-self-executing treaties and, if and when they do, the "violation" consists only of failure to enact implementing legislation and not the sorts of substantive violations of treaty principles that might be helpful to individual plaintiffs in tort actions under section 1350.

Judge Bork's entire analogy and his fears thus melt away. Not only is there no danger that non-self-executing treaties may be rendered self-executing if his "cause of action" reading of section 1350 is not upheld, but also there is no need to reconceptualize the entire body of customary international law to force it into a category of "providing no cause of action" on Judge Bork's analogy to non-self-executing treaties.

(3) If Judge Bork is mistaken about the parity between the law of nations and treaties in section 1350, he is also on very thin ice about what is left in section 1350, given his own theory that rules of customary international law must impliedly give rise to an individual cause of action before they can be invoked by individuals in United States courts. For under his restrictive interpretation of section 1350,

---

15. A non-self-executing treaty may nevertheless indirectly produce domestic private effects, including those of influencing the interpretation of a statute, evidencing federal foreign policy that may preempt the states, and generating a rule of customary law that in turn may apply to private parties. *See, e.g.,* Paust, Book Review, "Human Rights: From Jurisprudential Inquiry to Effective Litigation," 56 *N.Y.U. L. Rev.* 227, 239-42 (1981); A. D'Amato, *The Concept of Custom in International Law,* ch. 5 (1971).

it is hard to think of any rule of international law that would be available to an alien suing in tort. As Judge Edwards points out in criticism of Judge Bork's view of section 1350, even the three offenses recognized by Blackstone—violation of safe conducts, infringement of ambassadorial rights and piracy—are not now, and were not in 1789, rules that impliedly create a private right of action to secure their enforcement.[16] Hence, Judge Bork's reading of section 1350 completely guts the statute, even in its original intention as defined by Judge Bork himself.

More generally, Judge Edwards cites Professor Henkin for the proposition that "international law itself, finally, does not require any particular reaction to violations of law."[17] There is a variety of mechanisms by which international rules are enforced. Indeed, as I argued in Chapter 1, the very same mechanisms that give rise to international rules of law and ensure their survival over the years against potential competing rules are the mechanisms that account for their enforcement in given cases. To attempt to reshape all of international law through the particular post-1848 American mechanism of a "cause of action" is like trying to force a camel through the eye of a needle. The needle's-eye view is provincial as well as distorting, and ultimately is no more than a surrogate for Judge Bork's attempt to declare all international law irrelevant to decisions reached by American courts.

If we take the traditional meaning of "cause of action," none of this straining is necessary. Under this meaning, which I previously labeled as the first reading of the term given by the Supreme Court, a litigant has a cause of action when he refers to recognized legal rights that he claims have been invaded by the actions of the defendant. Since international law is a part of American law,[18] international law may well provide, in appropriate cases, such recognized legal rights. There are a huge number of cases in American law that have turned on rights founded in international law,[19] including nearly all the cases where the defendant has prevailed not because the plaintiff has failed to state a cause of action, but because the plaintiff's

---

16. 726 F.2d at 779 (Edwards, J., concurring).
17. L. Henkin, *Foreign Affairs and the Constitution*, 224 (1972), cited in id. at 777-78.
18. *The Paquete Habana*, 175 U.S. 677 (1900); *United States v. Smith*, 18 U.S. (5 Wheat.) 153 (1820).
19. I estimate some 5,700 cases cited in 1-20 *American International Law Cases* (F. Deák ed. 1971-1982).

action was barred by defensive doctrines such as sovereign immunity or act of state.[20] Thus, by departing from the traditional meaning of "cause of action," Judge Bork's restrictive secondary view of that term logically entails departing from the rule of decision in all of these cases throughout American history.

But what about this second meaning that Judge Bork ascribes to "cause of action," namely, to ask whether the plaintiff is a member of the class of litigants that may, as a matter of law, appropriately invoke the court's power? Judge Bork's argument, as I understand it, is that the proper class of litigants for nearly all rules of international law is the class of nations. International law is a creature of nations, and they may properly invoke it. Thus, individuals do not belong to this proper class of litigants and have no "cause of action" under nearly all rules of international law.

Whether or not this second meaning that Judge Bork gives to the notion of "cause of action" stands up under scrutiny,[21] let us for the moment assume it is correct and inquire whether, in fact, international law is addressed to nations and not to individuals. Judge Bork's authority for his viewpoint is Lassa Oppenheim, a prominent English positivist whose massive text on international law first appeared in 1905; its subsequent editions were last revised by Sir Hersch Lauterpacht in 1955.[22] (An examination of the works of some other writers cited by Judge Bork indicates that they, too, largely relied upon Oppenheim.) Was Oppenheim correct in saying that states are primarily the exclusive subjects of the rights and duties arising from international law?

In the first three editions of his book, Oppenheim expressed the view that states only and exclusively are the subjects of international law; later editions qualified this statement by phrases such as "prin-

---

20. *See, e.g.*, cases cited in Paust, "Federal Jurisdiction over Extraterritorial Acts of Terrorism and Nonimmunity for Foreign Violators of International Law under the FSIA and the Act of State Doctrine," 23 *Va. J. Int'l L.* 191 (1983).

21. It is very close to the notion of "standing," as Judge Bork admits in a footnote, 726 F.2d at 803 n.8. A careful reading of *Davis v. Passman*, 442 U.S. 226 (1979), indicates that the Supreme Court did not endorse in its text the idea of defining a cause of action according to the proper class of litigants, but did make an attempt to define it as such in a (possibly clerk-written?) footnote, 442 U.S. 240 n.18. Even in that footnote, it is hard to discern a real difference between "standing" and this second meaning of "cause of action."

22. 1 L. Oppenheim, *supra* note 11. Oppenheim himself acknowledged contrary views to the proposition that international law concerns only states. *See* 1 L. Oppenheim, *International Law: A Treatise*, 20 n.1 (2d ed. 1912). Professor Paust has labeled as "nonsense" the Oppenheim-based view that individuals were not in Oppenheim's time, and are not today, recognized as having the direct right under international law to sue or be sued. Paust, "Litigating Human Rights: A Commentary on the Comments," 4 *Hous. J. Int'l L.* 81, 89 (1981).

cipal," "primarily" and "as a rule." As Lauterpacht, his most recent reviser, writes at length in the eighth edition, individuals may directly be subjects of international law.[23] Piracy is a classic example; pirates are by definition outside the municipal laws of the various states, and are subject in the first instance directly to duties imposed by international law.[24]

To be sure, Oppenheim and other positivists at the turn of the century had some success in arguing that states alone were the subjects and objects of international law. The very phrase "international law," which had been invented by the leading positivist Jeremy Bentham in a book he published in 1789,[25] seemed to call for an exclusive state-oriented view of that body of law. The elaborate fiction was invented that when an alien is injured abroad, it is the alien's home state that is really injured under international law and not the alien himself. Thus, in the classic *Lotus* case,[26] although the person injured was Lieutenant Demons, in fact France "espoused" his claim and brought an action in the Permanent Court of International Justice against the state of Turkey. To carry the fiction through to its logical conclusion, one might suspect that if France had won that case, there would be a definite monetary amount awarded to France to redress France's "injury" and, in turn, the measure of that amount of money would conveniently be based on the damages suffered by Lieutenant Demons. This, indeed, is how the positivist fiction was embellished. We have already seen in this chapter the problems and confusions engendered by the notion of "espousal" of claims.

Oppenheim's state-oriented view of international law was largely fictitious, even in his day; certainly today it exists only to cloud the minds of people who aspire merely to a superficial view of "international law." The phrase "law *of* nations" in the Judiciary Act of 1789 is much more revealing of reality than Bentham's coinage of the term "international law." It suggests a law that is "of" the nations, like the Roman *jus gentium*. Even Blackstone, despite a prepositivist

23. 1 L. Oppenheim, *supra* note 11, 19-23.
24. *See* the good, but brief, discussion of Judge Edwards, 726 F.2d at 794 (Edwards, J., concurring). *See also* A. Rubin, *Piracy, Paramountcy and Protectorates*, 10-12, 34-46 (1974).
25. J. Bentham, *An Introduction to the Principles of Morals and Legislation*, 326 n.1 (Hafner ed. 1948). According to Professor Janis, Bentham deliberately changed Blackstone's fundamental assertion that the law of nations applied to individuals as well as states, Bentham opting positivistically for only the latter. Janis, "Jeremy Bentham and the Fashioning of 'International Law,'" 78 A.J.I.L. 405 (1984).
26. *The Case of S.S. "Lotus"* (Fr. v. Turk.), 1927 P.C.I.J., ser. A, No. 10.

streak in his writings, regarded the law of nations as "this great universal law collected from history and usage, and such writers of all nations and languages as are generally approved and allowed of."[27] As well summarized by Professor Alfred Rubin, "to Blackstone, the principal parts of the 'law of nations' were not those governing sovereigns in their relations with each other, but those rules of natural law which were, or should have been, identical in all states."[28]

As I suggested earlier in this chapter, in 1789 the term "nations" was a lot looser than it is today. Indeed, vast areas of Europe were not "nations" in today's sense, the Ottoman Empire was a loose federation of principalities, Germany and Italy were not yet unified, Africa was a "dark continent" and the term "nations" connoted "foreign lands" as well as "states" in the modern sense. The three Blackstonian categories of rules of the law of nations were recognized under the "law of nations" as applying to individuals, not just "states." An individual with a safe conduct had a right to be respected not only by States or nations, but also by principalities, duchies, groups, armed bands in de facto possession of territory, public organizations (such as the later Red Cross), nonpolitical entities such as the Holy See, capitulatory regimes and so forth. Indeed, the list of political, quasi-political and nonpolitical entities of 1789 was probably longer and more complex than it is today, given the recent spread of the modern state across the world's land surface. The law of nations in 1789, to be sure, applied to interstate transactions such as treaties, but it applied as well to nonstates (treaties could be made with the Vatican). A writer in 1789 would have boggled at the attempt to define the law of nations in terms of its subjects and objects. Instead, classical writers of that time sensibly confined their treatises to the content of the rules of the law of nations. It was simply understood that these rules would apply to whatever entities were appropriate (for example, individuals in the case of piracy, political entities in the case of treaties). All of this was severely distorted when Oppenheim came along and attempted to recast this sprawling and subtle law into the narrow mold of "states."

Yet in the 20th century, particularly among American and English writers who were more persuaded by positivism than their continental

---

27. 4 W. Blackstone, *Commentaries on the Laws of England*, 67 (1790).
28. Rubin, "U.S. Tort Suits by Aliens Based on International Law," 21 *Int'l Prac. Notebook* 19, 21 (1983).

colleagues, the state-oriented view of international law for a while made considerable headway. Recently, there has been a sharp reversal of the trend. The newly emerging laws of human rights have changed the perspective away from state-based claims; after all, some of the worst violations of human rights (genocide, torture) are perpetrated by states themselves. In the mid-1930s, when Stalin supervised the genocide of ten million Russian kulaks, the world took little notice; under positivist theory, what a nation did to its own citizens did not amount to a breach of "international law." Today, in the post-Nuremberg world, genocide is a crime that makes relevant, for international legal purposes, what a state does to its own citizens. It also makes relevant, in a way that Oppenheim possibly could not have thought, a claim by an outsider state on behalf of those persons subject to severe human rights deprivations. In the *Tel-Oren* case, it makes relevant to the real interests of the forum court an incident of torture and murder that occurred outside the territorial United States. Ironically, this recent turn to human rights law is in historical perspective a return to the pre-19th-century conception of the "law of nations." While "torture" in the *Filartiga* case may not itself have been part of the law of nations in 1789, the idea of including the concept of torture as part of the law of nations is a lot closer to the original climate of opinion behind section 1350 than Judge Bork's positivistic reluctance to give any real meaning to that statute.

Judge Bork, in sum, has seriously misunderstood the law of nations as it was meant to be understood in the jurisdictional provisions of the Judiciary Act of 1789. He views it through the distorting glasses provided by Oppenheim, and not the way it really was then or is now. But even if his view of "cause of action" were correct, a proper analysis of the concept "law of nations" would even fit into that narrow view and support standing for the plaintiffs.

Alas, *Tel-Oren* seems to have been ahead of its time. The plaintiffs did not even make the argument I have presented in this chapter—that the defendant's *assets* in the United States are protected by our laws, and those same laws should condition the continued ownership of property upon the nonviolation everywhere of basic human rights norms. But that idea, I fear, is not one the judiciary is willing to hear sympathetically these days.

And maybe judges will never get to it unless, as law students, they were exposed to courses in international law and human rights. Judge

Bork's view of international law is very much like that of law professors I know who think that it isn't "law" anyway and hence not a proper subject for American courts to deal with seriously. I hope that Chapter 1 of this book has made a beginning at answering *that* concern.

IV. Individual and State: Theory and Speculation

How should we conceptualize the relation between individual and state? Let me discuss the vision of Thomas Hobbes, and speculate as to its unfolding in the human-rights concerns of our troubled present-day world.

To Hobbes, a government was an unmitigated blessing; without the Leviathan, life was brutish and short. There is always an element of truth in this thesis. Any government that has ever existed has provided some security for some of the people, even if the government, like Idi Amin's in Uganda, engaged in a continual war against some of its citizens. The element of stability that any government provides can be inferred from, among other sources, Barbara Tuchman's account of fourteenth century Europe in her book *A Distant Mirror*. There were marauding bands in those days going from town to town, killing and torturing at will. But in time the bands got bigger until they became governments, and when that happened a certain amount of internal stability set in. The peasant's life was not as subject as it had been previously to random violent disturbance. To be sure, intergovernmental wars took the place of the previous scattered violence, and those wars got bigger and bigger (culminating eventually in World War II). But even the violence of the bigger wars was not as pervasive, and did not affect the average peasant, as much as did the wars of the pre-nation-state period.

Hobbes had proposed a trade: to get rid of continual civil strife, turn over all your guns to the government. At this point, as Hobbes recognized, the citizenry would be utterly powerless against the government. But Hobbes argued that the Leviathan, having absolute power, would not normally be inclined to exercise it ruthlessly. There was not much satisfaction in murdering and torturing one's own weaponless civilians. On the whole, Hobbes maintained that people would be better off giving away their ability to defend themselves than they would be by keeping it.

To be fair to Hobbes, we must remember that he did not prescribe the form of Leviathan that should necessarily be erected within the state. A representative parliamentary government would undoubtedly be less inclined to brutalize its own constituents than would a dictatorship. Hobbes was telling us that both kinds of government are more similar than dissimilar: they both have absolute power (and our more modern phrase "tyranny of the majority" acknowledges this fundamental fact). But he certainly argued for the desirability of representative government as the next step after setting up the Leviathan. Under Hobbes, any government is better than no government at all; but there are clear preferences of forms of government once one is established.

In today's world, there are governments which from time to time turn their inherent capability for brutality against their own citizens. More often their objects of wrath are those citizens who represent a political threat to officials within the government. The twentieth century certainly has seen the most massive genocides in human history in terms of total persons killed, although of course we are exponentially more populous today than ever before. But apart from these Hobbesian statistics, the necessities for most of the people in the world today are not freedom from arbitrary tyranny but rather civil freedoms such as the right to speak and criticize, freedom of worship, freedom of association, freedom from arbitrary arrest, freedom of movement within and among nations, and economic rights such as the right to subsistence, minimal clothing and shelter. Here perhaps the broadest and most abstract question we can ask is: With respect to these latter values, is the Hobbesian bargain good or bad? In other words, is government part of the problem or part of the solution?

What if a particular government is oppressing and brutalizing its people or minorities among its people? Does the rest of the world have to be bystanders to local tyranny? Is there a "Keep Out" sign on a nation's borders that insulates its government from any and all violations of human rights so long as they are directed against its citizens?

The Charter of the United Nations, for all its references to human rights and aspirations, is at bottom a collective-security pact designed to prevent the most recent war. Just as generals are sometimes accused of planning to fight the last war, so too the United Nations, in the perspective of forty years, can be seen as primarily a backward-looking institution. Nuclear weapons had already rendered the notion of collective security largely obsolete (though we can hardly criticize the framers of the U.N. for not immediately realizing this in 1945), and what would be important in years ahead would be matters of human rights that could not be conceptualized or dealt with by the infusion of massive military force. The U.N. was designed to enforce peace, not law. The law of the Charter attempts to put sacrosanct borders around all member states, only dimly recognizing the human-rights violations that could occur within those states.

Instead, what has happened since 1945 is an uneasy erosion of the sanctity of borders in the name of more universal concerns. Some local wars have occurred as the result of invitation to other governments to intervene (South Vietnam, Korea, and perhaps Afghanistan); other military actions have been for humanitarian intervention (Grenada, Central Africa, Uganda); and the United States policy toward Nicaragua is at least in principle said to attempt to prevent an irreversible tyranny of the left. We may today be witnessing an historically significant shift of attitude toward dictators in the reactions of the United States to the popular revolutions in Haiti and the Philippines. Perhaps it is too early to say, but it appears that the logic of interventionism is compelling a more coherent foreign policy on behalf of people who are oppressed by governments, whether of the right or of the left.

If so, international law is providing a corrective to Hobbes. Under Hobbesian theory, any government is better than no government. But we have found that some governments need to be checked if we care about the people they rule. Perhaps the diminishing importance of collective security, which is increasingly understood by the leaders of the major powers, has provided the relative luxury of being able to bypass the need for military alliances and accentuate the need for being friendly and humane to individuals in foreign lands. Perhaps in addition we are beginning to feel less relativistic about moral principles within nations, less willing to apply neutral principles of nonintervention, and less willing to look the other way when gross abuses of human rights take place within the confines of a foreign nation. Although we may be concerned lest one powerful nation, such as the United States, appears to be imposing its own standards of morality upon foreign countries, that caution appears to be rather formalistic compared to the substantive question of precisely what standards are being imposed. If the standards being imposed are those of freedom from governmental oppression (anti-genocide, anti-torture, anti-slavery, etc.) then maybe their imposition is worth the risk of allowing military and economic intervention in foreign countries that practice those gross violations of human rights. What may turn out to be decisively important is what happens *after* the intervention—does the intervening power become an annexing power (thus rendering the intervention a mere excuse for expansionism) or does it pull out? We are seeing increasing instances of the latter kind of unilateral international police action. Customary international law, which after all can and does change to reflect new state practice, seems clearly to be moving in the direction of permitting military intervention in order to provide the checks that appear necessary if the human rights of all people, in whatever countries they may find themselves, are our paramount concern. Let us consider in the next chapter, how these considerations play out with respect to the United States' support of the contras against the Sandinista government of Nicaragua.

10

NICARAGUA AND THE ACADEMIC VIEW OF INTERNATIONAL LAW

In this chapter I would like to take up some of the human-rights themes that have been essayed in previous chapters, and conjoin them to a discussion of what is "real" in international law and what may simply be ivory-tower theorizing. This latter issue goes to the matter of the epistemology of international law, and perhaps serves as a roundup to Chapter 1, which dealt with the ontology of international law.

The decision of the United States to withdraw from the International Court of Justice proceedings in *Nicaragua v. United States* had an unexpected consequence: candor. A month after the announced withdrawal, Secretary of State Shultz suggested, and President Reagan later confirmed in a press conference,[1] that the goal of U.S. policy was to *overthrow* the Sandinista Government of Nicaragua. Of course, this is precisely what Nicaragua all along had alleged to be the United States' goal. But while the case was actively *pending*, the United States could not concede that goal without serious risk of undermining its litigating position.

When the United States was still participating in the case, it argued strenuously to the Court that Nicaragua was engaged in an armed attack against its neighbors, carried out not only by supporting armed groups engaged in military and paramilitary activities in and against

---

1. President's News Conference, *N.Y. Times*, Feb. 22, 1985, A10, cols. 1, 3.

El Salvador (and on a smaller scale against Costa Rica, Honduras and Guatemala), but also by direct armed incursions across its border into Honduras and Costa Rica. Any military activity by the United States in response was within the exercise of its "inherent right of self-defense."[2]

Moreover, as Davis R. Robinson, Legal Adviser to the Department of State, summarized it, the self-defense nature of the U.S. position in turn meant that "[t]his is a classic case arising under chapter VII of the United Nations Charter."[3] As such, the case was a political question of resolution by the Security Council and not suitable for adjudication by the International Court of Justice. Professor Louis B. Sohn, who assisted in the drafting of the U.N. Charter and is considered a leading scholar of the United Nations, argued the political question position for the United States in the *Nicaragua* case. He surely knew that if the Court had accepted his argument and held that Nicaragua's Application was nonjusticiable, the United States would use its veto power in the Security Council to paralyze any U.N. action in the case.

In its Judgment on jurisdiction, the Court unanimously rejected the nonjusticiability argument. It pointed out that Article 24 of the Charter gives to the Security Council "primary responsibility for the maintenance of international peace and security," but that "primary" does not mean "exclusive."[4] It also reminded the United States that the Court was capable of dealing with the "legal" aspects of a case embedded necessarily within a "political" context, as the United States had successfully argued was the Court's proper role in the *Iranian Hostages* case.[5]

But the real props were knocked out of the U.S. litigation stance by President Reagan's statement that until the Sandinista Government says "uncle," the goal of U.S. policy is directly that of removing the "present structure" of that Government.[6] The President's candor was matched by an unnamed senior State Department official directly involved with the Nicaragua program, as reported by Joel Brinkley

---

2. *Counter-Memorial of the United States of America* (Nicar. v. U.S.) 220, para. 517 (submitted by the U.S. Government to the Court Aug. 17, 1984).
3. Davis R. Robinson, Letter to the Editor in Chief, 79 *A.J.I.L.* 423 (1985).
4. *Military and Paramilitary Activities in and against Nicaragua* (Nicar. v. U.S.), Jurisdiction and Admissibility, 1984 I.C.J. *Rep.*, para. 95 (Judgment of Nov. 26).
5. *United States Diplomatic and Consular Staff in Tehran* (U.S. v. Iran), 1980 I.C.J. *Rep.* 3, para. 37 (Judgment of May 24).
6. News Conference, *supra* note 1.

in the *New York Times*.[7] According to this official, arms interdiction *never was* the goal of aid to the contras. That would have been, he said, "a fool's errand."[8] In short, the entire notion of collective self-defense, of aiding Nicaragua's neighbors against armed aggression by Nicaragua and of supporting the contras in Nicaragua so as to stop Nicaragua from exporting its revolution to other countries has melted away as a legal rationale for U.S. policy.

Is there any legal rationale left? What is the purpose of a "legal rationale" anyway? These are profound questions raised by the recent events of the *Nicaragua* case, and will undoubtedly occupy many students of international law for many years.

There is only one basis in general customary international law to support the actual position of the United States with respect to Nicaragua. It is *not* to be found in positivist state-based conceptions of international law such as intervention in Nicaragua's internal affairs, sovereignty, territorial integrity or political independence.[9] *Nor* is it to be found in Professor Michael Reisman's proffered test of maintaining minimum world order. Professor Reisman would use that test to justify military intervention in support of the "right of peoples to determine their own political destinies,"[10] but I see no evidence—much as I would wish to see some—to show that democratically elected governments contribute more to international stability and order than, say, communist-bloc countries. Professor Reisman's attempt to tie self-determination to world public order has no empirical basis; internal forms of government do not necessarily correlate with foreign military adventurism. Instead, if any support for the U.S. position exists, it is to be found in the law of human rights, which both predated and postdated the statist conceptions of border impermeability reflected in Article 2(4) of the U.N. Charter.[11]

If we take human rights seriously, we cannot insulate a government's actions toward its own citizens by an artificial sovereign boundary. Professor Reisman was correct in likening the U.N. Charter

---

7. Brinkley, "Vote on Nicaraguan Rebels: Either Way, a Turning Point," *N.Y. Times*, Mar. 17, 1985, A1, col. 5.
8. Id., 6, col. 3.
9. This is how Nicaragua characterized the legal issues in its complaint. *See Application Instituting Proceedings, Military and Paramilitary Activities in and against Nicaragua* (Nicar. v. U.S.) (submitted by the Nicaraguan Government to the Court Apr. 9, 1984).
10. Reisman, "Coercion and Self-Determination: Construing Charter Article 2(4)," 78 *A.J.I.L.* 642, 643 (1984).
11. An argument that human rights predated positivist conceptions of the state has been given in Chapter 9. As to the impact of treaties on customary law, *see* Chapter 6.

to a "Wild West" town in the 19th century when a sheriff arrives announcing that he will enforce the law and that citizens no longer need carry weapons or resort to personal force to protect their rights.[12] However, if it later becomes clear that the sheriff is utterly incapable of maintaining order, Professor Reisman concludes that "even the best of citizens" will no longer refrain from the techniques of self-help that prevailed before the sheriff's arrival. Professor Oscar Schachter took sharp issue with Reisman's position. He replied that "[a] community might allow the citizen a gun to defend himself and his household, but it would not follow that he could legitimately use the weapon to impose behavior (however good) on another household."[13] We do not have to imagine the Wild West to refute Professor Schachter; recent news accounts and congressional testimony regarding severe child abuse make it clearly realistic to consider forcibly breaking into a neighbor's house or apartment to stop a parent from thrashing a helpless child to within an inch of its life. Certainly, the state now takes the position that parents may not brutalize their own children. This same concern with the rights of helpless children in domestic law has its analogue in concern for the rights of citizens helpless against torture and murder by their own government. Governments have a monopoly of armed power in their states, and the horrible 20th-century examples of genocide attest vividly to the necessity of foreign intervention to prevent brutal governments from getting away with mass murder.

The three paradigmatic cases justifying humanitarian intervention are genocide, slavery and widespread torture.[14] At the other extreme are violations of human rights that have no basis in customary or conventional international law for justifying intervention because the evil they represent is minor in comparison to the evil of military intervention (and the loss of life that usually accompanies military intervention). For example, if a state expels a minority group, the refugees' human rights have certainly been violated (and other states inherit an immigration burden), but there is no present basis in customary law to change the government's expulsion policy by means of an armed attack. Yet, although both ends of the human rights spectrum are clear, how can we deal with cases in the middle?

12. Reisman, *supra* note 10, at 643.
13. Schachter, "The Legality of Pro-Democratic Invasion," 78 *A.J.I.L.* 645, 646 (1984).
14. For a defense of this proposition *see* Chapter 6.

The simple answer is that students of international law can only look at state practice and draw conclusions from it. The danger of resorting to military intervention with its attendant risk of touching off a war erects a clear presumption against any transboundary use of force. Only the grossest abuses of human rights by a government against its own citizens would overcome the burden against external interference. Yet customary law can change, and state practice may add a fourth paradigmatic case to the list. The U.S. intervention in Grenada, which toppled a new government that had just machine-gunned its way into power, and the present policy to remove the Sandinista regime in Nicaragua may be steps along the way toward a new rule of customary international law. Historically, it is not so new; the Grenada intervention, as I suggested at the time it occurred,[15] was the reincarnation of Wilsonianism.

What Woodrow Wilson and Ronald Reagan have in common is the conviction that it is better to intervene sooner, rather than later, in an effort to prevent a nondemocratic government from seizing the reins of power and then perpetuating itself by its monopoly of armed power against its own citizenry. Whether one agrees with this philosophy or not, it is indeed grounded in human rights. An undemocratic government, according to all empirical evidence of the last several centuries, is far more likely to commit basic human rights violations against its citizens than a democratic government. I argued above that there was no correlation between democratic government and minimum world public order, but I doubt that anyone could dispute the very strong correlation between democratic government and respect for the fundamental human rights of the citizenry. One has only to look at the egregious cases of genocide (Stalinist Russia, Nazi Germany, Cambodia, the "disappeared" persons of dictatorial Argentina) for the obvious evidence. Philosophically, the proposition is logically compelling. As John Locke, Thomas Jefferson and Jeremy Bentham demonstrated, a government that depends upon the consent of the governed—exercised not just once but in periodic intervals, with free opposition parties—is extremely unlikely to brutalize its own citizens. To be sure, Aristotle long ago pointed out the danger that popular governments may become tyrannical, and "eternal vigilance" is a constant price that citizens have to pay in democracies.

---

15. D'Amato, "Intervention in Grenada: Right or Wrong?," *N.Y. Times*, Oct. 30, 1983, at E18, col. 3.

Nevertheless, the proposition is unassailable, both logically and empirically, that democratic governments are far less likely to tyrannize and brutalize their own citizens than are unaccountable governments.

Whether the Sandinista Government of Nicaragua is on its way toward becoming a totalitarian government capable of tyrannizing its own citizens is certainly hard to tell at present. Its violations of the human rights of its own Miskito Indian citizens count heavily against it, but the atrocities committed by the contras against Nicaraguan citizens indicate that the opposition in Nicaragua may not present a moral alternative. Yet this is the question that is really at issue. How enlightened it would have been for the International Court of Justice to hear argument addressed to this question, rather than to the spurious ones that filled the voluminous documents presented to the Court by both parties!

Apart from the specific question of Nicaragua, the real test of the Reagan administration will be whether it is willing to apply its interventionist philosophy, as did Wilson, to right-wing as well as left-wing governments.[16] There is surely no difference between human rights violations committed by undemocratic governments of either the right or the left. If we are truly trying to create a world that respects the fundamental rights and dignity of the person and attempts to clear away the debris of Hegelian state-based claims of right, we should expect a new American foreign policy that is as antagonistic to dictators of the right as it is to the Sandinista Government of Nicaragua.[17] And indeed there is some evidence of just such a possibility. The Reagan administration welcomed the overthrow of the Marcos dictatorship in the Philippines and the Duvalier dictatorship in Haiti, and unless this welcome evidences only temporary opportunism we may indeed find that human rights has become a powerful factor in an administration that came to office looking decidedly askance at Jimmy Carter's human-rights initiatives. (And Carter, to balance the record, showed nothing of the skill or human-rights sensitivity in the waning days of the dictatorship of the soon-to-be-deposed Shah of

---

16. When visiting King Juan Carlos of Spain, President Reagan referred to the "undemocratic governments" in Latin America of Paraguay, Chile, Cuba and Nicaragua, a statement which lumped together authoritarian and totalitarian regimes. CBS-TV Evening News, May 7, 1985.

17. For the argument that the best form of national security for the United States in the foreseeable future is the security that comes from having its citizens travel and trade abroad in countries that are committed to respecting human rights, see Chapter 7.

Iran that President Reagan showed in helping to prepare the ground for the bloodless revolution in the Philippines against America's "staunch old friend" Ferdinand Marcos.)

If the arguments on both sides that were made in *Nicaragua v. United States* were largely spurious, what is the *point* of international legal rationalization? It almost appears at times that governments invoke precisely those legal rationales in favor of their positions that they believe *academic* international lawyers want to hear. They may announce that they are following the X set of rules when the actions they take have a hidden agenda labeled Y; yet X is proclaimed because international legal scholars want to hear X and expect to hear X. By invoking the X set of rationales, governments appease the international legal community, which is one of many pressure groups governments attempt to accommodate by their verbal policies.

Not only do many international legal scholars accept these verbal rationalizations when they are made, but they also proclaim that it is important that governments invoke those rationales. If a government says X when it does Y, these scholars say that the government refrained from invoking Y because that would be tantamount to admitting a violation of international law. Hence, these scholars tell us, the government-invoked rules of international law (meaning set X) remain intact even though a government may have deviated from them in practice (in doing Y). Given this self-referential reinforcement of their own theories by scholars, one can hardly blame governments for going along with the game. One is reminded of La Rochefoucauld's observation, "L'hypocrisie est un hommage que le vice rend à la vertu."

When the United States intervened in Grenada, an interesting spectacle was played out in the scholarly literature. The government invoked the X set of rules in favor of its intervention, and academic critics also invoked the X set of rules to show that those rules, properly interpreted, proved instead that the U.S. intervention was illegal. But the real rationale, which in my opinion expressed at the time was a human-rights-based reason for intervention (the Y set of rules),[18] was not invoked by either side. To be sure, the Reagan administration did invoke Y in its more public, less legal-sounding statements, but these were overlooked both by the academic critics and by State Department attorneys charged with justifying the U.S. action ac-

---

18. D'Amato, *supra* note 15.

cording to the traditionally accepted X set of rules. Similarly, in *Nicaragua v. United States*, parties and critics alike debated the X set of rules until, a month after the United States withdrew from the case, President Reagan told us that the real rationale was Y.

The difference between X and Y is no simple dichotomy between what governments say and what they do. Rather, there is a profound challenge to the theory of international customary law to take into account the real difference between X and Y. The rules I have called X are those that governments profess and proclaim to be following when they undertake particular actions or restraints in the international arena. These governmental *statements* typically comport with academic versions of what international law requires. On the other hand, the rules I have called Y are those that actually cohere with the actions or restraints of the acting government. In scientific terms, Y is the "theory" that has a "better fit" with the facts than does X. As Wittgenstein, following the Skolem-Lowenheim theory, demonstrated, no theory is uniquely determined by a given set of facts or experiments, but theories that can be called "explanatory" must be consistent with all the data. The reason that *governments* typically do not proclaim the Y theory is that academics expect them to proclaim the X theory and would charge that the Y theory would be a governmental admission of violation of international law. But these are simply academic, or at best strategic, considerations; in fact, unbiased reasonable observers would agree that the operative theory is Y.

The insistence on what governments *say*, and an unwillingness to face up to the difficult task of inferring what they should have said from the facts of what they did, reached an apotheosis of sorts in an article by Dr. Michael Akehurst on customary international law.[19] The article, which has been widely cited, comes close to urging us to ignore totally what governments do and instead rely exclusively on what they *say*. Governmental *statements*, and not their actions (and the rules inferable from them), constitute what Dr. Akehurst calls custom. I have attempted to criticize the specifics of his approach in Chapter 6; here I mention it as a prominent illustration of the academic impulse to keep X as the set of rules regardless of what goes on in the real world. If Dr. Akehurst and the many who follow him have their way, their books will never be out of date because

---

19. Akehurst, "Custom as a Source of International Law," 47 *Brit. Y.B. Int'l L.* (1974-75).

they proclaim and set forth unchanging legal principles to which governments, regardless of what they actually do, pay lip service.

Instead, I would argue that customary law grows and changes over time as a result of the interactions of states in the international arena (the facts) and the rules we may infer from those interactions as the theory that best fits what the states did (even if it was not, or was only partly, what they said they were doing). It is surely more difficult to do this kind of international law research than to follow Dr. Akehurst and simply take governmental statements at face value. For what I am suggesting requires research into the *history* of governmental interactions, the *facts* that occurred, the *settlements* that were reached, the *agreements* that were entered into. At the same time, the researcher should be highly skeptical about the negotiating positions taken by the governments involved, their unilateral proclamations, the briefs they file in a court or arbitral tribunal, the opinions of their attorneys general or their foreign offices. The researcher should also be skeptical of *protests* by one government to another; the filing of a protest does not mean that the protesting government means or believes what it says.[20] And skepticism is also a good antidote to the all-too-easy tendency to view General Assembly resolutions, or Security Council condemnations of state actions, as expressive of international rules of law. Sometimes a Security Council condemnation that is not followed by any forcible action on the part of the Council is another way of saying to the ostensibly offending state, "We have to condemn you verbally, but don't worry, we're not going to do anything about it."[21] In such cases, the lack of action by the Security Council may be a more eloquent way of approving the Y set of rules than its verbal recommendation reciting the X set.

The truly operative rules generated by the customary practice of states, which I have labeled the Y set, are the rules that in reality accommodate the most deeply felt interests of the community of states. If concern for human rights is one of those deeply felt interests, that concern will be manifested in the emerging rules of custom even if those new rules are at variance with received wisdom. As Professor Thomas Franck has shown, new rules inferable from the practice of

---

20. Indeed, protest may have the counterproductive effect of articulating the very norm that the protesting government objects to. *See* A. D'Amato, *The Concept of Custom in International Law*, 101-02 (1971).

21. *See* B. H. Weston, R. A. Falk, and A. A. D'Amato (eds.), *International Law and World Order*, 94-101 (1980).

states have gone a long way toward undermining Article 2(4) of the Charter.[22] The Grenada and Nicaragua examples, as well as the Israeli raid upon the Iraqi nuclear reactor, add additional evidence to Professor Franck's thesis. The challenge to the international legal scholar is to dig beneath the verbiage, to peel off the ritual invocations of traditional rules in governmental press releases and to articulate the operative emerging rules of customary law. It is an exciting challenge because it is grounded in scientific objectivity and a commitment to "tell it like it is."

---

22. *See, e.g.*, Franck, "Who Killed Article 2(4)?," 64 *A.J.I.L.* 809 (1970); Henkin, "The Reports of the Death of Article 2(4) Are Greatly Exaggerated," 65 *A.J.I.L.* 544 (1971).

Postscript

International Law as a Career

I

Law students are likely at some point in their education to become fascinated with the idea of pursuing a career in public international law. "What species of law could possibly be more important?" they might ask. International law deals with the truly significant questions facing the world: war and peace, human rights, freedom of travel and emigration, terrorism and interventionism, international ecology and environmental preservation, and interesting new problems such as ocean mining and outer space exploration and exploitation. By comparison, the daily concerns of domestic lawyers, such as whether corporation A must pay corporation B a sum of money, do not seem vested with epochal significance. Yet immediately, the student encounters a fundamental paradox: Although international law seems to be the most important species of law in content and significance, it is clearly the least important in terms of career opportunities. Law firms do not appear to care about the prospective applicant who wants to work in public international law or who has taken law school courses and seminars in that field.

In brief, there exists an egregious case of market undervaluation. The most important field is the one least financially rewarded. This undervaluation also extends to law schools, which are creatures of the financial marketplace to a far greater extent than their apologists would concede. Although courses in international law do have some standing in law schools, perhaps more than their marketability would suggest, law faculties generally look upon them as "soft law" and consign them to a distinctly secondary place in the curriculum. The law school, as Duncan Kennedy and others have pointed out, is really a microcosm of the world of the large law firm, and students are trained to become cogs in the financially successful institutions of corporate America.[1]

Law firms exist and persist by skimming profits off the transactional costs of interactions among corporations, citizens, and the government.[2] Some lawyers *increase* the friction of those transactions so as to generate more work for themselves. A law school graduate may eventually become disillusioned with the pressure to increase friction by couching contracts, codes, statutes, regulations, warranties, and pleadings in complex legal jargon that ensures the hiring of more lawyers to read and interpret those works.[3]

I would like to address the question of why there is such a huge undervaluation of public international law in legal education and practice. I will also try to examine some implications of this inquiry for law students. Finally, I shall make some personal remarks, not because my own situation is an example of anything in particular, but because I acknowledge that it is necessary for the observer to recognize his own position in the field he describes. I could hardly expect the reader to accept my observations about a field unless I am willing to turn these observations inward and examine my own reasons and biases for choosing an economically irrational career in public international law.

---

1. *See* Duncan Kennedy, "Legal Education as Training for Hierarchy," in *The Politics of Law*, 40 (D. Kairys ed. 1982).

2. *See* R. Nader & M. Green, *Verdicts on Lawyers*, i, vii, xv (1976) (Nader's introductory overview); M. Green "The Gross Legal Product: 'How Much Justice Can You Afford?," in R. Nader & M. Green, Verdicts on Lawyers 65-77; *see also* J. Auerbach, *Unequal Justice: Lawyers and Social Change in Modern America*, 40 (1976) (noting the historical development of the American corporate legal elite); Swaine, "Impact of Big Business on the Profession," 35 *A.B.A.J.* 89, 169 (1949) (refuting various allegations of excessive business control over attorneys). *See generally*, P. Hoffman, *Lions of the Eighties* (1982) (offering the inside story of the "powerhouse law firms"); M. Green, *The Other Government* (1975) (describing large corporate Washington law firms as a form of other government).

3. *See* Mensch, "The History of Mainstream Legal Thought," in *The Politics of Law*, 21 (D. Kairys ed. 1982) (documenting the complexity of the common law that allowed lawyers to claim expertise beyond ordinary reason in early American society).

Professor David Kennedy has described the duality of international legal studies at Harvard Law School. On the one hand, "the international law library occupied pride of architectural place in a law school that offered an extremely wide variety of seminars on the law of far flung places."[4] But on the other hand, he perceived that international law was:

> not in the mainstream of my legal education . . . [the course offerings] were all upper level courses and yet did not seem to be related to first year domestic offerings in any hierarchical or progressive way. Although international law seemed to make some claim to be concerned with fundamental jurisprudential questions or jurisdictional priority, many of the courses presented international law as the specialized continuation of some domestic subject such as taxation or investment. . . . few if any of my professors "specialized" in international, comparative or historical legal studies.[5]

I can add from anecdotal experience that faculty members who microscopically examine Article 9 of the UCC or spend their lives researching advance sheets of cases brought under Rule 10-b5, tend to look at international law as parasitical on "real" law. They view international law as a hopeless attempt by quasi-lawyers (who are really political scientists) to claim that, somehow, international political decisions follow legal standards instead of those of national self-interest. It is not law, they say, because there are few international courts, fewer international decisions, and those decisions are not enforceable.

The more generous of these professors might say that if there is such a thing as international law, students are best trained for it by learning to "think like a lawyer" in all the conventional courses. Then, when those students must someday grapple with a public international law problem, they will be well equipped to handle it using the usual tools of legal analysis. A leading private practitioner of public international law reacted the same way when I asked him whether he would be interested in interviewing the best students in my international law classes. He responded that he was only interested in my best students period, and not those who had taken in-

---

4. David Kennedy, "International Legal Education," 26 *Harv. Int'l L.J.* 361, 366 (1985).
5. Id. at 366.

ternational law. "They'll get all the international law training they need from us," he explained; "just send me the top students and we'll teach them the rest."

All of these attitudes and arguments can be refuted decisively. Yet who will listen? What non-international law professors will read these remarks? What busy practitioner will care? Nevertheless, for the record, here are some brief refutations:

(1) That international law is "really law" is a topic I have addressed at length elsewhere.[6] Suffice it here to say that any legal system, domestic or international, defines the set of entitlements of its subjects and provides for enforcement of those entitlements by depriving the transgressor of one or more of them. The domestic legal system accomplishes this enforcement in familiar ways (courts, judgments, the sheriff), whereas the international system does it by less visible, but equally effective, entitlement deprivations that are carefully regulated by prescriptive norms. No observer can understand international relations without knowing how these norms define proper national interests and provide for their enforcement.

(2) When law professors say that international law is not really needed as a subject because all that is necessary is the ability to "think like a lawyer," the best answer is to ask them to pick any subject other than torts, contracts, or criminal law, and justify its independent status. Are not sales, tax, agency, bankruptcy, trusts and estates, and constitutional law simply variants of contract law? Can not family law, antitrust, regulated industries, administrative law, and just about any other course you can name be considered as simply admixtures of torts and contracts? What justifies all those courses?[7] Proponents of those courses will insist that there is something "extra" about their subject matter that cannot be deduced from the principles of torts and contracts, and which requires a specialized understanding of other kinds of intellectual issues. We reply that the same is true of international law. Not only are there special problems when nations, as well as individuals, are the creators and subjects of the same law, but international law also borrows from an amalgam of foreign legal systems those special procedures and arguments that have fused to make international law a distinct specialty. Finally, if

---

6. *See* Chapter 1, *supra*.
7. *Cf.* Duncan Kennedy, "Legal Education as Training for Hierarchy," in *The Politics of Law* 47 (D. Kairys ed. 1982) (challenging the dichotomy between those subjects considered "hard" and those considered "peripheral" in the law school curriculum).

not most importantly, there are jurisprudential issues, such as figuring out what customary international law consists of and how it is proved, that have no close analogues in domestic law. In terms of intellectual challenge, public international law should take a back seat to no other legal discipline.

(3) Practicing international lawyers who claim that junior associates need no law school training in international law so long as they have good minds, may unknowingly be wearing blinders. Their law firms may have missed decisive international law issues in their litigation and negotiations simply because no lawyer on the staff realized that those issues were present in the factual situations. Attorneys may engage in international law practice without recognizing potentially crucial arguments in their favor. Regardless of whether they win or lose those cases, they may never know what they have missed (unless the other side comes up with those "missing" arguments). I have read many decisions in which I could spot hidden and potentially decisive international law issues that neither side argued and the judge certainly failed to notice. Hence, the international lawyers who hire young law students with the attitude that they will learn whatever public international law they will need to know in the course of working for the firm, may be begging the question by adopting this in-bred attitude.

Yet, as I have said, these "refutations" conjure up the image of hitting one's head against the wall. It may take years before rational argument makes a dent in the minds of comfortable law professors and more than comfortable practicing attorneys. International law today may be to law what eighteenth century biology was to science, and it may take a paradigm shift before international law is given its proper status in the law school curriculum and in law firm placement.

II.

Unfortunately, if the market undervalues international law, it may remain undervalued for a long time. Law students cannot be blamed for turning their intellectual energies to the problem of getting corporation *A* to pay a sum of money to corporation *B*, because that sum of money includes the attorneys' livelihood. What advice can be given to a law student who wants to spend a lot of time thinking about and studying international law?

One possibility is to go to work for corporation A. The student, however, must make sure that corporation A is a multinational corporation with a great deal of business outside the United States. The fact that foreign business is involved does not guarantee that in-house counsel in the international legal affairs division of corporation A will practice *public* international law, but there remains that possibility. Dealings with foreign governments, foreign legal systems, choice-of-law problems, and questions of sovereign immunity, certainly can arise when one's client is a multinational corporation. Additionally, the attorney will be dealing with foreign attorneys and foreign bar associations. A variety of individual issues facing employees of the corporation will also arise including: the validity of marriages abroad, adoptions, immigration and emigration, passports, visas, false arrests and detentions, and civil liberties in foreign countries. Finally, corporation A might have operations in areas that directly come under international law: the oceans of the world (fishing, seabed mining, conservation, navigation), international rivers, harbors and straits, the polar regions, or even outer space technology.

I have advised many of my students to look for work in the legal departments of corporations that have an international business, and from time to time I hear from some of them that they enjoy a tremendous degree of responsibility for far-flung international business and legal matters. They say that public international law plays an important part in their professional lives. So there can be some public international law "success stories" in the legal department of the right corporation.

A second possibility is to work in the office of the Legal Adviser to the Department of State. These lawyers for the most part practice pure public international law. The work is obviously exciting and challenging, but the jobs are few and there is huge competition for limited positions.

Other branches of government have specialty divisions in their legal departments for international law, such as the Departments of Justice and Commerce. In addition, the entire Foreign Service field welcomes legally trained applicants for career positions.

The third possibility, joining a law firm, is unlikely to result in an international law practice except in special or "lucky" cases. Yet there are many international lawyers in law firms in New York and Washington D.C., and increasingly more in other major cities.

Fourth, many students interested in international law find that their first jobs do not include any work in that field. This is perhaps the most critical point of decision for young people interested in international law. Most people just tend to forget international law and become absorbed in the law practice they are in. It is difficult to keep in touch with a field when you are absorbed in entirely different matters. Sometimes, however, the best opportunities open up several years after you are doing nothing but domestic law.

Sometimes lightning will strike, as happened to a young lawyer working for a large law firm when, because of his knowledge of Spanish and his prior studies in international law, he was assigned to work on the project of a Latin American country. A year or two later, due to the volume of the work and the country's insistence, he left the firm and opened up his own practice devoted almost entirely to legal work for that country. He now has a highly successful small firm serving one satisfied client. Indeed, his example suggests a model for other countries—to have individual legal representation in the United States.

Young attorneys, however, should not wait for lightning to strike. The best thing for an attorney not practicing international law to do is to write an article or two on an international law subject. The best subjects are those that might interest your clients. For example, I suggested to a former student who is working for a large oil company that she write an article on deep-sea oil drilling. She is not involved with her company's international law division, but she could write an article that, a few years from now, might enable her to obtain an important position in that division. In general, I would suggest to young lawyers that they contact their former professors of international law from time to time and ask for ideas about topics of current interest. Writing an essay in a legal periodical is the best way for a young attorney to rise above the crowd, and perhaps to lay the groundwork for a later career in international law.

Finally, a broad category of career opportunity is to teach public international law in a law school. There are over one hundred and fifty law schools that have, or could be talked into having, a faculty member who specializes in public international law. By research and writing, teachers of public international law can build an international reputation which can lead to employment as an attorney on important international law cases. So long as this practical work coincides with the professor's research and teaching interests and does not interfere with class preparation, experience as counsel in this kind of case may enhance and enrich the professor's knowledge of the field. All seriously interested students should consult two excellent books of career opportunities in international law published by the American Bar Association and the John Bassett Moore Society of International Law.[8]

Nevertheless, adding up all these opportunities realistically does not produce an encouraging sum. It is very difficult to practice international law and make a living at the same time. You have to be convinced that sometimes the most important things in the world simply do not have much of a market value, and you must be prepared to make a financial sacrifice in order to do them. (Your friend's affection for you may be the single most valuable thing in your life, but does it have any market value? People who are demonstrating against the MX missile may—and I hope only "may"—be engaged in the single most important activity in the brief history of sentient life on the planet Earth, but they hardly are paid for their efforts. More likely, they are rounded up and thrown into jail.[9]) If making money makes life worth living, you should probably go into any field at all except public international law. On the other hand, if dedicating your life to the ideals of world peace and human rights gives your existence meaning, don't expect others to pay you much. For if others placed much value on world peace and human rights, then we would have already attained those ideals and there would be no need for your services now. Instead, most people place value on building up nuclear arsenals of planetary destruction and on in-groups exploiting out-groups. This global insanity is called the market system, so if you want to combat it, don't expect that very same system to reward you.

III.

Let me now make some personal observations about my career as a teacher and practitioner of public international law.

---

8. See generally "Career Preparation and Opportunities in International Law (J. Williams 2d ed. 1984); J. B. Moore Society of International Law Directory of Opportunities in International Law (7th ed. 1984).

9. See, e.g., United States v. Allen, 760 F.2d 447, 449, 453-54 (2d Cir. 1985) (upholding the convictions of MX Missile protestors after rejecting defendants' international claims); United States v. Montgomery, 772 F.2d 733, 737-38 (11th Cir. 1985) (involving protesters convicted for protesting the MX Missile and nuclear activities).

Postscript

The first dilemma I had to face was to reevaluate my relationship to the government. Putting it this way may strike the reader as grandiose, yet I believe studying international law is extremely liberating in terms of philosophical perspective. I was conscious of wanting to work in a discipline where the actors were nation-states, one of which was my own country. What should I think of the policies and preferences of the United States? As a citizen, could I possibly be an impartial observer? How could I write or advocate anything in international law if I could not genuinely treat all nations equally?

I wondered what it would be like for people who wanted to work in international law if they lived under dictatorships. No doubt they could not progress very far unless they served as justifiers and apologists for their governments. They would either have to absorb and internalize the values of their countries, or else be committed to a life of hypocrisy, but in either event they would have an all-powerful "client" whose policies they could not second-guess and whose actions they would have to justify by their legal arguments.

Fortunately for me, the United States is a free society. No one told me how I had to come out in my writings. When in the late 1960s my non-classroom time was spent entirely in research, writing, and active litigation contesting the legality of the Vietnam War, I was not muzzled or financially penalized in any way. I must add, however, that most of my colleagues were distinctly unsympathetic and that I was looked upon as a "nut." A few years later, when it became politically and academically respectable to oppose the Vietnam War, those social and collegial pressures abated.

My attitude toward the Vietnam War was itself a minority view. People were roughly divided into two main camps: the overwhelming majority (including academics) who supported the war for geopolitical reasons, and the minority (including draftees) who believed that the war was a geopolitical mistake and not in the best interest of the United States. I was in a very small third camp, opposed to the war for reasons of international human rights. It was quite clear long before "hard" evidence surfaced, that the United States engaged in war crimes atrocities in Vietnam that were not sporadic violations but endemic to our uncomfortable military situation there. Thrust into a guerrilla war, we responded the same way as the United States troops in the Philippines in 1900.[10] Of the many incidents I could recount, let me just give one. By 1969, American aircraft had engaged in thirty-nine distinct bombing attacks on the internationally renowned leper sanatorium in Quyuh Lap, North Vietnam. The roofs of the buildings in the sanatorium were painted with the Red Cross.[11] Nevertheless, this humanitarian, non-military target was a favorite among United States pilots, many of whom now captain your friendly domestic airplanes. In an interview at the time, one of the pilots explained the "psychology" of this kind of bombing mission:

> When you hit school buildings, or hospitals, or especially dams, you have a feeling of accomplishment. You see the effects below in terms of scattering adults and children, or water bursting and knocking down houses, or buildings caving in.[12]

Instead, to drop bombs in the leafy jungle would mean that there would be no visual results. Yet the bombs *had* to be dropped somewhere, because the pilots were sent out with full loads of bombs and told to come back after dropping them.

I thought long and hard whether I could blame the United States for these violations of human rights and I decided that I could not. In the first place, it seemed to me that other countries in the same position might do the same thing. (Many years later, this thought was confirmed by the Soviet atrocities in Afghanistan,[13] their own "Vietnam.") Secondly, the policy of the United States was subject to change. By bringing the atrocities to light, instituting lawsuits,[14] and

---

10. See W. Pomeroy, *American Neo-Colonialism: Its Emergence in the Philippines and Asia*, 88-92 (1970). In the so-called "Fil-American War" of 1898-1900, the United States conquered the Philippines in part to maintain commercial markets. Id. at 13-35, 190-200. American troops committed widespread atrocities against Filipinos, particularly after they faced increasing guerrilla resistance. Id. at 86, 88-96. As in Vietnam, the destruction of homes and even entire villages was common, and various methods of torture were used on peasants and soldiers alike. Id. at 89-95. Some U.S. troops were court-martialed for their abuses in this war. Id. at 91-92, 94; see also R. Barnet, *Intervention and Revolution: The United States in the Third World*, 99-100 (1968) (analogizing the American support of terrorism in the post-World War II Greek government to the American support of the Diem government in Vietnam).

11. See D'Amato, Gould, & Woods, "War Crimes and Vietnam: The 'Nuremberg Defense' and the Military Service Resister," 57 *Cal. L. Rev.* 1055, 1086 (1969), reprinted in 3 *The Vietnam War and International Law* 407, 438 (R. Falk ed. 1972).

12. N. Chomsky, *American Power and the New Mandarins*, 14 (1969).

13. See Senate Comm. on Foreign Relations & House Comm. on Foreign Affairs, 99th Cong., 1st sess., *Country Reports on Human Rights for 1984* 1159-69 (Joint Comm. Print 1985) (State Department Report chronicling abuses of human rights and atrocities committed in Afghanistan by the Soviet-backed regime).

14. See, e.g., J. N. Moore, *Law and the Indo-China War*, 570-98 (1972) (Chapter XIII. The Justiciability of Challenges to the Use of Military Force Abroad, citing cases, and discussing the basis of challenging American actions in the Vietnam War).

making it clear to military commanders that they were personally at risk for commanding or condoning war crimes, there was a chance, in a free society, to make a difference. Thus I found myself in an interesting logical trap: I could not blame the United States without blaming myself because I was a citizen of the United States. The only way I could avert self-blame was to campaign actively against the policy I deplored. So long as I did engage in such a campaign, I could not blame the United States as a whole for its policy! In brief, as a member of the state, the battle I had was not with the state itself but with other members of the state.

This perspective, which may seem simplistic now, was liberating for me at that time. I could fight the United States government's policies in Vietnam in the name of the United States! The government, after all, did not *represent* the United States any more than I did; though the government might have effective power, it was as subject to the Constitution as I was. Incidentally, a small but sweet moment for me was when the United States paid me as a public defender for a case where the court reversed the convictions of persons who had disrupted a draft board office, and held unconstitutional a part of the Military Selective Service Act.[15] Receiving that check provided a real lift to my spirits because the United States actually paid me for defeating the government in a case that the government went to great lengths to win.[16]

Out of the specific experiences I had regarding the Vietnam War,[17] I believe I developed an internationalist perspective. There are no "good nations" or "bad nations," but there are nations which from time to time violate the basic human rights of all peoples. One's moral perspective should be grounded, I believe, in these universal human rights. If one's own state violates these rights, one has a moral duty, I assert, to try to oppose effectively those policies. Effectiveness,

---

15. *United States v. Baranski*, 484 F.2d 556, 570-71 (7th Cir. 1973) (reversing convictions of draft resisters and holding part of the Military Selective Service Act unconstitutional).

16. Id. at 556. In the *Baranski* case, the defendants had poured blood on a number of files in the draft board office. The court sequestered these files for evidence in the case, and the potential draftees whose files were sequestered were never drafted. The government decided not to appeal the case to the U.S. Supreme Court even though the Seventh Circuit held part of the Military Selective Service Act unconstitutional. The Seventh Circuit's decision also contradicted the Fourth Circuit precedent in another case involving the pouring of blood on Selective Service files. *See United States v. Eberhardt*, 417 F.2d 1009, (4th Cir. 1969) (affirming convictions under the same provision held unconstitutional in *Baranski*) *cert. denied*, 397 U.S. 909 (1970).

17. *See generally* A. D'Amato & R. O'Neil, *The Judiciary and Vietnam* (1972) (recounting some personal experiences involving the Vietnam war).

I hasten to add, is not the same as joining in mass demonstrations or writing letters to Congress, though for some people such outlets may be all that are available. For people who have the training and opportunity to fight on a more effective basis, I believe that their moral obligation is commensurately greater.

In addition to the anti-Vietnam activities, I was fortunate to be involved as assistant counsel to Liberia and Ethiopia against South Africa in the World Court cases of the mid-1960s,[18] and in various individual human-rights cases throughout my teaching career.[19]

Not all professors of international law get these opportunities and I am grateful that a good number of them have come my way. To some extent these cases involved clashes with my own university and colleagues, but I must admit that the freedom of a professor of law to take unpopular positions, while not as great as that of a sole practitioner or a member of a very small law firm, is certainly not as restricted as that of a lawyer in a large law firm. Lawyers in large firms are tremendously shackled by the decisions of their partners concerning what is good for business and what would reflect adversely upon existing clients. Yet, even their freedom to take an unpopular human rights case is favorable compared to those attorneys who work as in-house counsel for corporations (who may rarely if ever get leave to work on such cases) or counsel for the Departments of State or Justice or other branches of the government (who would be totally barred from handling any private human rights cases).

As much as I would like to see good students become professors of international law, I would not want to paint an idyllic picture of the academic scene. There are petty satraps in the academic field as in any other, and small-minded people who are clever at in-fighting and office politics manage to puff themselves up into large dimensions on law school faculties.

When I read about Einstein or other great scientists whose work I admire, I find in their lives a great sympathy toward their students

---

18. South West Africa (Ethiopia v. S. Afr.; Liberia v. S. Afr.), 1966 I.C.J. 6 (Judgment of July 18, 1966) (narrowly rejecting challenges to South African administration of South West Africa (Namibia)). *See* G-M, Cockram, *South West Africa Mandate*, 317-43 (1976) (discussing the case before the International Court of Justice); S. Slonim, *South West Africa and the United Nations*, 278-309 (1973) (placing the I.C.J. 1966 judgment in the context of international efforts to solve the Namibian problem). *See generally* J. Dugard, *The South West Africa/Namibia Dispute*.

19. *See* A. D'Amato, *Litigating International Law* (to be published in 1987) (describing various human rights cases).

and a large-minded willingness to have their theories revised or improved by the next generation. In my own field, however, I have found instead a fear of new ideas and especially a fear of having one's pet theories be upset by one's own students. In part, I attribute this difference to a medieval sense of "priesthood" that still seems to permeate international law, though it has long since dissipated in physics, chemistry or biology. The elderly priests of international law have their legitimacy at stake; what they've pronounced as the truth depends on the validity of the theoretical arguments they have used to support their pronouncements. If someone challenges the validity and consistency of that intellectual scaffolding, their words of wisdom might tumble down. Hence some of them may view students as heretics rather than as fellow truth-seekers.

If international law, by means of good scholarly standards, can increase in precision and objectivity, and if its underlying theory can be made clearer and more intellectually satisfying, much of the "priesthood" attitude will necessarily fade away. The discipline will become stronger as it becomes more logically rigorous. In my view, prospects for the field of international law are extremely optimistic. If students approach the field realistically, I think they will be pleasantly surprised.

INDEX

Afghanistan invasion, 221, 242
Akehurst, Michael, 124, 131-36, 142, 230-31
Alien Tort Claims Act, 193-199-201, 208-19
Apartheid, vi, 165-91. See also Homelands
Aquinas, St. Thomas, 6
Argentina, see Falkland Islands invasion
Aristotle, 227
Armed attack, 31
Article 2(4), see "Territorial integrity" and "Political independence"
Asylum Case, 141
Austin, John 3, 4n
Axelrod, Robert 22n

Bantustans, see Homelands
Barkun, Michael, 7n
Baxter, Judge Richard R., 127, 129-30, 132-33
Begin, Menachem, 81
Bentham, Jeremy, 3n, 4n, 216, 227
Blackstone, William, 141n, 214, 216, 217n
Blockade
  land, 51
  pacific, 19, 43-47
  Venezuelan, 46
  war, 47
Borden, Sir Robert, 64
Bork, Judge Robert, 206-18
Boundaries
  sanctity of, 17-18
  stability of, v
Boxer rebellion, 36, 52-53
Boyle, Francis A., 80
Brierly, James, 98n
Brownlie, Ian, 32n, 80n, 102n
Buergenthal, Judge Thomas, 104n, 106n

Calabresi, Guido, 92
Calvo, Carlos, 196
Calvo clause, 197-98
Calvo Doctrine, 198-99
Caroline Case, 31-35
Carter, Jimmy, 150-228
Cause of action, 206-13, 215
Chapultepec, Act of, 69
Chayes, Abram, 47n, 53-54
Chen, Lung-chu, 11, 12n
Chomsky, Noam, 242n
Cicero, 6
Cocoyoc Declaration, 151, 158-59
Cognitive dissonance, 97
Collective security, 9, 85, 220
Communism, 156-58
Compensation, 77n, 83, 86-87, 206

Complementarity, see Prescriptions, complementarity of
Consensus, 103n, 122
Consent, 18-21, 142n
Constitutional law, enforcement of, 1-3
Constitutive laws, 91
Content analysis, 10-12
Continental Shelf cases, 17, 135-42
Contras, 52, 222, 228
Corfu Channel case, 39-41
Corfu incident, 43
Countermeasures, 24n
Covenant on Civil and Political Rights, 151n, 209n
Covenant on Economic, Social and Cultural Rights, 151
Criminal law, enforcement of, 2
Cuban missile crisis, 37, 44-45, 47n, 51, 53
Custom
  and entitlements, 112n
  and practice of states, 124-25
  articulation of
    by protest, 110-12
    by treaty, 132n
  duration of, 127-28, 134-35, 143-44
  opinio juris, 136-38, 141-42
  special, 141-42
  treaty generation of, 123-45
Cutler, Lloyd N., 117

DeVisscher, Charles, 94
Dugard, John, 99n, 120n, 244n
Dumbarton Oaks proposals, 70
Dworkin, Ronald, 95

Einstein, Albert, 244
Embargo, 47-48
Enforcement
  as hallmark of law, 1-10
  control of officials, 4-6
  distinguished from force, 27-28
  of constitutional law, 1-3
  of criminal law, 2-3
  of human rights, 55
  potential, 6-7
  See also Sanctions
Entitlements
  as human rights, 103-08
  and custom, 112n, 124
  compared with rights, 14-15, 92
  defined, 14, 92
  definition of "nation," v, 91
  distinguished from interests, 93-94
  each nation has same set, 94-95
  equal standing of, 95-96

247

equilibrium of, 96-98
examples of, 16-19, 92-94
in Iranian hostages situation, 110-20
in Namibian example, 120-22
preservation of, 98-103
reciprocal, 13-26
retaliation, 100
tit-for-tat strategy, 22-24
Epistemology of law, vi, 223
Equality
  marginal, 185
  mirror-image, 174-75
  strict, 175-77
  substantive, 177-85
  transitional, 185-91
Espousal of claims, 193-99, 216

Falk, Richard A., 1n, 76n, 81n, 82n, 111n, 118-20, 231n
Falkland Islands invasion, 35-36, 65
Farer, Thomas J., 142n
Fedayeen raids, 33, 36
Feinberg, Joel, 154
Feliciano, Florentino, 45, 80-81
Festinger, L., 97
Filartiga Case, 103n, 107n, 124n, 142n, 210
Finnis, John, 6n
Fisher, Roger, 1-3, 9, 100n, 102n, 111-12, 122n
Fisheries Case, 141
Force
  distinguished from enforcement, 27-28
  evolution of law of, 53-55
  "force against," 65-69, 79
  use of, 27-55
Forde, Francis M., 70
Fourteen Points, 62
Franck, Thomas M., 79n, 231-32
Fraser, Hon. Peter, 70
Freeze of assets, 115-17
Fuller, Lon L., 6n, 95n, 99n, 170-71

General Assembly resolutions, see Resolutions of the U.N.
Geneva Convention on the High Seas, 46
Genocide Convention, 124n, 128, 134, 209n
Genocide, crime of, 89-90, 123-24, 142-45, 226-27
Gewirth, Alan, 95n
Gordon, Edward, 103n
Greek frontier incidents, 37, 49
Grenada invasion, 221, 227, 229, 232
Guaranty, see Treaties
Guatemala invasion of 1954, 49
Hall, William, 126, 127n
Hart, H.L.A., 8n, 91, 96n, 132n
Havana Protocol, 68
Henkin, Louis, 2, 79n, 87, 101n, 106-07, 138n, 214

Hobbes, Thomas, 4n, 219-21
Homelands
  and border industries, 188
  and economic interdependence, 187
  "territorial apartheid," 121, 166-91
Hostages Case, see Tehran Hostages Case
Hostages in Iran, 22-24, 109-13
House, Edward M., 61, 63
Human rights
  and discrimination, 187-91
  and free markets, 162-64
  and individual standing, 193-99
  in customary law, 110
  nature of, 153-56
    See also Genocide, crime of; Slavery, crime of; Torture, crime of
Humanitarian intervention, 39
Hyde, Charles C., 42n

I'm Alone Case, 46
Indirect aggression, 48-50
Interests
  defined, 93
  distinct from entitlements, 93-94
International law
  as a career, 233-45
  as real "law," 1-26, 236-37
  as reciprocal entitlements, 13-26
  compliance with, 2, 8-9, 26
    See also Custom; Resolutions of the U.N.; Treaties
Invitation of military assistance, 51
Iran-Iraq war, 65, 117-20
Iraqi nuclear reactor
  Iraqi claims, 79-84
  Israeli air strike, 58-59, 75-87, 232
  Israeli justifications, 77-79, 85-87
Israeli air strike, see Iraqi nuclear reactor

Janis, Mark, 216n
Jefferson, Thomas, 43
Jus cogens, 96, 128
Jus gentium, 216-17
Just war, 9-10

Kaplan, Morton, 93n, 94
Katzenbach, Nicholas DeB., 93n, 94
Kellogg-Briand Pact, 28, 77, 84, 118
Kelsen, Hans, 64, 107
Kennedy, David, 235
Kennedy, Duncan, 234, 236n
Kennedy, John F., 45, 78n

Laffer curve, 158n
Lansing, Robert, 63
Lasswell, Harold, 11, 12n
Lauterpacht, Hersh, 9n, 128, 215

Index

Law
  as "enforcement," 1-10
  as "reciprocal entitlements," 13-26
  as "words," 10-13
  positivist view, 8
  See also Constitutional Law; International Law
Lebanon, intervention of 1958, 37, 50-51
Lillich, Richard, 80n
Lincoln, Abraham, v
Local custom, see Custom, special
Locke, John, 227
Lotus Case, 145, 216

MacChesney, Brunson, 78n
Mallison, Sally, 77n, 81, 82n, 85n
Mallison, Thomas, 77n, 81, 82n, 85n
Malvinas, see Falkland Islands invasion
Marbury v. Madison, 5
Marcos, Ferdinand, 161, 228-29
Marshall, John, 5, 202
Marx, Karl, 156
McDougal, Myres, 11-12, 45, 80-81, 94, 104n
McNair, Sir Arnold, 127
"Might makes right," v, 2-3
Miller, David Hunter, 62n, 63
Moore, John Norton, 242n
MX missile, 240

Namibian entitlement example, 120-22
Nation
  as bundle of entitlements, 16-19, 26, 91-95
  defined, v, 91
Nationality
  compared to "internationality," 105-06, 205
  meaning, 104-05
Nationals
  defined, 104-05
  protection abroad, 36-38
Nationals in Morocco Case, 141
Natural law, 6
Naulilaa incident, 42
Necessity
  land blockade, 51
  natural disasters, 50-51
Nicaragua Case (Nic. v. U.S.), vi, 223-29
Nixon, Richard M., 25, 78
Non-proliferation Treaty, 82-83
North Sea Continental Shelf Cases, see Continental Shelf Cases
Nuremberg Cases, 31, 77, 89, 149-50, 218

O'Connell, Daniel P., 127n

Odendaal Commission, 121, 166-91
O'Neil, Robert M., 243n
Ontology of law, v-vi, 223
Onuf, Nicholas, 12n, 99n, 144n
Opinio juris, see Custom
Oppenheim, Lassa, 9n, 43n, 89, 126-30, 201, 210, 215-17
Organization of American States, 38
Orwell, George, 4
Outer space, 18
Owen, Robert, 152
Owen, Roberts B., 115-16

Pacific blockade, see Blockade
Pacta sunt servanda, 96
Paquete Habana Case, 214n
Parry, Clive, 127n
Paust, Jordan, 102n, 213n, 215n
Piracy, 107-08, 200-01
Platt Amendment, 52
Policy-oriented jurisprudence, 11
"Political independence"
  contextual meaning, 58
  historical meaning, 59-61
  McDougal definition, 45
  travaux preparatoires, 69-77
Political question, 207, 213
Positivism
  and sanctions, 6-8
  and social disapproval, 7
  and sovereign immunity, 201-04
Prescriptions, complementarity of, 12
Proportionality, doctrine of, 31-36, 41, 52, 101-02

Rapaport, Anatol, 22n
Rawls, John, 158n, 160n
Reagan administration, 105, 160-64, 228
Reagan, Ronald, 223-24, 227, 229
Rebus sic stantibus, 17
Reciprocal entitlements, see Entitlements
Reisman, W. Michael, 7n, 11n, 81n, 225-26
Relatedness doctrine, 102, 111.
  See also Tit-for-tat strategy.
Reprisals, 19, 41-43
Resolutions of the U.N., 75-77, 231
Right of Passage Case, 51n, 141
Robinson, Davis R., 224
Roosevelt, Theodore, 39
Rovine, Arthur W., 120n
Rubin, Alfred, 216n, 217
Russell, Ruth B., 69

Sabbatino Case, 202-03
Sanctions
  against South Africa, 121
  as entitlement deprivations, 14-15

249

in natural law, 7n, 8n
in positivism, 7-8
  See also Enforcement.
Santissima Trinidad Case, 203
Schachter, Oscar, 107n, 138n, 226
Schooner Exchange Case, 202, 204
Schwarzenberger, Georg, 16n
Self-defense
  anticipatory, 79
  as enforcement, 28-29
  as self-help, 29-30, 39
  collective, 52, 224
  of nationals or property abroad, 36-38
  of ships and aircraft, 36
  of territory, 30-36
  of "vital interests," 38-39
Self-help
  and indirect aggression, 48-50
  and necessity, 50
  and removal of troops, 50
  collective, 52
  relation to self-defense, 30
  to get even, 41-47
  to secure justice, 39-41
Shultz, George, 223
Slavery, crime of, 123-24, 142, 144-45, 226
Skolem-Lowenheim theory, 230
Sohn, Louis, 104n, 127, 224
Sovereign immunity, 201-04, 215
Sovereignty
  over natural resources, 159-60
  vs. human rights, 158-60
  vs. individual, 193-204
Soviet Constitution, 156n
South West Africa Cases, 167, 174n, 176-80, 182-85, 187, 244.
Statements of governments
  and custom, 134-35
  as law, 229-31
Stein, Ted, 114n
Stone, Julius, 32n, 54-55, 79n
Story, Joseph, 203
Suez intervention of 1956, 37, 39
Surgical strike, see Iraqi nuclear reactor
Systemic stability, 16

Tampico incident, 42
Tehran Hostages Case, 24n, 109-20, 224
Tel-Oren Case, 194, 204-19
Territorial apartheid, see Apartheid
"Territorial integrity"
  and "inviolability," 60

contextual meaning, 58
historical meaning, 59-69
travaux preparatoires, 69-73
Terrorism
  in Tel-Oren Case, 204-05
  use of force against, 28-30
Tit-for-tat strategy
  and countermeasures, 24n
  and relatedness
  escalation potential, 102
  meaning of, 22-25
Torture, crime of, 123-24, 124n, 142-45, 200-01, 226
Transfer payments, 156-58
Treaties
  contract view of, 126-30, 143
  effect upon customary law, 123-45
  in insurance industry, 13
  of guaranty, 59-60
  reasonable time implication, 144
  self-executing, 209-13
  travaux preparatoires, 132-36
  See also Custom.
Troops, removal of, 50
Tuchman, Barbara, 219
Tunkin, G.I., 20n, 135n

Unilateral declarations, see Statements of governments

Van Hoof, G.J.H., 20n
Venezuela blockade of 1902, 46-47
Verwoerd, H.F., 182-83, 186, 190-91
Vienna Convention on the Law of Treaties, 17, 25n, 96n, 101n, 135-36
Vietnam war, 241-44
Vital interests, protection of, 38-39
von Bertalanffy, Ludwig, 98n
von Mehren, Robert B., vii, 27n

Walters, F.P., 61
Walzer, Michael, 9n
Watson, J.S., 20n, 90, 93-94, 99, 103-05, 108-09, 142n, 143, 146
Webster, Daniel, 31-35
West Rand Central Case, 126-27, 132n
Weston, Burns, 1n, 76n, 111n, 231n
Wiener, Norbert, 98n
Wilson, Woodrow, 42, 61-63, 227-28
Wittgenstein, Ludwig, 230
Wright, Quincy, 78n

Zipori, Mordechai, 78
Zoller, Elisabeth, 20n, 22n, 24n